Tuesday Nights

CHRISTOPHER KIMBALL'S

MILK STREET

Tuesday Nights

Christopher Kimball

J. M. Hirsch, Matthew Card, Michelle Locke,
Jennifer Baldino Cox and the
editors and cooks of Milk Street

Photography by Connie Miller

LITTLE, BROWN AND COMPANY

NEW YORK BOSTON LONDON

Little, Brown and Company
Hachette Book Group
1290 Avenue of the Americas, New York, NY 10104
littlebrown.com

First Edition: October 2018

Little, Brown and Company is a division of Hachette Book Group, Inc. The Little, Brown name and logo are trademarks of Hachette Book Group, Inc.

The publisher is not responsible for websites (or their content) that are not owned by the publisher.

The Hachette Speakers Bureau provides a wide range of authors for speaking events. To find out more, go to hachettespeakersbureau.com or call (866) 376-6591.

Photography credits: Connie Miller of CB Creatives.

ISBN 978-0-316-43731-8 (hardcover) / 978-0-316-42148-5 (signed edition) / 978-0-316-42149-2 (Barnes & Noble signed edition)
LCCN 2018942284

10 9 8 7 6 5 4 3 2 1

IM

Print book interior design by Gary Tooth / Empire Design Studio
Printed in China

Contents

Introduction

Albert Einstein may have shown that time is relative, but for as long as French cooking has ruled the world, we've been told it—and heat—were constants, the critical components of flavor. Turns out that's only true in European kitchens.

Look at cooking elsewhere in the world and you'll find that flavor is built with ingredients, not time. For anyone living outside Europe, this isn't much of a revelation. But for those of us raised on classic American cookery, heavily influenced by the cuisines of northern Europe, this is a watershed moment. Herbs, spices, fermented sauces, chilies, ginger, scallions, lemon grass, smoked meats and fish. These are the ingredients that make cooking quicker and easier. Likewise with pantry staples such as harissa, tahini, pomegranate molasses, salsas, chili paste and vinegars.

This quickly leads to a new way of thinking about dinner. Yellow lentils become a main course. Fried rice is the ultimate fast food. Stir-frying goes far beyond classic Chinese recipes, as in lomo saltado (a Peruvian stir-fry of beef and tomatoes) or Vietnamese shaking beef with soy sauce, sugar, garlic and watercress. Quick soups are made with stale bread, garlic, water and smoked paprika, or chickpeas and a soft-cooked egg. And, of course, there are endless variations on eggs for dinner, from frittatas to omelets to Turkish scrambles.

We've organized *Milk Street Tuesday Nights* by the way you cook. Some chapters focus on time—Fast, Faster and Fastest—others highlight easy methods or themes— Pizza Night, Easy Additions, Supper Salads, and Roast and Simmer.

We take familiar ingredients such as ground beef and spice them up. Add garam masala, ginger and garlic and you have keema matar. We dress pasta simply, but boldly, with ricotta and sage, for example. Spice rubs transform steaks, sautés and quick roasts. Meatballs are turned upside down with cashews and coconut. Sometimes we hew closely to the original inspiration. Sometimes we are inspired by our travels, as with chicken teriyaki donburi (a simple take on chicken teriyaki we learned from Elizabeth Andoh during our trip to Tokyo), or Thai rice soup, a classic recipe we picked up in Chiang Mai.

If you flip through these pages, you will notice two things: simplicity and big flavors. That is how you get supper on the table quickly on Tuesday nights while also delivering great food. No matter where you live. The secret is nothing new. This is how the world cooks. Milk Street is simply a translator, sifting through a world of spices, herbs, chilies and sauces that combine to put supper on the table quickly and easily.

Milk Street Tuesday Nights proves that culinary time is relative. It comes down to ingredients and how you define dinner. For millions of people let it be said that we offer nothing new. To them, we are late to the game. But we hope that this book offers the home cook a new beginning and a break from a past when *fast food* meant bad food.

In the kitchen, it turns out, time is indeed relative.

On the table in under 45 minutes

Beef Suya / 3

Glazed Salmon with Chili-Basil Sauce / 5

Kimchi and Bacon Fried Rice / 7

Pasta with Golden Onions and Breadcrumbs / 8

Salt-and-Pepper Shrimp / 11

Georgian Chicken with Walnut-Cilantro Sauce / 13

Sausage and Mushroom Ragu with Pappardelle / 15

Vietnamese Meatball Soup with Watercress (Canh) / 16

Curried Chicken and Rice with Cranberries / 19

Poached Cod in Tomato-Garlic Broth (Pesce all'Acqua Pazza) / 21

Frittata with Pasta, Thyme and Parmesan / 23

Indian Spiced Beef and Peas (Keema Matar) / 25

Pork Chops with Peanut-Guajillo Sauce / 27

Rigatoni with Ricotta-Sage Pesto / 28

Crispy Sichuan-Chili Chicken (La Zi Ji) / 31

White Beans with Sage, Garlic and Fennel / 33

Seared Strip Steak with Almond-Rosemary Salsa Verde / 35

Chicken Curry with Coconut and Tomatoes / 37

Soy-Steamed Japanese-Style Rice with Mushrooms and Tofu / 39

Spanish Eggs and Potatoes (Huevos Rotos) / 40

Taiwanese Five-Spice Pork with Rice (Lu Rou Fan) / 43

Pasta alla Norma / 45

Sumac-Spiced Chicken (Musakhan) / 47

Cantonese-Style Black Pepper Beef with Potatoes / 49

Ginger-Scallion Steamed Fish / 51

Spanish Ratatouille (Pisto Manchego) / 52

Ginger-Soy Steak with Pear-Cucumber Salad / 55

Tuscan Soup with Bread, Beans and Greens (Ribollita) / 57

Spicy Sichuan Tofu and Pork (Mapo Dofu) / 59

Whole-Wheat Penne with Broccolini and Chèvre / 61

Shrimp with Feta Cheese (Garides Saganaki) / 63

Cuban Picadillo / 65

Steamed Chicken and Shiitakes with Soy-Sake Sauce / 67

Shrimp with Tamarind and Cilantro / 69

Spice-Crusted Steak with Mashed Chickpeas / 70

Caramel-Braised Chicken with Ginger and Lime / 73

Linguini with Spiced Beef and Feta / 75

Cashew-Coconut Meatballs with Creamy Spiced Tomato Sauce / 77

Chicken Cutlets with Mango-Tomato Sauce / 79

Tibetan Curried Noodles with Beef and Cabbage / 81

Vietnamese Turmeric Fish with Wilted Herbs and Peanuts / 83

Milk-Poached Chicken with Tarragon Salsa Verde / 85

Yakiudon with Pickled Ginger / 87

Fast

If we're feeling frugal, we make this with boneless, skinless chicken thighs, which come out of the oven crispy outside and tender inside. Substitute an equal amount of chicken for beef and slice the thighs lengthwise into 1/2-inch strips.

Beef Suya

START TO FINISH:
45 minutes (30 minutes active)

SERVINGS:
4

½ cup unsalted dry-roasted peanuts

1 tablespoon sweet paprika

1 tablespoon ground ginger

1 tablespoon garlic powder

1 tablespoon onion powder

2 teaspoons packed light brown sugar

1 teaspoon cayenne pepper

Kosher salt and ground black pepper

3 tablespoons grapeseed or other neutral oil

1½ pounds flat iron steak, sliced against the grain into ½-inch-thick strips

1 tablespoon lime juice, plus lime wedges, to serve

Eaten on the spot with burning fingers and tongue or carried away wrapped in newspaper, the street snack known as suya is popular throughout Nigeria. Suya usually is made with thin strips of beef, but it's the spice rub that sets it apart—typically a blend of ground peanuts, red pepper and other seasonings. We like this with flat iron steak, which is easily cut into long, ½-inch-thick strips; look for a single 1½-pound piece. Blade steaks, also known as top blade, are a similar cut and are sometimes labeled flat iron; they are sold in smaller portions and a line of gristle runs down the center of each piece. Either cut worked, but if you opt for blade, choose the thickest you can find and remove the gristle (which means cutting each steak into two pieces) before slicing the meat into strips. The best way to check the meat for doneness is to cut into a piece at the center of a skewer; it should be medium-rare. We liked serving the suya with cucumber, tomato, cabbage and onion—cooling counterparts to the spicy beef.

Don't skip the lime wedges for serving. They provide a much-needed hit of acidity and freshness.

In a food processor, combine the peanuts, paprika, ginger, garlic powder, onion powder, sugar, cayenne, ¾ teaspoon salt and 1 teaspoon black pepper. Process until finely ground, about 20 seconds. Reserve ⅓ cup of the spice mix, then transfer the rest to a medium bowl; add the oil and stir to form a paste.

In a large bowl, combine the beef with 1 teaspoon salt. Toss and massage until evenly coated. Add the paste to the beef, tossing and massaging into the meat. Thread the beef tightly onto four 12-inch metal skewers, fitting multiple pieces of meat on each skewer; they should be tightly packed.

Place the skewers on a wire rack set in a foil-lined rimmed baking sheet. Heat the broiler with a rack set about 4 inches from the element. Broil until well-browned, about 5 minutes, flipping halfway through. Transfer to a plate and let rest for 5 minutes.

Brush the lime juice on both sides of the skewers, then sprinkle with the reserved spice mix. Serve with lime wedges.

Glazed Salmon
with Chili-Basil Sauce

START TO FINISH:	SERVINGS:
40 minutes	**4**

2 tablespoons chili-garlic sauce

2 tablespoons packed dark brown sugar

1 tablespoon fish sauce

2 teaspoons soy sauce

2 teaspoons cornstarch

3 tablespoons grapeseed or other neutral oil, divided

1 tablespoon finely grated fresh ginger

1 lemon grass stalk, trimmed to the lower 6 inches, dry outer layers discarded, minced

2 tablespoons lemon juice

½ cup chopped fresh basil, plus 1 tablespoon julienned basil, divided

Four 6-ounce center-cut salmon fillets (each 1 to 1¼ inches thick), patted dry

Kosher salt and ground black pepper

Lime juice might be more common in the Vietnamese-inspired sauce that accompanies this salmon, but lemon juice reinforces the flavor of the lemon grass. If you can find Thai basil—it's sold in many Asian markets—by all means use it; it packs a stronger, more savory punch than Italian basil. You'll need a 12-inch oven-safe skillet for cooking the salmon. Serve with steamed or stir-fried greens and rice.

Don't chop the basil until it's thoroughly dried or it will discolor almost instantly. When adding the fillets to the skillet, don't place them skin side down. Cooking them flesh side down for the entire time results in rich browning on the meat, which adds flavor and makes for an attractive crust.

Heat the oven to 400°F with a rack in the middle position. In a small bowl, stir together ⅔ cup water, the chili-garlic sauce, sugar, fish sauce and soy sauce until the sugar dissolves. In another small bowl, stir together the cornstarch and 1 tablespoon water.

In a medium saucepan over medium-high, heat 2 tablespoons of the oil until shimmering. Stir in the ginger and lemon grass and cook until fragrant, about 10 seconds. Pour in the chili-garlic sauce mixture and bring to a boil. Stir the cornstarch mixture to recombine, then stir into the sauce. Reduce to medium-low and simmer, stirring constantly, until thickened, about 3 minutes. Remove from the heat, stir in the lemon juice and ½ cup basil. Cover to keep warm.

Season the fillets on both sides with salt and pepper. In a 12-inch oven-safe skillet over medium-high, heat the remaining 1 tablespoon oil until barely smoking. Add the fillets flesh side down, reduce to medium and cook until golden brown, about 4 minutes. Transfer the skillet to the oven and cook until the thickest parts of the fillets register 115°F to 120°F, or are nearly opaque when cut into, 4 to 6 minutes. Remove from the oven.

Using tongs, carefully peel off and discard the skin from each fillet. With a wide metal spatula, transfer the fillets to a platter, turning them browned side up. Pour half of the sauce over the fish and sprinkle with the remaining 1 tablespoon julienned basil. Serve the remaining sauce on the side.

Kimchi and Bacon Fried Rice

START TO FINISH:
40 minutes

SERVINGS:
4

3¼ cups cooked Japanese-style short-grain rice, preferably chilled

6 ounces bacon, preferably thick-cut, chopped

1 medium yellow onion, finely chopped

2 cups well-drained napa cabbage kimchi, roughly chopped, plus 2 tablespoons kimchi juice

1 tablespoon soy sauce

1 cup frozen peas, thawed

2 teaspoons toasted sesame oil

4 scallions, thinly sliced on diagonal

Kosher salt and ground black pepper

4 large eggs

Furikake seasoning or nori cut into slivers, to serve (optional)

This fried rice is a great way to use up kimchi that has been languishing in your refrigerator. Spreading the seasoned rice in an even layer in the skillet and letting it cook undisturbed for a few minutes allows tasty charred bits to form on the bottom, so don't be impatient and stir too soon. The fried egg that tops each serving not only completes the dish with a hit of protein, but the yolk, when broken, flows onto the rice, adding a richness that heightens the flavors.

Don't use long-grain rice. Japanese-style short-grain rice gives the dish a satisfying stickiness and chew. Don't use a conventional skillet; a nonstick pan is needed to prevent the rice from sticking.

If the rice is chilled, use your fingers to break apart any large clumps. Set a mesh strainer over a small heatproof bowl and place near the stovetop.

In a 12-inch nonstick skillet over medium, cook the bacon until well browned, 10 to 12 minutes. Scraping the pan, pour into the strainer; reserve the bacon fat.

Return 1 tablespoon of the fat to the skillet, add the onion and cook over medium, stirring, until softened, 3 to 4 minutes. Stir in the rice and cook for 1 to 2 minutes. Drizzle the kimchi juice, soy sauce and 1 tablespoon of the bacon fat over the rice and stir. Spread the rice in an even layer, increase heat to high and cook until browned on the bottom, about 3 minutes.

Scrape along the bottom of the pan and flip the rice, then redistribute and cook until again browned on the bottom, another 2 to 3 minutes. Stir in the kimchi, bacon, peas, sesame oil and scallions. Cook, stirring, until hot, 1 to 2 minutes. Taste and season with salt and pepper. Transfer to a bowl and cover with foil.

Wipe out the skillet with paper towels. Add 1 tablespoon of the bacon fat and heat over medium-high until barely smoking. Swirl to coat the pan, then crack an egg in each quadrant. Immediately reduce to medium-low and sprinkle with salt and pepper. Cook until the whites are set but the yolks are still runny, 2 to 3 minutes. Remove the pan from the heat.

Serve the fried rice on individual plates, topped with a fried egg and sprinkled with furikake, if using.

Pasta with Golden Onions
and Breadcrumbs

START TO FINISH:	SERVINGS:
40 minutes	**4**

¼ cup extra-virgin olive oil

1 cup panko breadcrumbs

¾ cup lightly packed fresh flat-leaf parsley, finely chopped

2 teaspoons grated lemon zest, plus lemon wedges, to serve

Kosher salt and ground black pepper

12 ounces spaghetti or bucatini (see note)

3 tablespoons minced anchovy fillets, plus 4 teaspoons anchovy oil

2 large yellow onions, halved and thinly sliced

4 medium garlic cloves, finely chopped

1½ cups dry white wine or vermouth

¾ teaspoon red pepper flakes

2 tablespoons salted butter, cut into 4 pieces

This classic Venetian dish typically uses bigoli, a whole-wheat pasta shaped like fat spaghetti. We liked it with regular spaghetti, as well as with bucatini (also called perciatelli), a tubular spaghetti-like shape. The panko topping isn't traditional, but it adds a welcome crispness, toasted in olive oil and flavored with chopped parsley and lemon zest.

Don't rinse the anchovies before mincing, as this will wash away some flavor.

In a 12-inch skillet over medium, heat the olive oil until shimmering. Add the panko and cook, stirring, until golden, about 5 minutes. Transfer to a medium bowl. Let cool for a few minutes, then stir in the parsley, lemon zest and ¾ teaspoon salt. Wipe out the skillet.

In a large pot, bring 4 quarts of water to a boil. Add the pasta and 2 tablespoons salt; cook until al dente. Drain well, then return the pasta to the pot.

Meanwhile, set the skillet over medium-high and heat the anchovy oil until shimmering. Add the onions and cook, stirring, until lightly browned, about 8 minutes. Add the garlic and cook, stirring, until the onions are well browned and the garlic is golden, about 4 minutes. Stir in the anchovies, then add the wine, pepper flakes and ½ teaspoon black pepper. Bring to a boil over high and cook, stirring and scraping up any browned bits, until slightly thickened, about 5 minutes. Remove from the heat, add the butter and swirl until it blends into the sauce.

Add the sauce to the pasta and toss, then mix in ½ cup of the panko mixture. Transfer to a serving bowl, sprinkle with the remaining panko mixture and serve with lemon wedges.

Salt-and-Pepper Shrimp

START TO FINISH:
45 minutes

SERVINGS:
4

1½ pounds jumbo shrimp, peeled and deveined, tails left on

2 teaspoons Sichuan peppercorns

1 teaspoon white peppercorns

Kosher salt

2 tablespoons cornstarch

1 teaspoon white sugar

4 tablespoons grapeseed or other neutral oil, divided

1 large jalapeño or 2 serrano chilies, stemmed and thinly sliced crosswise into rings

6 medium garlic cloves, finely chopped

¼ cup finely chopped peeled fresh ginger

1 bunch scallions, thinly sliced

To make classic salt-and-pepper shrimp, the shrimp—with heads and shells intact—are deep-fried until crisp. This recipe is a much-simplified version that offers the same rich aromas and spicy, toasted-garlic flavor of the traditional recipe. Serve with rice and steamed or stir-fried greens.

Don't slice the scallions paper thin; they will scorch. About ¼ inch thick is best.

Pat the shrimp dry with paper towels and place in a large bowl. Use a spice grinder to grind the Sichuan and white peppercorns until medium-fine (about the coarseness of kosher salt). Transfer to a small bowl and stir in 1½ teaspoons salt. In another small bowl, stir together 2 teaspoons of the pepper mixture, the cornstarch and sugar, then sprinkle over the shrimp and toss. Set the remaining pepper mixture aside.

Line a baking sheet with paper towels. In a 12-inch nonstick skillet over medium-high, heat 1 tablespoon of the oil until barely smoking. Add half of the shrimp in an even layer and cook without stirring until deep golden brown, 1 to 2 minutes. Using tongs, flip and continue to cook until the second side is opaque, another 20 to 30 seconds. Transfer to the prepared baking sheet. Repeat with 1 tablespoon of the remaining oil and the remaining shrimp. Do not wash the skillet.

In the same skillet over medium-high, heat the remaining 2 tablespoons oil until shimmering. Add the jalapeño and cook, stirring, until the seeds begin to brown, about 1 minute. Add the garlic, ginger and all but 3 tablespoons of the scallions. Cook, stirring constantly, until the scallions and ginger have softened, about 2 minutes. Return the shrimp to the skillet and toss, then stir in the reserved spice mixture. Transfer to a platter and sprinkle with the remaining scallions.

Georgian Chicken
with Walnut-Cilantro Sauce

START TO FINISH:	SERVINGS:
40 minutes	**4**

4 teaspoons ground coriander, divided

Kosher salt

3 pounds bone-in, skin-on chicken thighs, trimmed

3 medium garlic cloves, peeled

3 tablespoons tomato paste

2 serrano chilies, stemmed and seeded

3 tablespoons pomegranate molasses, divided

¾ cup lightly packed fresh cilantro, divided

1 cup walnuts, toasted, divided

1¼ cups low-sodium chicken broth, divided

1 tablespoon grapeseed or other neutral oil

In the country of Georgia, chicken and fish often are served with a creamy walnut sauce. In our version, braised bone-in chicken thighs are accompanied by a walnut-cilantro puree that's lightly spiced and spiked with pomegranate molasses. If you like, scatter pomegranate seeds over the finished dish. You'll need an oven-safe 12-inch skillet for this recipe. Serve warmed flatbread alongside.

Don't fully submerge the chicken thighs in the sauce when returning them to the pan after browning. Keeping the skin dry and exposed helps it crisp and brown in the oven. Don't forget the skillet handle will be hot after it is removed from the oven, so be sure to use a pot holder.

Heat the oven to 450°F with a rack in the middle position. In a small bowl, stir together 2 teaspoons of the coriander and 1½ teaspoons salt. Season the chicken on both sides with this mixture; set aside.

In a blender, combine the garlic, tomato paste, chilies, 2 tablespoons of the pomegranate molasses, the remaining 2 teaspoons coriander, ½ cup of the cilantro, ¾ cup of the walnuts, ¾ cup of the broth and 1 teaspoon salt. Puree until smooth, 30 to 45 seconds, scraping the sides of the blender as needed.

In an oven-safe 12-inch skillet over medium-high, heat the oil until barely smoking. Add the chicken skin down in an even layer and cook undisturbed until crisp and golden brown, 5 to 7 minutes. Transfer, skin up, to a large plate. Pour off and discard any fat left in the pan.

Return the skillet to medium-low and add the remaining ½ cup broth, scraping up any browned bits. Add the walnut puree and bring to a simmer over medium. Return the chicken, skin up, to the pan, nestling the pieces into the sauce without submerging the skin. Cook, uncovered, in the oven until the chicken reaches 175°F, or a skewer inserted into the thickest piece meets no resistance, 12 to 15 minutes.

Transfer the chicken to a clean plate and let rest for 5 minutes. Set the skillet over medium and bring the sauce to a simmer. Stir in any accumulated juices from the chicken and cook until the sauce is smooth and thick, about 1 minute. Taste and season with salt.

Spoon the sauce onto a deep serving platter. Nestle the chicken, skin up, in the sauce. Drizzle with the remaining 1 tablespoon pomegranate molasses and sprinkle with the remaining ¼ cup walnuts and remaining ¼ cup cilantro.

Sausage and Mushroom Ragu
with Pappardelle

START TO FINISH:
45 minutes

SERVINGS:
4

2 tablespoons salted butter

5 medium garlic cloves, finely chopped

1 pound portobello mushrooms, stems and gills removed, caps finely chopped

2 large shallots, halved and thinly sliced

1 pound bulk sweet Italian sausage

1 cup dry red wine

1½ cups low-sodium chicken broth

½ teaspoon cinnamon

Kosher salt and ground black pepper

14½-ounce can crushed tomatoes

12 ounces dried pappardelle or tagliatelle pasta

This rich and hearty ragu was inspired by a recipe from Portland, Oregon, chef Vitaly Paley. Ground cinnamon, a hefty pour of red wine and crushed tomatoes build layers of flavor over a base of garlic, portobellos and Italian sausage. For the wine, choose something dry and full-bodied, such as cabernet sauvignon. Serve topped with grated Parmesan cheese.

Don't use Italian sausage links, even if the casings are removed. Bulk sausage is better because its grind tends to be finer than that of link sausage, allowing the meat to break apart more readily during cooking.

In a 12-inch skillet over medium, heat the butter and garlic until the butter has melted and the mixture begins to sizzle. Add the mushrooms and shallots and cook, stirring, until the mushrooms have released their liquid and the shallots have softened, about 5 minutes. Add the sausage and cook, stirring and breaking the meat into small pieces, until no longer pink, 8 to 10 minutes. Pour off and discard excess fat.

Increase to medium-high and add the wine. Bring to a boil and cook, stirring, until the wine has almost completely evaporated, about 5 minutes. Stir in the broth, cinnamon and ¾ teaspoon pepper. Continue to simmer until the broth has reduced by about half, 5 to 6 minutes. Reduce to medium, stir in the tomatoes and simmer until slightly thickened, about 5 minutes. Taste and season with salt and pepper. Cover and set aside.

While the sauce simmers, in a large pot bring 4 quarts of water to a boil. Add the pasta and 2 tablespoons salt and cook until the pasta is al dente. Reserve ½ cup of the cooking water, drain the pasta and return it to the pot. Add the sauce and toss. If needed, toss in a few tablespoons of the reserved cooking water to thin the sauce to coat the pasta.

Vietnamese Meatball Soup
with Watercress (Canh)

START TO FINISH:
40 minutes

SERVINGS:
4

1 pound ground pork

6 scallions, white parts finely chopped, green parts thinly sliced and reserved separately

1 large egg white, lightly beaten

3 tablespoons fish sauce, divided

4 teaspoons finely grated fresh ginger, divided

Kosher salt and ground white pepper

2 tablespoons grapeseed or other neutral oil

1 medium yellow onion, chopped

4 medium garlic cloves, thinly sliced

2 quarts (8 cups) low-sodium chicken broth

1 bunch watercress, cut into 1½-inch lengths (4 cups lightly packed)

2 tablespoons lime juice

This refreshing supper is a take on canh, a type of quick, brothy Vietnamese soup. The soup (pronounced KUN) can be sour, rich with vegetables or loaded with seafood. But whatever variety, the unifying factor is simplicity. Our version stays true to the simplicity, but scales up the ingredients so this can serve as a satisfying meal on its own. Watercress adds a peppery note; look for "live" watercress, which is packaged with its roots attached. It stays fresher longer and is easier to clean. To prep it, trim off and discard the roots, rinse and drain the greens, then cut them into 1½-inch lengths, discarding any stems that are thick or tough. If you prefer, substitute an equal amount of baby spinach for the watercress, but roughly chop the leaves before using. We also liked this soup made with chicken bouillon paste instead of chicken broth; use 2 tablespoons of paste dissolved in 2 quarts of water.

Don't leave the meatballs at room temperature after shaping them. Chilling firms them so they hold together in the simmering broth.

Line a rimmed baking sheet with kitchen parchment and mist with cooking spray. In a medium bowl, combine the pork, scallion whites, egg white, 1 tablespoon of the fish sauce, 2 teaspoons of the ginger, 1¼ teaspoons salt and 1 teaspoon white pepper. Mix with your hands. Lightly moisten your hands with water and form into 20 balls, each about a generous tablespoon. Set on the prepared baking sheet, cover and refrigerate.

In a large Dutch oven over medium, heat the oil until shimmering. Add the onion and cook, stirring, until beginning to soften, about 5 minutes. Add the remaining 2 teaspoons ginger and the garlic, then cook until fragrant, about 30 seconds. Add the broth and bring to a boil over high. Reduce heat to medium-low and simmer, uncovered, until the onion is fully softened, about 10 minutes.

Add the meatballs, then bring to a simmer over medium-high. Reduce heat to maintain the simmer and cook undisturbed until the meatballs are cooked through, 8 to 10 minutes; they should reach 160°F at the center. Off heat, stir in the watercress and remaining 2 tablespoons fish sauce. Let stand until the greens are wilted and tender, about 1 minute. Stir in the lime juice. Taste and season with salt and pepper, then stir in the scallion greens.

Our director of recipe development, Diane Unger, prefers to shape the meatballs for this soup by forming 10 larger meatballs, then cutting them in half with a bench scraper. No need to reshape them.

Curried Chicken and Rice
with Cranberries

START TO FINISH:	SERVINGS:
45 minutes	**4**

3 tablespoons grapeseed or other neutral oil, divided

2 tablespoons finely grated fresh ginger

1 tablespoon curry powder

½ teaspoon ground cardamom

Kosher salt and ground black pepper

1½ pounds boneless, skinless chicken thighs, trimmed and cut into 1-inch pieces

1½ cups basmati rice, rinsed and drained

2½ cups coconut water, divided

4 large shallots, halved lengthwise and thinly sliced

½ cup chopped dried cranberries

2 tablespoons lime juice

2½ cups lightly packed fresh cilantro, roughly chopped

South Asian biryani, a mixture of rice, spices and meat, inspired this aromatic, flavor-packed recipe. We use coconut water to cook the rice; it adds just a touch of richness and a savory-sweet quality that works perfectly with the curry and cardamom. Mango chutney is a great complement for this dish.

Don't stir too much *after adding the rice to the skillet. If allowed to cook undisturbed for a few minutes, the mixture forms a crisp, flavorful crust on the bottom. A wide metal spatula is ideal for scraping up the browned bits.*

In a medium bowl, mix together 1 tablespoon of the oil, the ginger, curry powder, cardamom, 2½ teaspoons salt and 1 teaspoon pepper to form a paste. Transfer 1 tablespoon of the paste to a large saucepan and set aside. Add the chicken to the bowl with the remaining paste and stir to coat. Marinate at room temperature while you cook the rice.

Stir the rice and 1¾ cups of the coconut water into the paste in the saucepan. Bring to a simmer over medium-high. Cover, reduce to low and cook until mostly tender but still slightly firm, about 10 minutes. Remove from the heat, uncover and fluff the rice with a fork. Set aside.

In a 12-inch skillet over medium-high, heat the remaining 2 tablespoons oil until shimmering. Add the shallots and cook, stirring, until golden brown, about 5 minutes. Push the shallots to the side, then add the chicken in an even layer. Cook, without stirring, until golden brown on the bottom, about 3 minutes. Stir the shallots into the chicken, add ¼ cup of the remaining coconut water and, using a metal spatula, scrape up any browned bits. Cook, stirring constantly, until the liquid has evaporated, about 20 seconds.

Add the rice, the remaining ½ cup coconut water and the cranberries. Stir, then cook undisturbed over medium-high until the rice begins to crisp and brown on the bottom, about 3 minutes. Off heat, add the lime juice. Using the spatula, stir to combine while scraping along the bottom to loosen the crust. Stir in 2 cups of the cilantro, then taste and season with salt and pepper. Transfer to a serving platter and sprinkle with the remaining ½ cup cilantro.

Poached Cod

in Tomato-Garlic Broth (Pesce all'Acqua Pazza)

START TO FINISH:
45 minutes

SERVINGS:
4

Four 6- to 8-ounce skinless cod fillets

Kosher salt and ground black pepper

3 tablespoons extra-virgin olive oil

1 teaspoon finely chopped anchovy fillets

4 medium garlic cloves, finely chopped

¼ teaspoon red pepper flakes

1 medium yellow onion, finely chopped

½ cup dry white wine or vermouth

1 pound grape tomatoes, halved

½ cup pitted Kalamata olives, halved

2 tablespoons drained capers

⅓ cup lightly packed torn fresh basil

There are many versions of pesce all'acqua pazza, or "fish in crazy water," but all involve poaching or simmering fish in a tomato broth or sauce. For our version, anchovies, black olives and capers bring bold, punchy flavor to mild-flavored fillets. Though this recipe calls for cod, any firm, meaty, white fish would work. Be sure to have some crusty bread for serving—or even better, toast some baguette slices, then rub them with garlic and brush with olive oil.

Don't worry if the cod at the grocery store is sold as a single fillet. Cut the fillet into as many pieces of a similar thickness as you need for even cooking—it may be as many as five or six—and if some pieces are very thin, fold them in half or thirds to approximate the thickness of the thicker pieces. When cooking the fish, check it frequently for doneness and remove the pieces as they finish.

Season the cod fillets on both sides with salt and pepper. In a 12-inch skillet over medium, heat the oil until shimmering. Add the anchovies and cook, stirring and mashing, until the bits dissolve, about 1 minute. Add the garlic and pepper flakes and cook, stirring, until the garlic begins to brown, 45 to 60 seconds. Add the onion and ½ teaspoon salt, then cover and reduce to medium-low. Cook, stirring, until the onion is softened, 3 to 4 minutes.

Pour in the wine, bring to a simmer over medium-high and cook, uncovered, until the liquid is almost fully evaporated, 1 to 2 minutes. Add the tomatoes and cook, uncovered and stirring occasionally, until they begin to break down, about 3 minutes. Stir in 1 cup water, the olives and capers, then bring to a simmer.

Nestle the fish in a single layer in the sauce and reduce to medium-low. Cover and cook until the centers of the fillets reach 120°F or the flesh flakes easily when cut, 5 to 8 minutes. Use a slotted spatula to transfer them to individual bowls or plates.

Set the skillet over medium-high and cook the sauce, stirring, until slightly thickened, 2 to 3 minutes. Taste and season with salt and pepper. Spoon around the fish, dividing it evenly, then sprinkle with the basil and black pepper.

Frittata

with Pasta, Thyme and Parmesan

START TO FINISH:
45 minutes

SERVINGS:
4

4 ounces spaghetti or bucatini, broken in half

Kosher salt and ground black pepper

8 large eggs

2 ounces shredded white cheddar cheese (½ cup), divided

½ ounce finely grated Parmesan cheese (¼ cup)

½ cup finely chopped fresh flat-leaf parsley

2 teaspoons minced fresh thyme leaves

6 tablespoons extra-virgin olive oil, divided

8 medium garlic cloves, thinly sliced

1 medium leek, white and light green parts thinly sliced

Italians are known to use leftover pasta as a filling for frittatas. In this recipe, we use spaghetti or bucatini (a tubular pasta similar to spaghetti) for a frittata enriched with cheese and seasoned with parsley and thyme. For the best flavor and texture, we used two kinds of cheese: Parmesan for its salty-sweet nuttiness and sharp or extra-sharp white cheddar for its creaminess. Gruyère is a good alternative to cheddar.

Don't forget to rinse the pasta after draining. Rinsing halts the cooking so the pasta won't continue to soften as it waits to go into the skillet. And don't use a conventional skillet. A nonstick coating allows the frittata to slide out of the pan. Make sure the skillet is oven-safe, as the frittata finishes cooking in a 350°F oven.

Heat the oven to 350°F with a rack in the upper-middle position. In a large saucepan, bring 2 quarts of water to boil. Add the pasta and 1 tablespoon salt, then cook until the pasta is al dente. Drain, then rinse under cold water. Spread on a paper towel-lined plate and set aside. In a large bowl, whisk the eggs and ½ teaspoon each salt and pepper. Stir in ¾ cup of the cheddar, the Parmesan, parsley and thyme.

In an oven-safe 10-inch nonstick skillet over medium, heat 3 tablespoons of the oil until shimmering. Add the garlic and cook, stirring constantly, until fragrant, about 30 seconds. Add the leek and ½ teaspoon salt. Cook, stirring, until softened and lightly browned, about 6 minutes. Transfer to another plate and let cool for 2 minutes, then fold into the egg mixture.

Wipe out the skillet, add the remaining 3 tablespoons oil and heat over medium until shimmering. Add the pasta and stir to coat. Pour the egg mixture over the pasta and fold with a silicone spatula. Continue to gently fold and scrape the sides of the pan, allowing the uncooked egg to flow to the sides. Once the eggs begin to thicken and set, after about 1 minute, smooth the top and cook the frittata undisturbed until the bottom is deep golden brown, another 3 minutes. Sprinkle with the remaining ¼ cup cheddar and transfer to the oven. Bake until the eggs are set at the center, 10 to 15 minutes.

Let cool for 5 minutes. Run a silicone spatula around the edge and underneath the frittata to loosen, then slide onto a serving plate and cut into wedges.

Indian Spiced Beef and Peas

(Keema Matar)

START TO FINISH:	SERVINGS:
40 minutes	**4**

14½-ounce can whole peeled tomatoes

2 tablespoons tomato paste

3 tablespoons grapeseed or other neutral oil

1 large red onion, finely chopped

4 medium garlic cloves, finely grated

4 teaspoons finely grated fresh ginger

3 tablespoons garam masala

Kosher salt and ground black pepper

1 pound 90 percent lean ground beef

2 cups frozen peas

¼ cup plain whole-milk yogurt, plus more to serve

⅓ cup chopped fresh cilantro

Keema is often made with ground lamb or mutton and potatoes, but we use ground beef and green peas. The garam masala adds robust spiciness, but not much chili heat. If you'd like the bite of chili in the dish, serve it with hot sauce or minced fresh jalapeños or serranos. Warm naan is the perfect accompaniment to keema, but basmati rice is also good.

Don't stir in the yogurt without first letting the keema matar cool for about 5 minutes. Adding the yogurt while the mixture is piping hot increases the chances the yogurt will curdle.

In a medium bowl, use your hands to crush the tomatoes into small pieces. Stir in ½ cup water and the tomato paste, then set aside. In a 12-inch skillet over medium-high, heat the oil until shimmering. Measure out and reserve ¼ cup of the onion, then add the remainder to the skillet. Cook, stirring, until softened and beginning to brown, about 6 minutes. Add the garlic and ginger and cook, stirring constantly, until fragrant, about 1 minute.

Reduce to low, add the garam masala and ½ teaspoon pepper, then cook, stirring constantly, until fragrant, about 30 seconds. Stir in the tomato mixture. Bring to a simmer over medium and cook, stirring and scraping up any spices, until the mixture is slightly thickened, about 5 minutes.

Break the ground beef into 1- to 2-inch pieces and add to the skillet on top of the tomato mixture, but do not stir. Sprinkle 4 teaspoons salt over the beef, then cover, reduce to medium-low and cook without stirring until the beef is no longer pink on the exterior, about 6 minutes.

Stir in the peas and cook, uncovered and breaking up the bits of beef, until the meat is no longer pink, another 4 minutes. Remove from the heat and let stand, covered, for 5 minutes. Stir in the yogurt. Serve topped with the cilantro, the reserved chopped onion and with additional yogurt.

Pork Chops

with Peanut-Guajillo Sauce

START TO FINISH:	SERVINGS:
40 minutes	**4**

4 large guajillo chilies
(1 ounce), stemmed, seeded
and torn into 2-inch pieces

1 árbol chili, stemmed

2 medium garlic cloves,
smashed and peeled

¾ cup unsalted, dry-roasted
peanuts

2 tablespoons extra-virgin
olive oil

2 teaspoons agave syrup

1 tablespoon lime juice

Kosher salt and ground
black pepper

2 tablespoons fresh oregano,
plus more to serve

1 tablespoon chili powder

4 center-cut, bone-in pork
chops, each about 1 inch thick,
patted dry

2 tablespoons grapeseed or
other neutral oil

Guajillo chilies and roasted peanuts produce a rich, earthy sauce for bone-in pork chops. We especially liked the deep color and bright flavor of guajillo chilies, but New Mexico chilies were good, too. Whichever you use, look for pods that are soft and pliable, an indicator of freshness. The árbol chili supplies the heat; you can omit it if you like, or substitute ¼ to ½ teaspoon red pepper flakes (pepper flakes do not need to be toasted, so add them directly to the blender). You will need a 12-inch oven-safe skillet for this recipe.

Don't use the chilies without first toasting them. *Toasting enhances their flavor and crisps the skins, resulting in a smoother puree.*

Heat the oven to 450°F with a rack in the middle position. In a small saucepan over medium, bring 1½ cups water to a simmer. Cover and reduce to low. In a 12-inch oven-safe skillet over medium-high, toast both varieties of chili and the garlic, pressing with a wide metal spatula and flipping halfway through, until fragrant, about 1 minute. Transfer to the saucepan, pressing to submerge them in the water. Remove the pan from the heat, cover and let stand until the chilies have softened, about 10 minutes. Set the skillet aside.

In a blender, combine the peanuts, olive oil, agave, lime juice and 1 teaspoon salt. Using a slotted spoon, transfer the chilies and garlic to the blender, then add ¾ cup of the soaking liquid. Puree until smooth, 1 to 2 minutes, scraping the sides as needed. If necessary to achieve a smooth texture, add the remaining soaking liquid, 1 tablespoon at a time. Add the oregano and pulse until roughly chopped, about 3 pulses. Transfer to a serving bowl and set aside.

In a small bowl, stir together 1 tablespoon salt, the chili powder and 1 teaspoon pepper. Use to season the pork chops on all sides. In the 12-inch skillet over medium-high, heat the grapeseed oil until barely smoking. Add the chops and cook until deeply browned on the bottoms, about 5 minutes. Using tongs, flip, then transfer the skillet to the oven. Cook until the meat near but not touching the bone reaches 140°F, or is just slightly pink when cut into, 6 to 8 minutes.

Transfer the chops to a wire rack set over a rimmed baking sheet and let rest for 10 minutes. Place the chops on a serving platter and sprinkle with oregano. Serve with the sauce.

Rigatoni with Ricotta-Sage Pesto

START TO FINISH:
40 minutes

SERVINGS:
4

6 tablespoons extra-virgin olive oil

⅓ cup chopped fresh sage

3 cups lightly packed fresh flat-leaf parsley

2 teaspoons grated lemon zest

1 ounce finely grated Parmesan cheese (½ cup), plus more to serve

½ cup whole-milk ricotta cheese

Kosher salt and ground black pepper

12 ounces short, tubular pasta with ridges, such as rigatoni or penne rigate

½ cup walnuts, toasted and coarsely chopped

This ricotta-based pesto gets its pale green hue from an abundance of parsley. Its deep flavor comes from sage that has been gently cooked in olive oil. We used the microwave to make the sage–oil infusion because it does the job quickly. But take care not to overheat the mixture or both the sage and the oil will become bitter. The ideal pasta for this dish is a short, tubular shape with ridges that catch the pesto; we liked rigatoni and penne rigate.

Don't cook the pasta before preparing the pesto, as the pasta must be hot when tossed with the sauce. Also, don't forget to reserve 1 cup of the cooking water before draining the pasta; you'll need to add at least some of it to the pasta and pesto as you toss them together.

In a small microwave-safe bowl, stir together the oil and sage, making sure the sage is completely submerged. Microwave on high just until the oil is hot and the sage is fragrant, about 1 minute, checking after 30 seconds; it should not sizzle. Cool to room temperature.

In a food processor, combine the sage-oil mixture and the parsley. Process until finely chopped, about 15 seconds. Add the lemon zest and Parmesan and process until well incorporated, about 5 quick pulses. Transfer to a large bowl. Stir in the ricotta, 1 teaspoon salt and ¾ teaspoon pepper.

In a large pot, bring 4 quarts of water to a boil. Add the pasta and 2 tablespoons salt and cook until the pasta is al dente. Reserve 1 cup of the cooking water, then drain the pasta.

Add the pasta to the ricotta mixture and toss to coat, then stir in ½ cup of the reserved cooking water. The mixture should be creamy; if needed, adjust with additional cooking water. Serve sprinkled with walnuts and additional Parmesan.

This was inspired by a dish we enjoyed at Sichuan Gourmet in Framingham, Massachusetts. The chicken is not dry-fried, a classic Sichuan technique in which food is fried without batter, thereby drying out and browning it. Instead, it has a thin, crispy cornstarch coating.

Crispy Sichuan-Chili Chicken
(La Zi Ji)

START TO FINISH:	SERVINGS:
45 minutes	**4**

⅓ cup soy sauce or tamari

3 tablespoons unseasoned rice vinegar

2 large egg whites, lightly beaten

4 tablespoons, plus 2 teaspoons white sugar

2 pounds chicken tenders, halved crosswise

1 cup cornstarch

½ cup Sichuan peppercorns, toasted and finely ground, divided

Kosher salt

2 cups peanut oil

6 tablespoons Sichuan chili oil, plus more to serve

4 scallions, thinly sliced

Sweet and salty, crispy and juicy, spicy and numbing, la zi ji—literally, chicken with chilies–checks all the boxes of Sichuan cuisine. In this version, we use chicken tenders and coat them with cornstarch and egg whites so they fry up with a lightly crisp crust. Sichuan peppercorns, toasted and ground, flavor the cornstarch coating and a seasoning salt that's sprinkled onto the chicken at the table. To toast the peppercorns, heat them in a small skillet over medium, shaking the pan frequently, until fragrant, about 2 minutes. Transfer to a bowl and let cool, then finely grind in a spice grinder. To remove any large, fibrous bits, sift the ground pepper through a mesh strainer. Serve with steamed rice and stir-fried or steamed bok choy, broccoli or green beans.

Don't shake off too much of the cornstarch *before frying; the chicken should be fully covered and coated.*

In a large bowl, stir together the soy sauce, vinegar, egg whites and 2 table-spoons of the sugar until the sugar dissolves. Add the chicken and toss to coat. Cover and let stand at room temperature for 15 minutes.

Meanwhile, set a wire rack in a rimmed baking sheet. In a large shallow bowl, stir together 2 tablespoons of the remaining sugar, the cornstarch, 3 table-spoons of the Sichuan pepper and 2 teaspoons salt; set aside. In a small bowl, stir together the remaining 2 teaspoons sugar, the remaining Sichuan pepper and 1 teaspoon salt; set aside.

Drain the chicken in a colander. Add half the chicken to the cornstarch mixture and toss to coat, pressing the pieces into the cornstarch so that it adheres. Transfer the chicken to the prepared rack in a single layer, gently shaking off excess cornstarch. Repeat with the remaining chicken.

Set another wire rack in a rimmed baking sheet. In a large Dutch oven, heat the peanut oil over medium-high to 375°F. Add half of the coated chicken and cook until golden brown on the first sides, 2 to 3 minutes. Using tongs, flip the chicken and cook until golden brown on the second sides, another 2 to 3 minutes. Carefully transfer the chicken to the second rack. Allow the oil to return to 375°F, then repeat with the remaining chicken.

In a small microwave-safe bowl or measuring cup, microwave the chili oil on high until just warm, about 30 seconds. In a large, shallow bowl or 13-by-9-inch baking dish, combine the chicken and scallions. Drizzle with the chili oil, sprinkle with 2 tablespoons of the seasoning salt and toss. Serve with additional chili oil and the remaining seasoning salt.

White Beans

with Sage, Garlic and Fennel

START TO FINISH:	SERVINGS:
45 minutes	**4**

6 tablespoons extra-virgin olive oil, divided

1 large fennel bulb, trimmed, halved, cored and finely chopped

1 medium yellow onion, finely chopped

4 medium garlic cloves, finely chopped

3 tablespoons finely chopped fresh sage, plus 20 whole leaves

¼ teaspoon red pepper flakes

Kosher salt and ground black pepper

14½-ounce can diced tomatoes

Two 15½-ounce cans white beans (see note), 1 can rinsed and drained

Shaved or grated Parmesan cheese, to serve

This is a simplified version of classic Tuscan fagioli all'uccelletto. For complexity, we flavor the beans with three layers of sage—finely chopped leaves, sage-infused oil and crumbled fried leaves. Any variety of canned white beans will work, though Great Northern and navy beans held their shape better than cannellini. This dish is hearty enough to serve as a main—it's excellent with grilled rustic bread—but is also a good accompaniment to roasted chicken or pork.

Don't drain both cans of beans. *The liquid from one of the cans creates a sauce-like consistency that keeps the beans succulent.*

In a large Dutch oven over medium, heat 3 tablespoons of the oil until shimmering. Add the fennel, onion, garlic, chopped sage, red pepper flakes and 1 teaspoon salt. Cover and cook, stirring occasionally, until the vegetables have softened, about 15 minutes.

Stir in the tomatoes and beans. Cook, uncovered, stirring occasionally and adjusting the heat to maintain a gentle simmer, for 10 minutes. Taste and season with salt and pepper.

Meanwhile, line a plate with paper towels. In a 12-inch skillet over medium-high, heat the remaining 3 tablespoons oil until shimmering. Add the whole sage leaves and cook, flipping once, until the edges begin to curl, about 1 minute. Transfer to the prepared plate; reserve the oil.

Transfer the beans to a serving bowl, then drizzle with the sage oil. Coarsely crumble the sage leaves over the beans. Top with Parmesan.

Seared Strip Steak

with Almond-Rosemary Salsa Verde

START TO FINISH:
40 minutes

SERVINGS:
6

1 cup lightly packed fresh
flat-leaf parsley

½ cup sliced almonds, toasted
and cooled, divided

¼ cup drained capers

3 anchovy fillets, rinsed

1 tablespoon minced
fresh rosemary

2 teaspoons finely grated
lemon zest, plus 2 tablespoons
lemon juice

1 medium garlic clove, peeled

Ground black pepper

½ cup extra-virgin olive oil

Kosher salt

Two 14- to 16-ounce strip
steaks (about 1½ inches thick),
halved crosswise and patted
dry

1 tablespoon grapeseed or
other neutral oil

We dress rich and savory seared strip steak with a robust salsa verde spiked with anchovies, capers and a bit of fresh rosemary. Be sure to let the steak rest on a wire rack or the bottom will steam and lose its crisp crust. If your steaks have an extra-generous layer of fat, trim the fat to be no thicker than ¼ inch. We liked the steaks medium-rare; keep in mind that they should be removed from the pan one stage shy of desired doneness, as their temperature continues to rise as they rest. Pair this with something absorbent, such as crusty bread or steamed rice, the better to soak up the beef juices and herb sauce. The sauce can be made up to a day ahead and refrigerated, but allow it to come to room temperature before serving. Both quick and versatile, this sauce also is good served with roasted poultry or fish and makes an excellent sandwich spread.

Don't use steaks *that are thinner than 1½ inches or they will overcook before they brown. Don't forget to rinse the capers and anchovies, which otherwise can make the salsa verde too salty.*

In a food processor, combine the parsley, ¼ cup of the almonds, the capers, anchovies, rosemary, lemon zest, garlic and ½ teaspoon pepper. Process until finely chopped, about 1 minute. With the processor running, slowly add the olive oil and process, scraping the bowl as needed, until smooth. Add the remaining almonds and pulse until coarsely chopped, about 10 pulses. Transfer to a bowl and stir in the lemon juice. Taste and season with salt and pepper.

Season the steaks on both sides with salt and pepper. In a 12-inch skillet over medium-high, heat the grapeseed oil until barely smoking. Add the steaks, reduce to medium and cook until well browned on both sides and 120°F at the center for medium-rare, 10 to 15 minutes.

Transfer the steaks to a wire rack set over a rimmed baking sheet and let rest for 10 minutes. Thinly slice the steaks, arrange on a platter or serving plates and pour over any accumulated juices. Serve with the salsa verde.

Chicken Curry

with Coconut and Tomatoes

START TO FINISH:	SERVINGS:
40 minutes	**4**

½ cup unsweetened shredded coconut, finely chopped

2 tablespoons poppy seeds

2 teaspoons ground fennel seeds

2 teaspoons ground coriander

1 teaspoon ground cardamom

Kosher salt and ground black pepper

2 tablespoons unrefined coconut oil

1½ pounds boneless, skinless chicken thighs, cut into 1½-inch pieces

1 medium yellow onion, finely chopped

2 Fresno chilies, stemmed, halved and thinly sliced

1 tablespoon finely grated fresh ginger

2 pounds firm plum tomatoes, grated (see note)

This dish was inspired by chicken Chettinad, a robustly spiced curry from southern India made with chilies, poppy seeds and coconut. To grate the tomatoes, first cut them in half. Place the cut side of each half against the large holes of a box grater and grate until you're left with just the skin; discard the skin. If you like, garnish the dish with cilantro and serve with lemon wedges and basmati rice or naan.

Don't forget to finely chop *the shredded coconut; its texture can be tough and fibrous if left whole.*

In a 12-inch skillet over medium, combine the coconut, poppy seeds, fennel seeds, coriander, cardamom and 1 teaspoon black pepper. Toast, stirring, until the coconut is golden and the mixture is fragrant, about 4 minutes. Transfer to a small bowl and set aside.

Set the skillet over medium-high, add the coconut oil and heat until shimmering. Add the chicken in an even layer and cook without stirring until light golden brown on the bottom, about 3 minutes. Add the onion and 1½ teaspoons salt, then cook, stirring occasionally, until the onion begins to brown, 4 to 5 minutes.

Stir in the chilies, ginger, ½ cup water, 1¾ cups of the tomatoes and the coconut-spice mixture, scraping up any browned bits. Cover and cook over medium-low, stirring occasionally, until a skewer inserted into a piece of chicken meets no resistance, about 15 minutes. Stir in the remaining tomatoes, then taste and season with salt and pepper.

Soy-Steamed Japanese-Style Rice

with Mushrooms and Tofu

START TO FINISH:	SERVINGS:
45 minutes	**4**

1½ cups Japanese-style short-grain rice, rinsed and drained

5 tablespoons soy sauce, divided

Kosher salt and ground white pepper

14-ounce container extra-firm tofu, drained and cut into ½-inch cubes

8 ounces fresh shiitake mushrooms, stemmed, caps thinly sliced

2 medium carrots, peeled and shredded

4 teaspoons finely grated fresh ginger

2 tablespoons mirin

2 tablespoons unseasoned rice vinegar

3 scallions, thinly sliced on diagonal

This recipe is a simplified take on takikomi gohan, a Japanese dish in which rice is cooked in a flavorful liquid, with additional ingredients scattered over it. Be sure to use Japanese-style short-grain rice; if it's not alongside the other varieties of rice at the grocery store, check the Asian foods aisle. Kokuho Rose and Nishiki are two widely available brands. Tofu makes this vegetarian dish a satisfying main course, but it's also great as a side to meat, poultry or fish.

Don't forget to rinse the rice. Rinsing removes surface starch that would otherwise cause excessive stickiness. When adding the tofu-mushroom mixture, work quickly to minimize the loss of heat and steam.

In a large Dutch oven over medium-high, stir together the rice, 2 cups water and 2 tablespoons of the soy sauce. Bring to a simmer, then cover, reduce to low and cook without stirring for 10 minutes; the rice will have absorbed most of the liquid and be almost tender.

Meanwhile, in a large bowl, toss together the tofu, mushrooms, carrots, ginger, mirin, vinegar, the remaining 3 tablespoons soy sauce, and ¼ teaspoon each salt and white pepper.

After the rice has cooked for 10 minutes, quickly scatter the tofu mixture evenly over the rice; do not stir. Cover and continue to cook over low until the rice is tender, about 5 minutes.

Remove from the heat and let stand, covered, for 10 minutes. Uncover and stir the rice. Taste and season with salt and pepper. Spoon into bowls and sprinkle with the scallions.

Spanish Eggs and Potatoes
(Huevos Rotos)

START TO FINISH:	SERVINGS:
45 minutes	**4**

1½ pounds small potatoes (about 1½ inches in diameter), quartered

2 tablespoons extra-virgin olive oil

1 large yellow onion, finely chopped

2 tablespoons sherry vinegar

Kosher salt and ground black pepper

4 medium garlic cloves, minced

8 ounces Spanish chorizo, quartered lengthwise and sliced ¼ inch thick

1 large poblano chili, stemmed, seeded, quartered lengthwise and cut crosswise into thin strips

6 large eggs

1 scallion, thinly sliced on diagonal

Hot sauce, to serve

In traditional Spanish huevos rotos, or "broken eggs," fried eggs are served on top of fried potatoes, along with serrano ham or chorizo. The yolks are broken so they flow onto the food below, creating a rich sauce. For our simplified version, we precook the potatoes in the microwave, then crisp them in olive oil; the eggs are cooked in the skillet directly on top of the potatoes. Use small red or white potatoes, as their skins add flavor without toughness. If you can find only large potatoes, choose a thin-skinned variety, such as Yukon Gold, and cut them, unpeeled, into ¾-inch pieces.

Don't cook the eggs to the point where the yolks set. The key to this dish is the rich, runny yolk that coats the potatoes.

Place the potatoes in a large microwave-safe bowl. Cover and microwave on high until tender, about 10 minutes, stirring halfway through. Let cool slightly and, using a potato masher, gently crush them until slightly flattened but still in large chunks. If the potatoes are too firm to flatten, cover and microwave on high until tender, then crush.

In a 12-inch nonstick skillet over medium-high, heat the oil until barely smoking. Add the potatoes in an even layer and cook without stirring until crisp on the bottom, about 5 minutes. Stir, redistribute in an even layer and cook until crisp on the bottom, another 5 minutes. Stir in the onion, vinegar and ½ teaspoon salt. Cook, stirring, until the onion has softened, about 5 minutes. Add the garlic, chorizo and chili, then cook, stirring constantly, until fragrant, about 30 seconds. Distribute the mixture in an even layer and reduce to medium-low.

Using the back of a large spoon, make 6 evenly spaced indentations in the potatoes, each about 2 inches in diameter. Crack 1 egg into each, then sprinkle with salt and pepper. Cover and cook until the egg whites are set but the yolks are still runny, 4 to 6 minutes.

Sprinkle the scallion over the top. Using a paring knife, cut a small X in the top of each egg and allow the yolk to flow out. Serve with hot sauce.

Taiwanese Five-Spice Pork
with Rice (Lu Rou Fan)

START TO FINISH:
40 minutes

SERVINGS:
6

1½ pounds ground pork

1 cup low-sodium soy sauce, divided, plus more as needed

¼ cup grapeseed or other neutral oil

12 ounces shallots, halved and thinly sliced

10 medium garlic cloves, minced

1¼ cups dry sherry

⅓ cup packed dark brown sugar

2 tablespoons five-spice powder

1 tablespoon unseasoned rice vinegar

Steamed rice, to serve

3 scallions, thinly sliced

This Taiwanese dish, called lu rou fan, is a one-bowl meal consisting of richly flavored, soy-simmered pork served over steamed rice. Pork belly is traditional, but we found ground pork faster and just as delicious. Hard-cooked eggs are common, but we preferred soft-cooked eggs for their runny yolks. To make soft-cooked eggs, bring 2 cups of water to a simmer in a large saucepan fitted with a steamer basket. Add the eggs, cover and steam over medium for 7 minutes. Transfer the eggs to ice water to stop the cooking, then shell and halve the eggs before serving. We liked serving steamed or stir-fried bok choy or broccoli alongside, a nice balance to the richness of the pork.

Don't use regular soy sauce; when reduced during cooking in this recipe it will become too salty. And don't use cooking sherry, which contains added salt; use an inexpensive dry sherry.

In a medium bowl, mix the pork with ¼ cup of the soy sauce. Cover and refrigerate until needed.

In a large Dutch oven over medium, heat the oil until shimmering. Add the shallots and cook, stirring, until deeply browned, 15 to 20 minutes. Add the garlic and cook, stirring constantly, until the garlic is fragrant and just beginning to brown, about 1 minute.

Add the sherry, sugar, five-spice and remaining ¾ cup soy sauce. Stir until the sugar has dissolved, then increase to high and bring to a boil. Cook, stirring, until reduced and syrupy and a spoon leaves a clear trail, about 5 minutes.

Reduce to low and allow the simmering to subside. Add the pork, breaking it into small pieces. Cook, stirring, until the meat is no longer pink, 5 to 7 minutes. Stir in the vinegar, then taste and add soy sauce, if needed. Spoon steamed rice into individual bowls, top with the pork and sprinkle with the scallions.

Pasta alla Norma

START TO FINISH:
45 minutes

SERVINGS:
4

1-pound eggplant, peeled and cut into ¾-inch cubes

Kosher salt

6 tablespoons extra-virgin olive oil, divided

12 ounces penne rigate or mezze rigatoni pasta

8 medium garlic cloves, finely chopped

½ teaspoon red pepper flakes

2 pints grape tomatoes

2 tablespoons white balsamic vinegar

½ cup lightly packed fresh basil, roughly chopped

2 ounces ricotta salata cheese, shredded (1 cup)

This classic Sicilian dish of eggplant and pasta in tomato sauce is said to take its name from a 19th-century Bellini opera. The eggplant is usually fried before being added to the sauce, but we opted to roast it to concentrate its flavor and condense its porous texture. The eggplant is in the oven for about 30 minutes unattended; use that time to prep the other ingredients, cook the pasta and simmer the tomatoes to make the sauce. Ricotta salata is a firm cheese with a milky, salty flavor. Do not substitute fresh ricotta; a mild feta is a more appropriate substitute.

Don't forget to reserve about ½ cup of the pasta cooking water before draining. You'll need the starchy, salted liquid to help bring together the eggplant, pasta and sauce during the final simmer.

Heat the oven to 475°F with a rack in the upper-middle position. Line a rimmed baking sheet with kitchen parchment. In a large bowl, toss the eggplant with 1½ teaspoons salt and 4 tablespoons of the oil. Spread in a single layer on the prepared baking sheet and roast until browned and tender, 30 to 35 minutes, stirring midway through.

Meanwhile, in a large pot, bring 4 quarts of water to a boil. Stir in the pasta and 2 tablespoons salt; cook until the pasta is al dente. Reserve about ½ cup of the cooking water, then drain the pasta.

While the eggplant roasts and the water heats, in a 12-inch skillet over medium-high, heat the remaining 2 tablespoons oil until shimmering. Add the garlic and pepper flakes and cook, stirring, until fragrant, about 30 seconds. Add the tomatoes and 1½ teaspoons salt, then cover and cook, occasionally shaking the pan, until the tomatoes begin to release their liquid, about 1 minute. Stir in the vinegar, then use the back of a large spoon to crush the tomatoes. Cover, reduce to medium and cook, stirring, until the mixture breaks down into a lightly thickened sauce, 8 to 9 minutes.

Add the drained pasta, eggplant and ¼ cup of the reserved pasta water to the tomatoes. Cook over medium, stirring constantly, until the sauce begins to cling to the pasta, 2 to 3 minutes. Taste and season with salt. Stir in half of the basil and transfer to a serving bowl. Sprinkle with the remaining basil and the ricotta salata.

We tried substituting more affordable walnuts and almonds for the pricey pine nuts, but none of the alternatives had the sweet, buttery flavor and softer chew we wanted. The 1/2 cup called for here might seem indulgent, but it's worth it.

Sumac-Spiced Chicken

(Musakhan)

START TO FINISH:
40 minutes

SERVINGS:
4

2 pounds boneless, skinless chicken thighs, trimmed, cut into 2-inch pieces, patted dry

Kosher salt and ground black pepper

6 tablespoons extra-virgin olive oil, divided

1 large yellow onion, halved and thinly sliced

4 medium garlic cloves, thinly sliced

½ cup toasted pine nuts (¼ cup chopped, ¼ cup whole)

4 tablespoons ground sumac, divided

2 teaspoons sweet paprika

Four 8-inch pita bread rounds

½ cup lightly packed fresh flat-leaf parsley, chopped

Tahini, to serve

Ground sumac is the star of this deeply savory Palestinian chicken dish that is eaten spooned onto soft pita breads. Its tart, citrusy flavor is balanced by the sweetness of the sautéed onion and rich pine nuts. Look for sumac in well-stocked grocery stores, spice shops and Middle Eastern markets; it can also be ordered online.

Don't crowd the chicken in the pot or stir it as it browns; both hinder the caramelization that builds complexity in the dish. Don't skip the tahini for drizzling at the table. Its nutty flavor and richness complement the chicken. And since tahini separates on standing, don't forget to stir it well before serving.

Heat the oven to 250°F with a rack in the middle position. Season the chicken with salt and pepper. In a large Dutch oven over high, heat 1 tablespoon of oil until barely smoking. Add half the chicken in a single layer and cook undisturbed until well browned, about 5 minutes. Transfer to a bowl. Repeat with another 1 tablespoon of oil and the remaining chicken.

Add 2 tablespoons oil to the pot and heat over medium until shimmering. Add the onion and cook, stirring, until softened, about 5 minutes. Add the garlic, chopped pine nuts, 3 tablespoons of the sumac and the paprika. Cook, stirring, until fragrant, about 30 seconds.

Stir in 3 cups water and bring to a simmer. Return the chicken and any accumulated juices to the pot. Cover, reduce to medium-low and cook until a skewer inserted into the chicken meets no resistance, about 10 minutes. While the chicken simmers, wrap the pita tightly in foil and place in the oven to warm.

Using tongs, transfer the chicken to a bowl. Bring the liquid to a simmer over medium-high and cook, stirring, until most of the moisture has evaporated, 10 to 15 minutes. Meanwhile, use 2 forks to shred the chicken into bite-size pieces. When the sauce has reduced, return the chicken to the pot and stir in the ¼ cup whole pine nuts. Taste and season with salt and pepper. Cover to keep warm.

Remove the pita from the oven and unwrap. Brush on both sides with the remaining 2 tablespoons oil and sprinkle with the remaining 1 tablespoon sumac. Cut each pita in half. Stir the parsley into the chicken and transfer to a serving bowl. Serve with the pita and tahini for drizzling.

Cantonese-Style Black Pepper Beef
with Potatoes

START TO FINISH:	SERVINGS:
45 minutes	**4**

3 tablespoons grapeseed
or other neutral oil, divided

3 tablespoons soy sauce

5 medium garlic cloves,
finely grated

4 teaspoons finely grated
fresh ginger

2 teaspoons cornstarch

Kosher salt and coarsely
ground black pepper

1 pound beef sirloin tips or
tri-tip, patted dry and cut into
1-inch pieces

12 ounces Yukon Gold
potatoes, cut into 1-inch pieces

6 ounces sweet potato, peeled
and cut into 1-inch pieces

1 medium yellow onion,
chopped

1 red, yellow or orange bell
pepper, stemmed, seeded and
cut into ½-inch pieces

6 tablespoons finely chopped
fresh cilantro

Stir-fried beef with black pepper sauce is a Cantonese classic. But taking the dish in a westerly direction, we followed the example of London chef Jeremy Pang and threw Yukon Gold and sweet potatoes into the mix. Steaming the potatoes in the microwave saves time and another pot. Be sure to use black pepper that has been coarsely ground so it adds texture to the finished dish.

Don't chop the garlic and ginger. Rather, use a wand-style grater to grate them to a paste so they mix easily into the marinade and readily release their flavors.

In a small bowl, whisk together 1 tablespoon of the oil, the soy sauce, garlic, ginger, cornstarch and 1 teaspoon pepper. In a medium bowl, toss the beef with 2 tablespoons of the soy sauce mixture, then let stand at room temperature for 15 minutes. Whisk 3 tablespoons water into the remaining soy sauce mixture; set aside.

In a medium microwave-safe bowl, toss both types of potatoes with 1 teaspoon salt. Cover and microwave on high until just shy of tender (a fork inserted should meet just a little resistance), about 8 minutes, stirring halfway through. Set the potatoes aside.

In a 12-inch nonstick skillet over medium-high, heat 1 tablespoon of the remaining oil until shimmering. Add the beef in a single layer and cook, turning about every minute, until well-browned and the center of the thickest piece reaches 120°F (for medium-rare), about 4 minutes total. Transfer to a plate and set aside.

In the same skillet, heat the remaining 1 tablespoon oil over medium-high until shimmering. Add the potatoes and cook, stirring occasionally, until tender and browned, about 3 minutes. Add the onion and bell pepper and cook, stirring, until slightly softened, about 4 minutes. Reduce to medium and return the beef and accumulated juices to the skillet, then pour in the reserved soy sauce mixture. Cook, folding gently, until the juices have reduced slightly and the ingredients are well-coated, about 2 minutes. Stir in ¼ teaspoon pepper and 5 tablespoons of the cilantro. Transfer to a platter and sprinkle with the remaining cilantro.

Ginger-Scallion Steamed Fish

START TO FINISH:
45 minutes

SERVINGS:
4

3 tablespoons chopped fresh cilantro, plus ¼ cup whole leaves, divided

6 scallions, 3 minced and 3 thinly sliced on diagonal, divided

2 tablespoons finely grated fresh ginger

6 tablespoons soy sauce, divided

3 tablespoons grapeseed or other neutral oil, divided

6 large green cabbage leaves, plus 2 cups thinly sliced green cabbage

Four 6-ounce skinless cod, haddock or halibut fillets

2 tablespoons unseasoned rice vinegar

2 teaspoons white sugar

1 teaspoon ground white pepper

1 serrano chili, stemmed and sliced into thin rings

1 tablespoon toasted sesame oil

In southern China, cooks have a worry-free method for cooking delicate, flaky white fish to perfection: steaming the fish whole over aromatic-spiked water. The mild heat slowly firms the protein, allowing it to stay moist. We adapted the technique, using skinless cod fillets for convenience and lining our steamer basket with cabbage leaves to mimic the skin of the whole fish. Rubbing the fillets with a seasoning paste of ginger, cilantro, scallions and soy sauce produced deep flavor. We drew on another classic Cantonese technique for a flavorful finish—topping the fillets with raw chopped scallions and serrano chilies, then pouring sizzling-hot oil over them to bring out the flavors and aromas. Because fillets vary in thickness, a general guide is to steam them for about 8 minutes per 1-inch thickness.

Don't let the steaming water reach a full boil. A gentle heat cooks the fish slowly and evenly, helping it stay moist.

In a wide, shallow bowl, stir together the chopped cilantro, minced scallions, ginger, 2 tablespoons of soy sauce and 1 tablespoon of grapeseed oil. Add the fish and coat on all sides. Let stand at room temperature for 10 minutes.

Place a steamer basket in a large Dutch oven. Add enough water to fill the bottom of the pot without reaching the basket. Remove the basket. Cover the pot and bring to a simmer over medium-high. Line the basket with 4 of the cabbage leaves. Place the fish fillets on the leaves, then cover with the remaining 2 leaves. Turn off the heat under the pot, then set the basket in it. Cover and return to a simmer over medium. Steam until the fish flakes easily, 8 to 12 minutes.

Meanwhile, in a small bowl, whisk the remaining 4 tablespoons soy sauce, the rice vinegar, sugar and white pepper. Transfer 3 tablespoons to a medium bowl, add the sliced cabbage and toss. Arrange on a serving platter. Reserve the remaining dressing.

When the fish is ready, discard the cabbage leaves covering it. Use a spatula to set the fillets on the sliced cabbage. Sprinkle with sliced scallions and the serrano.

In a small skillet over medium-high, heat the remaining 2 tablespoons grapeseed oil until barely smoking. Pour the oil over the fillets. Drizzle with sesame oil and sprinkle with the cilantro leaves. Serve with the reserved dressing on the side.

Spanish Ratatouille

(Pisto Manchego)

START TO FINISH:	SERVINGS:
40 minutes	**4**

One 12-ounce zucchini

Two 8-ounce Chinese or Japanese eggplants, peeled and cut into 1-inch cubes

Kosher salt and ground black pepper

8 tablespoons extra-virgin olive oil, divided

1 large yellow onion, quartered lengthwise and thinly sliced

2 medium bell peppers (red or yellow), stemmed, seeded and cut into ½-inch pieces

8 medium garlic cloves, thinly sliced

¾ teaspoon ground cumin

1½ teaspoons dried oregano

14½-ounce can diced tomatoes

¼ cup chopped fresh flat-leaf parsley

2 ounces manchego cheese, shaved

Pisto manchego, Spain's colorful combination of sautéed summer vegetables, is similar to France's ratatouille. As is, it makes a wonderful side. When topped with a poached or fried egg, it's a delicious main course. The flavorful tomato juices make crusty bread almost obligatory, but the dish would also pair wonderfully with rice or a baked potato. If you can't find Japanese or Chinese eggplant, a pound of globe eggplant will do, but you may need to increase the covered cooking time by a few minutes.

Don't use the seedy core of the zucchini, as it turns soft and mushy with cooking.

Trim off the ends of the zucchini, then slice lengthwise into planks, leaving behind and discarding the seedy core. Cut the zucchini planks into ½-inch cubes and set aside. In a medium bowl, toss the eggplant with 1 teaspoon salt and ½ teaspoon pepper.

In a large Dutch oven over medium-high, heat 6 tablespoons of the oil until shimmering. Add the eggplant in an even layer and cook, undisturbed, until golden brown, 3 to 5 minutes. Stir, cover and reduce to medium. Cook, stirring, until tender but not falling apart, another 3 to 5 minutes. Using a slotted spoon, transfer to a paper towel-lined medium bowl and set aside.

To the same pot, add 1 tablespoon of the remaining oil and heat over medium-high until shimmering. Add the zucchini in an even layer and cook undisturbed until well-browned, about 4 minutes. Cook, stirring, until browned on all sides and tender, another 1 to 2 minutes. Using the slotted spoon, transfer to the bowl with the eggplant.

To the same pot, add the remaining 1 tablespoon oil and heat over medium-high until shimmering. Add the onion and ½ teaspoon salt. Cook, stirring, until golden brown, 3 to 5 minutes. Stir in the bell peppers, 1 teaspoon salt and ½ teaspoon pepper. Cover and cook, stirring, until the peppers soften, 3 to 5 minutes. Stir in the garlic, cumin and oregano, then cook until fragrant, about 30 seconds. Stir in the tomatoes with their juice, then cover and simmer over medium until the flavors meld, 5 to 7 minutes.

Reduce to low and stir in the eggplant-zucchini mixture. Cook until heated through, 1 to 2 minutes. Stir in the parsley, then taste and season with salt and pepper. Transfer to a platter and top with manchego.

Ginger-Soy Steak

with Pear-Cucumber Salad

START TO FINISH:
40 minutes

SERVINGS:
4

½ cup soy sauce

2 tablespoons finely grated fresh ginger

2 tablespoons white sugar, divided

1 tablespoon toasted sesame oil

4 medium garlic cloves, finely grated

Kosher salt and ground white pepper

1½ pounds sirloin tips, cut into 2-inch pieces

6 tablespoons unseasoned rice vinegar

1 English cucumber, quartered lengthwise, thinly sliced on the bias

1 firm pear, quartered, cored and thinly sliced crosswise

1 tablespoon toasted sesame seeds

Broiled steak gets big flavor, but remains weeknight-friendly by using sirloin tips cut into quick-cooking chunks that get a 15-minute soak in a ginger-garlic-soy sauce marinade. The rich, beefy steak is balanced with a cool salad of sliced cucumber and pear dressed with a tangy dressing. And no need to hunt for the elusive, perfectly ripe pear. We liked slightly underripe fruit for their firm, crisp texture; any variety will work. Sirloin tips are sometimes labeled steak-house-style steak tips; the cut also goes by "sirloin flap meat." If it isn't available, flat iron steak is a good alternative, but make sure it is about 1 inch thick. To make this recipe gluten-free, substitute an equal amount of tamari for the soy sauce; be sure to double-check that your tamari does not contain gluten.

Don't marinate the steak longer than 30 minutes or it will be too salty.

In a medium bowl, stir together the soy sauce, ginger, 1 tablespoon of the sugar, the sesame oil, garlic and 1 teaspoon pepper until the sugar dissolves. Add the beef and stir to coat. Cover and let sit at room temperature for 15 minutes.

Meanwhile, in a separate medium bowl, combine the vinegar, the remaining 1 tablespoon of sugar and 1 teaspoon salt. Stir in the cucumber and pear. Cover and refrigerate until ready to serve.

Heat the broiler with an oven rack about 4 inches from the heat. Remove the beef from the marinade and pat dry with paper towels. Place the pieces on a wire rack set in a rimmed baking sheet. Cook until 125°F at the center for medium-rare, 7 to 10 minutes, flipping the pieces halfway through. Transfer to a plate and let rest for 10 minutes.

Drain the cucumber mixture and transfer to a large platter, arranging it on one side. Sprinkle with the sesame seeds. Arrange the steak opposite the salad.

Tuscan Soup

with Bread, Beans and Greens (Ribollita)

START TO FINISH:	SERVINGS:
40 minutes	**4**

5 tablespoons extra-virgin olive oil, divided, plus more to serve

1 teaspoon sweet paprika

Kosher salt and ground black pepper

5 ounces crusty white bread, such as ciabatta, cut into 1-inch cubes (4 cups)

1 medium red onion, finely chopped

1 red bell pepper, stemmed, seeded and finely chopped

1 bunch red Swiss chard, stems removed and sliced ¼ inch thick, leaves cut crosswise into 1-inch pieces and reserved separately

6 medium garlic cloves, minced

2 teaspoons fennel seeds

1½ quarts low-sodium chicken broth

Two 15½-ounce cans Great Northern beans, drained and rinsed

In Italian, ribollita means "reboiled," a reference to this dish's origins as peasant food—leftover bread, beans and inexpensive vegetables were thrown into a pot and simmered to make a hearty stew-like soup. For our version, we cut the bread into cubes, toasted it in olive oil and used it as a garnish so the bread retained its texture. We liked red Swiss chard for the color it added, but any variety worked. Great Northern beans held their shape nicely, but feel free to use cannellini instead. If you like, top with grated Parmesan cheese.

Don't discard the chard stems. They're chopped and cooked with the onion and bell pepper for added texture and flavor.

In a medium bowl, stir together 2 tablespoons of the oil, the paprika, and ¾ teaspoon each salt and pepper. Add the bread and toss to coat. Heat a 12-inch skillet over medium, then add the bread and cook, stirring, until crisp and brown, about 7 minutes. Transfer to a plate.

In a large Dutch oven over medium-high, heat the remaining 3 tablespoons of oil until shimmering. Add the onion, bell pepper and chard stems. Cook, stirring, until the vegetables are softened and beginning to brown, about 5 minutes. Stir in the garlic and fennel seeds and cook until fragrant, about 30 seconds.

Add the chard leaves and cook, stirring, until beginning to wilt, 1 to 2 minutes. Add the broth and bring to a simmer, then reduce to medium. Stir in the beans, cover and cook until the chard leaves are tender, 7 to 9 minutes.

Off heat, taste and season with salt and pepper. Ladle into bowls, drizzle with oil and sprinkle with the croutons.

"The softness of the tofu means you can really shovel this down at alarming speeds," says contributing editor, Dawn Yanagihara, who developed this recipe.

Spicy Sichuan Tofu and Pork

(Mapo Dofu)

START TO FINISH:
40 minutes

SERVINGS:
6

4 teaspoons cornstarch

2 tablespoons chili oil

1 tablespoon grapeseed or other neutral oil

2 tablespoons finely grated fresh ginger

8 medium garlic cloves, finely grated

6 scallions, white and light green parts minced, dark green tops thinly sliced

1 tablespoon Sichuan peppercorns, finely ground

12 ounces ground pork

3 tablespoons chili-bean sauce (toban djan, see note)

2 tablespoons oyster sauce

Two 14-ounce containers silken tofu, drained and cut into rough ¾-inch cubes

This is our take on the Sichuan classic mapo dofu, a braise of tofu and ground pork in a sauce flavored with chili oil and tingling Sichuan peppercorns. Toban djan, a fermented chili-bean paste, supplies much of the rich, savory flavor here; it's sold in jars in Asian markets. If you can't find it, substitute 2 tablespoons white miso mixed with 4 teaspoons chili-garlic sauce and 2 teaspoons soy sauce. You can tone down the heat by omitting the chili oil and using a total of 3 tablespoons peanut oil, but don't cut back on the toban djan. Serve this dish with steamed rice. Leftovers taste even better, though the tofu will release water, slightly thinning the sauce.

Don't use chili-sesame oil or sesame oil infused with chili. The sesame flavor will overpower the dish. Don't forget to drain off the excess water from the tofu before adding it to the sauce.

In a small bowl, stir together the cornstarch and 1 tablespoon water. In a 12-inch nonstick skillet over medium-high, heat the chili oil and grapeseed oil until shimmering. Add the ginger, garlic, minced scallions and Sichuan peppercorns. Cook, stirring, until the aroma of the garlic and ginger has mellowed slightly but the mixture has not browned, about 2 minutes.

Add the pork and cook, breaking it into small bits, until the pork is no longer pink, 4 to 5 minutes. Stir in the chili-bean sauce. Add 1¾ cups water and scrape the bottom of the pan to loosen any browned bits. Stir in the oyster sauce, bring to a simmer and cook, stirring occasionally, until the flavors meld, about 5 minutes.

Stir the cornstarch mixture to recombine. While stirring the pork mixture, pour in the cornstarch mixture. Return to a simmer, stirring constantly, and cook until thickened, about 1 minute. Pour off and discard any water released by the tofu, then add the tofu and half of the sliced scallions. Cook until the tofu is heated through, 3 to 5 minutes. Sprinkle with the remaining sliced scallions.

Whole-Wheat Penne

with Broccolini and Chèvre

START TO FINISH:	SERVINGS:
40 minutes	**4**

12 ounces whole-wheat penne rigate

Kosher salt and ground black pepper

4 ounces chèvre (fresh goat cheese), room temperature

8 tablespoons extra-virgin olive oil, divided

¾ cup panko breadcrumbs

1 tablespoon grated lemon zest, plus lemon wedges, to serve

1 medium yellow onion, finely chopped

8 medium garlic cloves, minced

6 anchovy fillets, minced

1 teaspoon red pepper flakes

12 to 16 ounces Broccolini, trimmed, large stalks halved lengthwise, cut into 1-inch pieces

This combination of pasta and Broccolini is tied together with a blend of tangy fresh goat cheese and fruity extra-virgin olive oil for a light but creamy sauce. Olive oil doesn't just add flavor, it also helps the cheese melt smoothly. Lemony toasted breadcrumbs add a pleasing and crunchy contrast as well as a bright flavor accent. If you can't find Broccolini, sometimes called "baby broccoli," substitute an equal weight of broccoli florets.

Don't use cold goat cheese; it needs to be room temperature to combine with the oil. And don't boil the pasta until al dente; it should still be very firm when drained, as it will continue cooking in the skillet with the Broccolini.

In a large pot, bring 4 quarts of water to a boil. Stir in the pasta and 2 tablespoons salt, then boil until barely cooked and still quite firm. Reserve 2 cups of the cooking water, then drain and set aside.

Meanwhile, in a small bowl, use a fork to mix the goat cheese, 5 tablespoons of the oil, and ½ teaspoon each salt and pepper. Set aside. In a 12-inch nonstick skillet over medium, combine 1 tablespoon of the remaining oil and the panko. Cook, stirring, until light golden brown, 6 to 8 minutes. Stir in ½ teaspoon each salt and pepper, then transfer to a small bowl. Let cool, then stir in the lemon zest. Set aside.

Return the skillet to medium and heat the remaining 2 tablespoons oil until shimmering. Add the onion and cook, stirring, until beginning to brown, about 5 minutes. Stir in the garlic, anchovies and pepper flakes; cook until fragrant, about 30 seconds. Stir in the Broccolini and ¼ cup of the reserved pasta cooking water. Cover and cook until the Broccolini turns bright green, 30 to 60 seconds. Add the cooked pasta and 1 cup of the reserved pasta water. Cook, stirring, until al dente and the Broccolini is crisp-tender, 3 to 4 minutes.

Off heat, add the goat cheese mixture and ⅓ cup of the remaining reserved pasta cooking water. Stir until the pasta is evenly coated, adding more pasta water as needed. Taste and season with salt and pepper. Transfer to a serving platter and sprinkle with the panko mixture. Serve with lemon wedges.

Shrimp with Feta Cheese

(Garides Saganaki)

START TO FINISH:
45 minutes

SERVINGS:
4

3 tablespoons extra-virgin olive oil, divided

1¼ pounds jumbo shrimp, peeled, deveined, tails removed, patted dry

4 medium garlic cloves, finely chopped

4 teaspoons fennel seeds, finely ground

¼ teaspoon red pepper flakes

⅓ cup dry white wine

1½ pounds small tomatoes, such as Campari, chopped, plus ¼ cup finely diced

⅓ cup pitted Kalamata olives, chopped

2 tablespoons plus 2 teaspoons chopped fresh oregano

Kosher salt and ground black pepper

4 ounces feta cheese, coarsely crumbled (1 cup)

¼ cup chopped Peppadew peppers (optional)

This classic Greek dish pairs plump, sweet shrimp with briny feta cheese. We added chopped Kalamata olives for added savoriness, as well as ground fennel for a hint of anise. Our preferred tomatoes for this recipe are Campari (or cocktail) tomatoes, as they tend to be sweet and flavorful year-round; they're larger than cherry tomatoes but smaller than standard round tomatoes and usually sold on the vine in containers. We tried cherry and grape tomatoes, but found their skins to be tough and unpleasant in the finished sauce. Chopped Peppadew peppers are an unconventional ingredient, but their mild, sweet heat makes them a welcome addition. Serve with crusty bread to sop up the sauce.

Don't use pre-crumbled feta. The cheese plays a prominent role in this dish, so good-quality feta sold in blocks and packed in brine is important.

In a 12-inch nonstick skillet over medium-high, heat 1 tablespoon of the oil until shimmering. Add half the shrimp in an even layer and cook without disturbing until deep golden brown on the bottoms, 1 to 2 minutes. Stir and cook until pink and opaque on all sides, another 20 to 30 seconds. Transfer to a medium bowl. Repeat with 1 tablespoon of the remaining oil and the remaining shrimp. Set aside.

Add the remaining 1 tablespoon oil to the pan and heat over medium-high until shimmering. Add the garlic, fennel and red pepper flakes and cook, stirring constantly, until the garlic is light golden brown, about 20 seconds. Add the wine and cook, stirring, until the liquid is almost evaporated, 30 to 60 seconds. Add the chopped tomatoes, olives and 1½ teaspoons salt. Cook, stirring, until the tomatoes have broken down into a sauce, 6 to 7 minutes.

Remove the pan from heat. Stir in 2 tablespoons of the oregano, then taste and season with salt and pepper. Return the shrimp to the skillet, along with any accumulated juices. Cover and let stand until the shrimp are heated through, about 1 minute. Transfer to a serving dish. Sprinkle with the feta, finely diced tomatoes, the Peppadews (if using) and the remaining 2 teaspoons oregano.

Cuban Picadillo

START TO FINISH:
45 minutes

SERVINGS:
4

2 tablespoons extra-virgin olive oil

2 medium yellow onions, finely chopped

Kosher salt and ground black pepper

6 medium garlic cloves, minced

1½ pounds 90 percent lean ground beef

½ cup raisins, chopped

1 tablespoon cumin seeds

1 teaspoon dried oregano

2 tablespoons tomato paste

½ cup pimiento-stuffed green olives, roughly chopped, plus 3 tablespoons olive brine

½ cup minced fresh cilantro

3 plum tomatoes, cored, seeded and finely chopped

Picadillo—a ground beef dish popular in Cuba, the Caribbean and Latin America—combines tangy, sweet and salty flavors. There are many variations, but the essentials are a stew of ground meat and tomatoes with raisins for sweetness and chopped olives for a balancing touch of brine. For an optional, finishing touch, chopped hard-cooked egg makes an attractive and delicious garnish. Serve the picadillo with white rice or fried potatoes or on a mound of french fries. Or serve with a stack of warm corn tortillas and use it as a taco filling.

Don't use 80 or 85 percent lean ground beef or the picadillo may end up slick and greasy.

In a 12-inch nonstick skillet over medium-high, heat the oil until shimmering. Add the onions and ½ teaspoon salt. Cook, stirring, until beginning to brown, about 5 minutes. Add the garlic and cook until fragrant, about 30 seconds. Add the beef and cook, breaking it up, until no pink remains, 5 to 7 minutes.

Stir in the raisins, cumin, oregano, tomato paste and 1½ teaspoons salt, then cook until fragrant, about 30 seconds. Stir in ¾ cup water and bring to a simmer. Reduce to medium and cook, stirring occasionally, until most of the water has evaporated, 7 to 9 minutes.

Stir in the olives and cook until heated through, about 1 minute. Off heat, stir in the brine, cilantro and tomatoes. Taste and season with salt and pepper.

Steamed Chicken and Shiitakes
with Soy-Sake Sauce

START TO FINISH:	SERVINGS:
40 minutes	**4**

¼ cup sake

3 tablespoons soy sauce

2 tablespoons unseasoned rice vinegar

1 tablespoon toasted sesame oil

1 tablespoon finely grated fresh ginger

1 tablespoon chili-garlic sauce

1½ pounds boneless skinless chicken thighs, trimmed and patted dry

Kosher salt

6 ounces shiitake mushrooms, stems removed, caps sliced ¼ inch thick

3 radishes, halved and thinly sliced

3 scallions, thinly sliced on diagonal

Steaming is a simple cooking method that results in clean, pure flavors. In this recipe, we layer sliced fresh shiitake mushrooms in a steamer basket under briefly marinated chicken thighs. The mushrooms soak up the cooking juices, becoming deeply flavorful. Drizzling the chicken with a few tablespoons of sauce after steaming but before slicing allows the sake-soy mixture to better permeate the meat. Serve with steamed rice.

Don't steam the chicken over high heat. Gentle steaming over medium heat keeps the meat tender and succulent.

In a medium bowl, combine the sake, soy sauce, vinegar, oil, ginger and chili-garlic sauce. Set aside ⅓ cup in a small bowl. Season the chicken generously on both sides with salt, then toss in the bowl with the remaining sake-soy mixture. Marinate at room temperature for 15 minutes.

Meanwhile, in a covered large Dutch oven over medium-high, bring 1 inch of water to a simmer. Arrange the mushrooms in an even layer in a steamer basket, then set the chicken thighs in an even layer over them. Turn off the heat under the pot, then set the basket in it. Cover and return to a simmer over medium and cook until the thickest part of the chicken registers 170°F and a skewer inserted into the thickest part of the chicken meets no resistance, 10 to 12 minutes.

Transfer the chicken and mushrooms to a serving platter. Whisk 2 tablespoons of the steaming liquid into the reserved sake-soy mixture. Drizzle 3 tablespoons of the mixture over the chicken and mushrooms, tent with foil and let rest for 5 minutes.

Cut the chicken crosswise into ¼-inch slices and return to the platter. Sprinkle with the radishes and scallions and serve with the remaining sauce.

Shrimp with Tamarind
and Cilantro

START TO FINISH:
40 minutes

SERVINGS:
4

3 tablespoons tamarind paste

2 tablespoons grapeseed or other neutral oil

1½ pounds extra-large shrimp, peeled, deveined, tails removed and patted dry

1 medium yellow onion, chopped

Kosher salt and ground black pepper

2 tablespoons salted butter

1 cup finely chopped fresh cilantro, divided

3 tablespoons tomato paste

2 teaspoons ground coriander

¾ teaspoon ground turmeric

Tart tamarind and a generous amount of cilantro complement the natural sweetness of shrimp, while coriander and turmeric add fragrance and complexity in this recipe inspired by a Persian seafood stew called galieh mahi. Tamarind paste, available in Asian markets, is sold in dense blocks packed in plastic; it should be soft and pliable, not hard and brittle. For this dish, we liked extra-large shrimp, but slightly smaller or larger shrimp will work, too. If the shrimp are smaller, brown them for less time; if larger, leave them in the skillet a bit longer.

Don't sear all the shrimp at once. It's important to work in batches and distribute them in an even layer in the pot so they brown without overcooking. Also, don't sear both sides of the shrimp; they finish cooking in the sauce.

In a 2-cup glass measuring cup or small microwave-safe bowl, combine the tamarind paste and ½ cup of water. Microwave on high until warm, about 1 minute, then whisk to combine. Let stand for 10 minutes, then pour the mixture through a fine mesh strainer set over a bowl and press on the solids to extract as much liquid as possible; discard the solids. You should have about ⅓ cup of strained tamarind.

In a large Dutch oven over medium-high, heat the oil until barely smoking. Add half the shrimp in an even layer and cook without stirring until lightly golden on the bottom, about 45 seconds. Using a slotted spoon, transfer to a plate. Repeat with the remaining shrimp; set aside.

In the same pot over medium-low, add the onion and cook, stirring, until softened and lightly golden, 6 to 8 minutes. Stir in 2 teaspoons salt and the butter, then add ½ cup of the cilantro. Cook, stirring frequently, until the cilantro has darkened and the onion is deep golden brown, 5 to 6 minutes.

Add the tamarind and tomato paste and cook, stirring constantly, until slightly darkened, about 1 minute. Stir in the coriander, turmeric, ¾ teaspoon pepper and 2 cups water. Bring to a simmer over medium and cook, stirring, until the sauce has slightly thickened, about 10 minutes.

Add the shrimp and stir to coat with the sauce. Cook, stirring, until the shrimp are opaque throughout, 1 to 2 minutes. Off heat, stir in ¼ cup of the remaining cilantro, then taste and season with salt. Transfer to a serving dish and sprinkle with a few tablespoons of the remaining cilantro or more as desired.

Spice-Crusted Steak

with Mashed Chickpeas

START TO FINISH:
45 minutes

SERVINGS:
4

1½ pounds flat iron steak, cut into 3 or 4 pieces

¼ cup soy sauce

2 tablespoons cumin seeds, coarsely ground

2 tablespoons fennel seeds, coarsely ground

Kosher salt and ground black pepper

Two 15½-ounce cans chickpeas, drained

6 tablespoons extra-virgin olive oil, divided, plus extra to serve

1 bunch scallions, thinly sliced

2 teaspoons grated lemon zest, plus ¼ cup lemon juice, plus lemon wedges to serve

1 cup lightly packed fresh flat-leaf parsley

A warm salad of roughly crushed chickpeas and scallions provides the perfect foil for our cumin- and fennel-crusted flat iron steak. We were inspired by a similar dish from Moro, the London restaurant of chefs Sam and Sam Clark. They serve their steak over hummus, but our simpler approach keeps the dish weeknight ready. When grinding the cumin and fennel seeds, be sure to keep them coarse—don't pulverize them to a powder. We liked the flavor and texture of flat iron steak, but if you can't find this cut, hanger steak or sirloin tips (also called flap meat) are good substitutions. Add a dollop of plain yogurt and warmed pita bread to round out the meal.

Don't skip the soy sauce marinade for the steak; it gives the meat a deep, savory flavor. But don't marinate for longer than 20 minutes or it will be too salty.

In a shallow baking dish, combine the steak and soy sauce, turning to coat. Set aside for 15 to 20 minutes. Meanwhile, in a small bowl combine the cumin, fennel and 2 teaspoons each salt and pepper.

Remove the steak from the baking dish and pat dry with paper towels. Use all but 1 tablespoon of the seasoning mixture to coat the steak all over. Set aside. In a large bowl, use a potato masher to roughly mash about ¾ of the chickpeas; stir in the remaining whole chickpeas.

In a 12-inch nonstick skillet over medium-high, heat 2 tablespoons of the oil until barely smoking. Add the chickpeas and cook, stirring occasionally, until heated through, 2 to 3 minutes. Stir in half of the scallions, another 2 tablespoons of the oil and the lemon juice. Off heat, stir in the lemon zest and parsley. Taste and season with salt and pepper, then transfer to a platter, mounding it to one side.

Wipe out the skillet. Heat the remaining 2 tablespoons oil over medium-high until barely smoking. Add the steak and cook until well browned on both sides and 120°F at the center for rare, 125°F for medium rare, 6 to 10 minutes, flipping halfway through. Transfer to a wire rack set over a rimmed baking sheet and let rest for 10 minutes.

Thinly slice the steak against the grain, then arrange the slices on the platter next to the mashed chickpeas. Pour over any accumulated juices and sprinkle with the remaining scallions and reserved spice mixture. Drizzle with oil and serve with lemon wedges.

In the Vietnamese kitchen, nuoc mau is a dark, smoky caramel used to flavor dishes much like this one. The savory-sweet braising liquid for the chicken is also great with fish.

Caramel-Braised Chicken

with Ginger and Lime

START TO FINISH:
45 minutes

SERVINGS:
4

½ cup plus 1 tablespoon coconut water, divided

¼ cup white sugar

3 tablespoons fish sauce

2 medium shallots, peeled, halved and thinly sliced (½ cup)

2-inch piece fresh ginger, peeled and cut into ⅛-inch matchsticks (⅓ cup)

2 pounds boneless, skinless chicken thighs, trimmed, cut into 1½-inch chunks

¼ cup chopped fresh cilantro

1 small jalapeño chili, stemmed and sliced into thin rings

1 tablespoon grated lime zest, plus 1 tablespoon lime juice

Lime wedges, to serve

Vietnamese caramel chicken is a dish with multiple layers of flavor: salty, sweet, smoky, bitter and meaty. For our take, we used coconut water as the cooking liquid. It added a subtle salty-sweet richness that brought even more complexity to the dish. The generous amount of ginger, cut into matchsticks, mellows and softens as it cooks, and it adds a brightness that perks up the deeper flavors.

Don't get distracted once you begin cooking the caramel. Have the fish sauce measured out so that when the caramel turns mahogany it can be added immediately to stop the cooking.

In a 12-inch skillet over medium-high, combine the 1 tablespoon coconut water and the sugar. Bring to a boil and cook, stirring occasionally, until the mixture turns golden at the edges, about 3 minutes. Reduce to medium and continue to cook, swirling the pan but without stirring, until the caramel is mahogany in color and smokes lightly, another 4 to 5 minutes.

Off heat, add the fish sauce and stir; the mixture will steam and bubble vigorously. Set the pan over medium, pour in the remaining ½ cup coconut water and stir until fully incorporated. Add the shallots and ginger and bring to a simmer, then cover, reduce to low and cook for 5 minutes.

Stir in the chicken. Cover and cook over medium, stirring once or twice, until a skewer inserted into the chicken meets no resistance, 15 to 20 minutes, adjusting the heat as needed to maintain a steady simmer. Uncover, increase to medium-high and simmer vigorously (the sauce will form large bubbles), stirring occasionally, until the chicken is glazed and the sauce is syrupy, about 8 minutes.

Off heat, stir in half of the cilantro, the jalapeño, lime zest and lime juice. Top with the remaining cilantro and serve with steamed rice and lime wedges.

Linguini with Spiced Beef
and Feta

START TO FINISH:
45 minutes

SERVINGS:
4

1½ pounds 90 percent lean ground beef

2 tablespoons ground cumin

2 teaspoons sweet paprika

2 teaspoons cinnamon

Kosher salt and ground black pepper

2 large yellow onions, finely chopped

8 medium garlic cloves, minced

28-ounce can whole peeled tomatoes, crushed by hand

12 ounces linguini

8 ounces feta cheese, crumbled

1 cup chopped fresh mint

This savory pasta dish was inspired by kawarma, the spicy ground beef topping spooned over hummus in Israel. We decided it would work equally well over noodles with just a few adjustments. The result is a ground beef sauce seasoned with fragrant spices and generous amounts of onion and garlic, all lightened with a good dose of mint. Rather than sprinkle the feta as a garnish, we toss the just-cooked noodles with most of the cheese so it melts and coats the strands. If you like, you could serve the sauce with warmed flatbread instead of noodles.

Don't use ground beef *fattier than 90 percent lean or the sauce will be greasy.*

In a medium bowl, combine the beef, cumin, paprika, cinnamon, 1 teaspoon each salt and pepper and ¼ cup water. Mix with your hands.

Add the beef mixture, onions and garlic to a 12-inch skillet. Set over medium-high and cook, stirring and breaking up the meat, until the onion has softened and the beef is no longer pink, 8 to 10 minutes. Stir in the tomatoes with juices and bring to a simmer, then reduce to medium and cook, stirring, until most of the liquid has evaporated and the sauce has thickened, 10 to 15 minutes.

Meanwhile, in a large pot, bring 4 quarts water to a boil. Stir in the pasta and 2 tablespoons salt; cook until the pasta is al dente. Reserve about 1 cup of the cooking water, then drain the pasta. Return the pasta to the pot. Add about ¾ of the feta and toss. Taste and season with salt and pepper, then transfer to a platter.

Stir the mint into the sauce, then taste and season with salt and pepper. Pour the sauce over the pasta and sprinkle with the remaining feta.

Cashew-Coconut Meatballs

with Creamy Spiced Tomato Sauce

START TO FINISH:
45 minutes (30 minutes active)

SERVINGS:
4

½ cup unsweetened shredded coconut

3 tablespoons grapeseed or other neutral oil, divided

1 large yellow onion, finely chopped

5 medium garlic cloves, minced

1¼ cups unsalted roasted cashews

2 cups lightly packed fresh cilantro, divided

1 pound 85 percent lean ground beef

¾ cup coconut milk, divided

1 large egg plus 1 large egg yolk, beaten

2 teaspoons garam masala, divided

Kosher salt and ground black pepper

14½-ounce can crushed tomatoes

Tender and flavorful, these meatballs are a take on southern Indian kofta, balancing the sharp, green flavor of fresh cilantro with warm spices. Roasted cashews and toasted coconut add richness and texture. We amplified those flavors by using coconut milk in the meatball mixture, as well as in the creamy, spicy tomato sauce in which they are simmered. The meatballs can be shaped up to an hour in advance and refrigerated until ready to cook. Steamed basmati rice or warmed flatbreads are ideal accompaniments.

Don't skip the step of toasting the shredded coconut. Toasting brought out its nuttiness and subtle sweetness.

In a 12-inch skillet over medium, toast the coconut, stirring frequently, until golden, about 2 minutes. Transfer to a large bowl and set aside. In the same skillet over medium, heat 2 tablespoons of the oil until shimmering. Add the onion and garlic and cook, stirring, until lightly golden, 7 to 9 minutes. Transfer to a small plate and set aside, reserving the skillet.

In a food processor, pulse the cashews until finely ground, about 10 pulses. Set aside ¼ cup. To the remaining cashews, add 1½ cups of the cilantro and process until finely chopped, about 30 seconds. Transfer to the bowl with the toasted coconut, then add ⅓ cup of the cooked onion mixture, the beef, ¼ cup coconut milk, the eggs, 1 teaspoon of garam masala, 2 teaspoons of salt and ½ teaspoon of pepper. Mix well, then shape into sixteen 2-inch meatballs and place on a large plate. Cover with plastic wrap and refrigerate for 10 minutes.

In the same skillet over medium, heat the remaining 1 tablespoon oil until shimmering. Add the meatballs in a single layer and cook until browned on the bottoms, 2 to 3 minutes. Add the remaining onion mixture, the remaining ½ cup coconut milk, the remaining 1 teaspoon garam masala, 1 teaspoon salt, ¼ teaspoon pepper and the tomatoes. Stir gently, loosening the meatballs from the pan. Bring to a boil over medium-high. Cover, reduce to medium-low and cook at a gentle simmer until cooked through, 12 to 15 minutes.

Transfer to a serving platter and sprinkle with the remaining ½ cup cilantro and the reserved cashews.

Chicken Cutlets
with Mango-Tomato Sauce

START TO FINISH:
45 minutes

SERVINGS:
4

12- to 14-ounce ripe mango, peeled, pitted and finely diced (about 1 cup)

1 teaspoon honey

2 tablespoons lime juice, divided

Four 5- to 6-ounce chicken breast cutlets, pounded to an even ¼-inch thickness

Kosher salt and ground black pepper

2½ teaspoons garam masala, divided

3 tablespoons grapeseed or other neutral oil

1 medium yellow onion, finely chopped

1 tablespoon finely grated fresh ginger

1 jalapeño chili, stemmed and minced

1½ cups cherry or grape tomatoes, halved

⅓ cup chopped fresh cilantro

Curry spices and a lightly spicy mango-tomato relish infuse these quick-cooking chicken cutlets. We speed up the process by pounding the cutlets ¼ inch thick. We then seasoned them with garam masala, an aromatic Indian spice blend, before sautéing. The finished cutlets are paired with a mix of mangoes and cherry tomatoes brightened with ginger and jalapeño. If you prefer milder heat, remove the jalapeño seeds before mincing. If you can't find cutlets, prepare your own from boneless, skinless chicken breasts that weigh about 7 ounces each. Remove the tenderloin from the breast using kitchen shears, saving for another use, such as chicken fingers. Use a sharp knife or the shears to trim away any fat. Place on a cutting board and lay a sheet of plastic wrap on top. Use a meat mallet or small, heavy skillet to gently but firmly pound the chicken to the proper thickness.

Don't pound the cutlets *if they're ¼ inch thick right out of the package. They can be used as they are.*

In a small bowl, toss the mango with the honey and 1 tablespoon of the lime juice. Set aside. Season the chicken on both sides with 1½ teaspoons salt and 1½ teaspoons of the garam masala.

In a 12-inch skillet over medium-high, heat the oil until shimmering. Add the chicken in a single layer and cook until golden, 2 to 3 minutes. Flip the cutlets and cook until the second sides are golden, another 2 to 3 minutes. Transfer to a platter and tent with foil to keep warm.

Pour off and discard all but 1 tablespoon of fat from the skillet and return the pan to medium. Add the onion, ½ teaspoon salt, the remaining 1 teaspoon garam masala and 2 tablespoons water. Cook, stirring occasionally and scraping up any browned bits, until the onion has softened, about 4 minutes. Add the ginger and jalapeño, then cook, stirring constantly, until the moisture has evaporated and the mixture begins to stick to the pan, about 1 minute.

Stir in the tomatoes and the mango and its juices. Cover and cook over medium-low, stirring occasionally, until the mango has softened, about 3 minutes. Off heat, stir in the remaining 1 tablespoon lime juice and the cilantro. Taste and season with salt and pepper. Spoon the mango-tomato mixture over the cutlets.

Tibetan Curried Noodles
with Beef and Cabbage

START TO FINISH:	SERVINGS:
40 minutes	**4**

3 tablespoons soy sauce, divided

2 tablespoons white sugar, divided

12-ounce flank steak

6 ounces dried medium-thick Asian wheat noodles (see note)

2 tablespoons grapeseed or other neutral oil, divided

8 scallions, whites finely chopped, greens sliced, reserved separately

8 medium garlic cloves, minced

1 tablespoon finely grated fresh ginger

1 tablespoon curry powder

1½ pounds napa cabbage, cut lengthwise into 3-inch wedges, then crosswise into thin strips (about 7 cups)

Kosher salt

Lime wedges, to serve

Tibet shares much of its border with India and Nepal, and centuries of trade have made curry blends an important element in Tibetan cuisine. Use dried Asian wheat noodles about ⅛ inch in diameter; the noodles must have enough heft to stand up to the beef and cabbage. Japanese udon is a good, widely available option, but don't use Italian pasta—it didn't give us the right texture for the dish. To use your time efficiently, season the steak first and let it stand while prepping the rest of the ingredients.

Don't forget to rinse the cooked and drained noodles under running cold water. This stops the cooking, preventing them from turning mushy, and washes away excess starch.

In a medium bowl, stir together 2 tablespoons of the soy sauce and 1 tablespoon of the sugar. Cut the steak in half with the grain, then cut each piece across the grain into ¼-inch slices. Add the steak to the soy mixture and toss. Marinate at room temperature for 15 minutes.

In a large pot bring 4 quarts water to a boil. Add the noodles and cook until tender. Drain and rinse under cold water until cool. Set aside.

In a 12-inch nonstick skillet over medium-high, heat 1 tablespoon of the oil until shimmering. Add the steak and any accumulated juices and cook, stirring constantly, until no longer pink, about 2 minutes. Transfer to a small bowl.

To the same skillet, add the remaining 1 tablespoon oil and heat over medium until shimmering. Add the scallion whites, garlic, ginger and curry powder. Cook, stirring constantly, until fragrant, about 30 seconds. Stir in the cabbage, the remaining 1 tablespoon soy sauce, the remaining 1 tablespoon sugar and ½ teaspoon salt. Cook, stirring and scraping up any browned bits, until the thick rib pieces of the cabbage are crisp-tender, about 4 minutes.

Add the noodles and toss. Add the steak and any accumulated juices and toss again. Off heat, taste and season with salt, then stir in the scallion greens. Serve with lime wedges.

Vietnamese Turmeric Fish

with Wilted Herbs and Peanuts

START TO FINISH:	SERVINGS:
40 minutes	**4**

2 tablespoons white sugar

¼ cup lime juice

2 tablespoons fish sauce

1½ pounds tilapia fillets (about ½ inch thick), cut into 2-inch pieces, patted dry

Kosher salt and ground black pepper

⅓ cup cornstarch

1½ teaspoons turmeric

6 tablespoons grapeseed or other neutral oil, divided

6 scallions, thinly sliced

¾ cup dry-roasted salted peanuts, roughly chopped

1 cup chopped fresh cilantro

½ cup chopped fresh dill

This dish draws inspiration from a Hanoi restaurant, Cha Ca La Vong, renowned for its fish—the only item on the menu—seasoned with turmeric and dill. For our version, cornstarch and ground turmeric form a delicate crust on tilapia fillets that are quickly sautéed. Other firm white fish, such as snapper or cod, would work well here, but you'll need to increase the cooking time for fillets thicker than ½ inch. Generous fresh herbs—we use dill and cilantro, but mint is great, too—along with a sauce of lime juice and fish sauce brighten the dish. To add spice, stir red pepper flakes into the sauce or offer Sriracha at the table. Serve with rice noodles.

Don't overcook the herb mixture. Transfer it to the platter with the fish as soon as the cilantro and dill are stirred in.

In a small bowl, stir together ⅓ cup water, the sugar, lime juice and fish sauce until the sugar dissolves. Set aside. Season the fish with salt and pepper. In a gallon zip-close bag, mix together the cornstarch, turmeric, 1 tablespoon salt and 1 teaspoon pepper. Add the fish, seal the bag and shake to coat. Transfer to a plate, shaking off any excess coating.

In a 12-inch nonstick skillet over medium-high, heat 2 tablespoons of the oil until barely smoking. Add half the fish and cook, flipping the fillets once, until golden and opaque throughout, 2 to 3 minutes per side. Transfer to a platter. Repeat with 2 tablespoons of the remaining oil and the remaining fish.

Wipe out the skillet. Heat the remaining 2 tablespoons oil over medium until shimmering. Add the scallions and peanuts and cook until sizzling and fragrant, about 1 minute. Off heat, stir in the cilantro and dill, then immediately distribute over the fish. Serve with the lime-fish sauce mixture for drizzling.

Milk-Poached Chicken

with Tarragon Salsa Verde

START TO FINISH:
40 minutes

SERVINGS:
4

Four 8- to 10-ounce boneless, skinless chicken breasts, pounded ½ inch thick

Kosher salt and ground black pepper

1 quart (4 cups) whole milk

1 cup lightly packed fresh tarragon, plus 4 sprigs

4 medium garlic cloves, lightly smashed and peeled

2 tablespoons salted butter

1 teaspoon black peppercorns

½ cup lightly packed fresh flat-leaf parsley

2 tablespoons drained capers

3 anchovy fillets

2 tablespoons red wine vinegar

⅔ cup extra-virgin olive oil

We love the Italian trick of gently simmering pork in milk, not water, to produce meat that is tender and succulent; we adapted the technique for chicken breasts. Before poaching, we pounded the breasts until they were ½ inch thick, which keeps the cooking quick and even. If your chicken breasts have tenderloins attached, remove them before pounding; they can be reserved for another use, such as stir-frying. While the chicken rests, make a simple tarragon sauce in the food processor to add both flavor and color. Serve with buttered egg noodles, boiled potatoes or toasted pearl couscous tossed with fruity extra-virgin olive oil and lemon.

Don't use low-fat or nonfat milk; both will curdle during cooking. And don't allow the poaching liquid to reach a full simmer. Gentle cooking is needed for the chicken to remain tender and moist.

Season the chicken on both sides with salt and pepper. In a 12-inch skillet over medium-high, combine the milk, tarragon sprigs, garlic, butter, peppercorns and 2 teaspoons salt. Bring to a simmer, stirring, then reduce to low and submerge the chicken breasts in an even layer. Cover and cook, adjusting the heat to maintain a gentle simmer (only a few bubbles), until the breasts are opaque throughout, 18 to 24 minutes, flipping halfway through.

Transfer the chicken to a cutting board. Pour the poaching liquid through a fine mesh strainer set over a medium bowl; reserve 2 garlic cloves and 3 tablespoons of the strained poaching liquid; discard the remaining solids and liquid.

In a food processor, combine the tarragon leaves, parsley, capers, anchovies, vinegar, reserved garlic and reserved poaching liquid. Pulse until finely chopped, about 15 pulses. Add the oil and process until well combined, about 20 seconds.

Cut the chicken breasts crosswise on the bias into ½-inch slices and arrange on a platter. Spoon the sauce over them.

We opted for store-bought pickled ginger for weeknight ease, but homemade is a treat. Combine 3/4 cup unseasoned rice vinegar, 1/4 cup water, 2 tablespoons sugar, 1 teaspoon salt and 4 ounces peeled, thinly sliced fresh ginger. Cover and refrigerate for 30 minutes.

Yakiudon with Pickled Ginger

START TO FINISH:
45 minutes

SERVINGS:
4

12 ounces dried udon noodles

2 tablespoons plus 2 teaspoons grapeseed or other neutral oil, divided

¼ cup soy sauce

2 tablespoons mirin

1 teaspoon white sugar

3 small dried shiitake mushrooms, broken in half

8 ounces fresh shiitake mushrooms, stemmed, halved if large, thinly sliced

1 small yellow onion, halved and thinly sliced

2 medium garlic cloves, minced

12 ounces baby bok choy, trimmed and sliced crosswise ½ inch thick

½ teaspoon ground white pepper

2 scallions, thinly sliced on diagonal

1 tablespoon sesame seeds, toasted

Pickled ginger, to serve

This Japanese noodle dish is all about the chew, which comes from hearty wheat udon noodles. We got the dense chew we wanted by using an Italian technique of cooking them only until al dente—still quite firm. Japanese noodles often are rinsed after cooking, and chilling helps firm their texture. We streamlined the process by adding ice to the strainer as we rinsed the udon under cold water. Soy sauce, dried shiitake mushrooms and mirin went into our sauce, balanced by a little sugar. To balance the savoriness, we turned to pickled ginger. You can find this, jarred, in the Asian foods section of grocery stores.

Don't fully cook the udon. Check for doneness well before the suggested cooking time.

In a large pot, bring 4 quarts of water to a boil. Add the udon, stir well and cook until al dente. Drain using a colander, then add 2 cups of ice to the noodles. Run under cool water, tossing, until they are chilled. Drain well, then transfer to a large bowl. Toss with 2 teaspoons of the oil, then set aside.

In a small saucepan over medium, combine the soy sauce, ¼ cup water, mirin and sugar. Bring to a simmer, stirring, then add the dried mushrooms, pushing them into the liquid. Remove from the heat, cover and set aside until the mushrooms have softened and cooled, 20 to 30 minutes.

Remove the mushrooms from the soy sauce mixture, squeezing them to allow any liquid to drip back into the pan. Remove and discard the stems, then finely chop. Transfer to a medium bowl and set aside.

In a large nonstick skillet over medium-high, heat 1 tablespoon of the remaining oil until barely smoking. Add the fresh mushrooms and cook, stirring, until lightly browned and slightly shrunken, about 3 minutes. Add the onion, drizzle with the remaining 1 tablespoon oil and cook, stirring occasionally, until softened, about 3 minutes. Stir in the garlic and cook until fragrant, about 30 seconds. Add the bok choy and cook, stirring, until the leaves are wilted and the stem pieces are crisp-tender, about 2 minutes. Transfer to the bowl with the chopped dried shiitakes.

Set the now-empty skillet over medium and add the udon, gently tossing with tongs. Add the vegetable mixture, gently toss, then add the soy sauce mixture and white pepper. Cook, tossing constantly, until the noodles are heated and have absorbed most of the liquid, about 2 minutes. Transfer to serving bowls and sprinkle with scallions and sesame seeds. Serve with pickled ginger.

Ready in 30 to 35 minutes

Faster

Stir-Fried Chicken
with Snap Peas and Basil

START TO FINISH:
30 minutes

SERVINGS:
4

1 pound boneless, skinless chicken breasts, cut into 1-inch pieces

1 tablespoon soy sauce

3 tablespoons fish sauce, divided

Ground white pepper

3 tablespoons peanut oil, divided

¼ cup chopped fresh basil, plus 3 cups torn and lightly packed

2 tablespoons white vinegar

4 ounces sugar snap peas, strings removed, halved on diagonal

8 scallions, white and light green parts finely chopped, dark green tops cut into 1-inch pieces

2 or 3 serrano chilies, stemmed and thinly sliced

4 medium garlic cloves, thinly sliced

1 tablespoon white sugar

A double dose of basil adds herbal flavor and fragrance to this stir-fry. Inspired by Thailand's popular chicken-and-basil dish known as gai pad krapow, we follow the Thai approach of using herbs by the fistful. Chopped leaves are added to the freshly cooked chicken; the leaves gently wilt, their flavor mellowing and seasoning the meat. Just before serving, 3 cups of lightly torn leaves go into the dish to add fresh, peppery flavor. Sugar snap peas bring crunch and sweetness. To prepare the chicken, cut each breast lengthwise into ½-inch strips, then cut the strips crosswise into 1-inch pieces.

Don't begin cooking until all ingredients are prepared. The stir-fry comes together quickly, so make sure everything is ready and close at hand.

In a medium bowl, stir together the chicken, soy sauce, 1 tablespoon of the fish sauce and ½ teaspoon white pepper. Let sit for 15 minutes, then drain and pat dry with paper towels.

In a 12-inch nonstick skillet over medium-high, heat 1 tablespoon of the oil until barely smoking. Add the chicken in an even layer. Cook, stirring occasionally, until well browned and cooked through, 5 to 7 minutes. Transfer to a clean bowl, then stir in the chopped basil and vinegar. Set aside.

Add the remaining 2 tablespoons oil to the skillet and heat over medium-high until barely smoking. Add the snap peas, scallion whites/light greens and chilies. Cook, stirring, until the peas are lightly browned, about 3 minutes. Add the garlic and cook, stirring, until fragrant, about 30 seconds. Stir in the sugar. Add the scallion tops and the chicken with any accumulated juices and cook, stirring, until most of the juices have evaporated, about 1 minute.

Off heat, add the remaining 2 tablespoons fish sauce and the torn basil. Stir until the basil is wilted. Taste and season with white pepper.

The macadamia nuts are a substitute for candlenuts, chickpea-shaped nuts with a waxy texture commonly used as a thickener in Southeast Asian curries. They got their name thanks to their high oil content: They have so much they can burn like a candle.

Coconut—Lemon Grass Shrimp

START TO FINISH:
30 minutes

SERVINGS:
4

1 cup coconut milk

½ cup unsalted, roasted macadamia nuts

3 stalks lemon grass, trimmed to the lower 6 inches, dry outer layers discarded, roughly chopped

2-inch piece fresh ginger, peeled and cut into 3 pieces

1 tablespoon ground turmeric

1 teaspoon packed light brown sugar

1½ pounds extra-large shrimp, peeled, deveined, tails removed and reserved, patted dry

Kosher salt and ground white pepper

2 tablespoons coconut oil (preferably unrefined), divided

2 Fresno chilies, stemmed, halved, seeded and sliced into thin half rings

2 teaspoons grated lime zest, plus 2 tablespoons lime juice

This quick shrimp curry draws inspiration from a dish from Singapore's Candlenut restaurant. Lemon grass, turmeric and ginger are pureed with coconut milk for a sauce that is flavorful but not heavy. You can buy peeled shrimp, but make sure they have the tails attached; they are used to infuse the sauce. We preferred unrefined coconut oil because of its pronounced coconut flavor, but refined worked well, too. Fresno chilies are fresh red chilies with mild heat; if you can't find them, substitute fresh cherry peppers. Steamed rice makes a good accompaniment; for a quick and easy flavor boost, make the rice with half coconut milk, half water.

Don't fully cook the shrimp when searing them. They finish cooking in the sauce.

In a blender, combine the coconut milk, 1 cup water, macadamia nuts, lemon grass, ginger, turmeric and sugar. Blend until smooth, about 1 minute. Set aside.

Season the shrimp with salt and pepper. In a 12-inch nonstick skillet over medium-high, heat 1 tablespoon of the coconut oil until barely smoking. Add half the shrimp in a single layer; cook without stirring until golden on the bottom, about 45 seconds. Transfer to a bowl. Repeat with 2 teaspoons of the remaining oil and the remaining shrimp. Set the shrimp aside; do not wipe out the skillet.

Add the chilies to the skillet and cook, stirring, until beginning to brown and soften, about 1 minute. Transfer to the bowl with the shrimp and stir.

Add the remaining 1 teaspoon coconut oil to the skillet and heat over medium-high until barely smoking. Add the shrimp tails and cook, stirring, until pink and beginning to blister, about 1 minute. Off heat, stir in the coconut milk mixture. Bring to a simmer over medium and cook, stirring constantly to prevent sputtering, until beginning to thicken, 3 to 5 minutes.

Set a fine mesh strainer over a medium bowl. Pour the mixture through it and press firmly on the solids to extract as much liquid as possible; you should have about 1½ cups. Discard the solids and return the liquid to the skillet. Bring to a simmer over medium. Pour in any accumulated shrimp juices (do not add the shrimp) and cook, stirring occasionally, until the liquid has thickened and a silicone spatula leaves a trail when drawn through the sauce, about 5 minutes.

Reduce to low, stir in the shrimp and chilies, then cover and cook until the shrimp are opaque, 2 to 4 minutes. Stir in the lime zest and juice, then taste and season with salt and pepper.

Maque Choux

with Andouille Sausage

START TO FINISH:	SERVINGS:
30 minutes	**4**

1 tablespoon grapeseed or other neutral oil

12 ounces andouille sausage, halved lengthwise and cut into ½-inch pieces

2 tablespoons salted butter

1 small yellow onion, finely chopped

1 small red bell pepper, stemmed, seeded and finely chopped

1 Anaheim chili, stemmed, seeded and finely chopped

Kosher salt and ground black pepper

2 medium garlic cloves, minced

½ teaspoon dried thyme

3 cups corn kernels

1 tablespoon cider vinegar

4 scallions, thinly sliced

Pronounced "mock shoe," this Creole classic from Louisiana is said to get its name from a French inflection of a Native American word for the dish. We swapped the standard green bell pepper for an Anaheim chili, which has a bright yet earthy flavor and mild heat. If you can't find an Anaheim chili, a small poblano is a good alternative. Fresh, sweet summer corn is best, but frozen works, too. If using frozen corn, use a 1-pound bag directly from the freezer.

Don't forget to salt the vegetables *immediately after adding them to the skillet. This helps draw out moisture so they soften faster.*

In a 12-inch skillet over medium-high, heat the oil until shimmering. Add the sausage and cook, stirring, until well browned, about 3 minutes. Transfer to a paper towel–lined plate and discard any fat in the skillet.

Set the skillet over medium and melt the butter. Add the onion, bell pepper, Anaheim chili and ½ teaspoon salt. Cook, scraping up any browned bits and stirring occasionally, until the vegetables are softened, 5 to 7 minutes. Stir in the garlic and thyme and cook until fragrant, about 30 seconds. Increase to medium-high and add the corn, ¾ teaspoon salt and ¼ teaspoon pepper. Cook, stirring, until the corn is crisp-tender, 3 to 5 minutes.

Return the sausage to the skillet, stir and cook until heated through, about 1 minute. Stir in the vinegar, then taste and season with salt and pepper. Stir in the scallions.

Black Bean Noodles
with Pork and Mushrooms

START TO FINISH:
30 minutes

SERVINGS:
4

12 ounces dried wide, thick Asian wheat noodles (such as udon)

2 tablespoons grapeseed or other neutral oil

8 ounces fresh shiitake mushrooms, stemmed and finely chopped

12 ounces ground pork

4 scallions, white and light green parts minced, dark green tops thinly sliced

4 medium garlic cloves, minced

½ teaspoon red pepper flakes

½ cup dry sherry

3 tablespoons black bean garlic sauce

1 tablespoon hoisin sauce

1 tablespoon low-sodium soy sauce

2 tablespoons plus 1 teaspoon unseasoned rice vinegar, divided

½ English cucumber, thinly sliced on the diagonal, then cut into matchsticks

This riff on Chinese zha jiang mian—or noodles with pork and fermented bean sauce—substitutes prepared black bean garlic sauce for the traditional and harder-to-find fermented yellow or brown bean paste. On its own, the sauce tastes intense, but its boldness is balanced by the neutral flavor of the noodles and the freshness of the cucumber. You can find it in the Asian aisle of most larger grocery stores. Make sure to thoroughly drain the noodles before portioning them; excess water clinging to them will dilute the sauce.

Don't salt the water when cooking the noodles; the sauce provides plenty of salt for the dish. And don't forget to reserve 1 cup of the cooking water before draining the noodles.

In a large pot, bring 4 quarts of water to a boil. Add the noodles and cook until al dente, 5 to 6 minutes. Reserve 1 cup of the cooking water, then drain the noodles and rinse under cool water until cold. Drain well, then set aside in the colander.

Meanwhile, in a 12-inch skillet over medium-high, heat the oil until shimmering. Add the mushrooms and cook until softened and the bits clinging to the bottom of the pan begin to brown, about 3 minutes. Add the pork and cook until crispy and caramelized, about 6 minutes.

Stir in the minced scallions, garlic and pepper flakes, then cook until fragrant, about 1 minute. Add the sherry and cook, scraping the pan, until evaporated. Stir in the reserved cooking water, black bean sauce, hoisin and soy sauce. Bring to a simmer and cook over medium, stirring occasionally and breaking up any large bits of pork, until the sauce has the consistency of thin gravy, 4 to 5 minutes. Off heat, stir in 2 tablespoons of the vinegar.

While the sauce simmers, season the cucumber with the remaining 1 teaspoon of rice vinegar. Divide the noodles among serving bowls, then spoon the sauce over them. Top with sliced scallion greens and cucumber.

Braised Chickpeas and Spinach
with Smoked Paprika and Garlic (Guisat de Cigrons)

START TO FINISH:	SERVINGS:
35 minutes	**4**

¼ cup smoked almonds

½ cup panko

½ teaspoon fresh thyme leaves

Kosher salt and ground black pepper

5 tablespoons extra-virgin olive oil, divided

2½ teaspoons smoked paprika, divided

Three 15½-ounce cans chickpeas, 2 cans rinsed and drained

5 large garlic cloves, minced

1 teaspoon finely chopped fresh rosemary

14½-ounce can diced fire-roasted tomatoes

⅛ teaspoon cayenne pepper

10-ounce bunch spinach, stemmed

This Spanish-inspired chickpea stew gets deep flavor from fire-roasted tomatoes and a good dose of smoked paprika and garlic. Toasted panko and chopped smoked almonds sprinkled on just before serving add nice textural contrast.

Don't use baby spinach in place of mature bunch spinach. We found that bunch spinach became tender when wilted, but baby spinach turned mushy in the stew. Don't drain all three cans of chickpeas. One is used with its liquid.

In a food processor, pulse the almonds until coarsely chopped, about 8 pulses. Transfer to a small bowl. Process the panko until slightly finer in texture, about 10 seconds, then add the thyme, ¼ teaspoon each salt and black pepper, 1 tablespoon of the oil and ¾ teaspoon of the paprika. Process until well combined, about 10 seconds. Transfer the panko mixture to a 12-inch skillet and set aside. Pulse 1 cup of the drained chickpeas until coarsely ground, about 5 pulses, then transfer to another small bowl.

Set the skillet with the panko mixture over medium and cook, stirring, until crisp and browned, 4 to 5 minutes. Stir in the chopped almonds, then scrape the mixture onto a plate; set aside.

In a large saucepan over medium-low, heat 3 tablespoons of the remaining oil until shimmering. Add the garlic and cook, stirring occasionally, until pale golden, about 2 minutes. Stir in the remaining 1¾ teaspoons paprika and the rosemary; cook until fragrant, about 1 minute. Add the tomatoes and cook, stirring, until slightly thickened, about 3 minutes. Stir in the ground chickpeas, the remaining drained chickpeas, the remaining 1 can chickpeas (with its liquid), 1 teaspoon salt and the cayenne. Bring to a simmer over medium-high, then reduce to low, cover and cook, stirring occasionally, about 10 minutes.

Stir in the spinach, then cover and cook until wilted, about 1 minute. Transfer to a serving bowl, sprinkle with several tablespoons of the panko-almond mixture and drizzle with the remaining 1 tablespoon oil. Offer the rest of the topping on the side.

Mushroom Pork Omelet

START TO FINISH:	SERVINGS:
30 minutes	**4**

8 ounces ground pork

1 tablespoon plus 1 teaspoon soy sauce, divided

1 tablespoon fish sauce

2 teaspoons white sugar

2 teaspoons finely grated fresh ginger

Ground white pepper

8 large eggs

1 tablespoon chili-garlic sauce

3 tablespoons peanut oil

6 ounces fresh shiitake mushrooms, stems discarded, caps finely chopped

8 scallions, finely chopped

Cilantro leaves, to serve

Lime wedges, to serve

For Radish-Cucumber Pickle

½ cup unseasoned rice vinegar

1 tablespoon white sugar

1½ teaspoons fish sauce

1 teaspoon chili-garlic sauce

4 radishes, halved and thinly sliced

½ English cucumber, quartered lengthwise and thinly sliced on the bias

This rich, frittata-like omelet is delicious hot, but we also liked it at room temperature. It's particularly good with pickled radishes and cucumbers, which provide contrast and crunch. They are easily made in the time needed to make the omelet. To round out the meal, steamed jasmine rice makes a good accompaniment.

Don't use a conventional skillet. A nonstick coating is key, allowing the omelet to easily slide out of the pan.

Heat the oven to 400°F with a rack in the upper-middle position. In a medium bowl, mix together the pork, 1 tablespoon soy sauce, the fish sauce, sugar, ginger and ½ teaspoon white pepper. In a separate medium bowl, beat the eggs, chili-garlic sauce and remaining 1 teaspoon soy sauce.

In a 12-inch oven-safe nonstick skillet over medium-high, heat the oil until barely smoking. Add the pork mixture and the mushrooms and cook, stirring occasionally and breaking up the meat, until the pork is no longer pink and the mushrooms are tender, about 5 minutes.

Stir in the scallions and cook until fragrant, about 30 seconds. Pour the egg mixture over the pork mixture and cook, pushing and stirring from the edges to the center, until the eggs just begin to set, 2 to 3 minutes. Transfer the skillet to the oven and bake until the top is set, about 5 minutes.

Set the skillet on a wire rack and let cool for 5 minutes. Run a silicone spatula around the edge and under the omelet to loosen, then slide the omelet on to a cutting board. Cut into 8 wedges and transfer to a serving platter. Serve with cilantro leaves and lime wedges.

RADISH-CUCUMBER PICKLE

START TO FINISH:	MAKES ABOUT:
10 minutes	**1½ cups**

In a medium bowl, whisk the vinegar, sugar, fish sauce and chili-garlic sauce until the sugar dissolves. Stir in the radishes and cucumber. Cover and refrigerate for at least 30 minutes, or up to 24 hours.

Pistachio-Mint Beef Kofta

START TO FINISH:
35 minutes

SERVINGS:
4

1 cup roasted and salted pistachio meats (shelled)

2½ teaspoons dried mint

1½ pounds 85 percent lean ground beef

5 tablespoons chopped fresh dill, divided

4 tablespoons chopped fresh mint, divided

4 medium garlic cloves, minced

1 teaspoon ground allspice

¾ teaspoon cayenne pepper

Kosher salt and ground black pepper

1 large egg plus 2 large egg yolks, beaten

1 cup plain whole-milk yogurt

2 tablespoons grapeseed or other neutral oil

Pistachios—lots of them—give these beef kofta a rich, toasty flavor that's balanced by the sweetness of dried mint and the grassiness of fresh dill. Most supermarkets sell shelled pistachios that are already toasted and salted. If you start with raw ones, toast them in a 400°F oven for about 8 minutes, stirring once, and increase the salt in the meat mixture by ¼ teaspoon. Serve with shredded romaine lettuce, thinly sliced red onion and warmed flatbreads.

Don't worry about overmixing the beef. Processing for a full minute yields a mixture with a spreadable consistency that, when cooked, has a texture that's pleasantly springy, yet soft and tender.

In a food processor, pulse the pistachios and dried mint until the nuts are coarsely chopped, about 3 pulses. Set aside 2 tablespoons, then process the remaining mixture until finely ground, about 20 seconds.

Add the beef, 3 tablespoons of the dill, 1 tablespoon of fresh mint, the garlic, allspice, cayenne, 1½ teaspoons salt and ¾ teaspoon pepper. Process until well combined, 1 to 1½ minutes, frequently scraping the bowl. Add the eggs and process until the mixture has a spreadable, sticky consistency, about 1 minute.

Shape into 12 patties, each about ½ inch thick. Place on a large plate, cover and refrigerate for 15 minutes.

Meanwhile, in a small bowl, stir together the yogurt, the remaining 2 tablespoons dill, the remaining 3 tablespoons fresh mint, ½ teaspoon salt and ¼ teaspoon pepper. Set aside.

In a 12-inch nonstick skillet over medium, heat 1 tablespoon of the oil until shimmering. Add half of the patties in a single layer and cook, turning once, until golden brown on both sides, about 3 minutes per side. Transfer to a platter and tent with foil. Repeat with the remaining 1 tablespoon oil and patties. Sprinkle the reserved pistachios over the patties and serve with yogurt sauce.

A traditional Spanish tortilla is cooked on both sides by inverting it in the pan, a tricky and intimidating process. We found it easier to cook the bottom on the stovetop and finish the top in the oven.

Tortilla Española

with Potato and Eggplant

START TO FINISH:	SERVINGS:
30 minutes	**4**

8 large eggs

Kosher salt and ground black pepper

½ cup roughly chopped fresh flat-leaf parsley

5 tablespoons extra-virgin olive oil, divided

1 medium yellow onion, chopped

1 pound Yukon Gold potatoes, peeled and cut into ½-inch cubes

8 ounces Chinese or Japanese eggplant, cut into ¾-inch cubes

2 medium garlic cloves, thinly sliced

In Spain, a tortilla is a thick, hearty, frittata-like omelet, usually made with potatoes and onion. We make it even more substantial with the addition of eggplant and garlic. Chinese and Japanese eggplants—the varieties called for in this recipe—have thinner skins and fewer seeds than large globe eggplants. If you can't find either, you can substitute Italian or globe, but remove the peel before cutting it into cubes. Aioli or mayonnaise is a great accompaniment to any tortilla.

Don't use a conventional skillet; nonstick is essential for the tortilla to slide easily out of the pan. Also, the skillet must be oven-safe, as the tortilla finishes cooking in a 350°F oven.

Heat the oven to 350°F with a rack in the middle position. In a large bowl, whisk together the eggs, 1 teaspoon salt and ¼ teaspoon pepper. Stir in the parsley.

In a 12-inch oven-safe nonstick skillet over medium-high, heat 4 tablespoons of the oil until shimmering. Stir in the onion, potatoes, eggplant, garlic and 1 teaspoon salt. Cover and cook, stirring occasionally, until the vegetables are browned and tender, about 10 minutes.

Pour the egg mixture over the vegetables and cook, stirring constantly with a silicone spatula, until almost set, about 2 minutes. Using the spatula, tuck in the eggs around the perimeter to form a neat circle. Transfer the skillet to the oven and bake until set, 5 to 10 minutes.

Run the spatula around the edge and under the tortilla to loosen, then carefully slide onto a cutting board. Serve warm or at room temperature.

Soupy Rice with Chicken,
Bok Choy and Mushrooms (Pao Fan)

START TO FINISH:
30 minutes

SERVINGS:
4

8 ounces boneless, skinless chicken thighs, cut into rough ¼-inch pieces

1½ tablespoons oyster sauce

Kosher salt and ground white pepper

1 quart low-sodium chicken broth

1½ cups jasmine rice, rinsed and drained

1 tablespoon grapeseed or other neutral oil

8 ounces fresh shiitake mushrooms, stems removed and caps thinly sliced

1 tablespoon finely grated fresh ginger

1 pound baby bok choy, trimmed and cut crosswise into ½-inch pieces

5 scallions, thinly sliced

Toasted sesame oil or chili oil, to serve

Soupy rice, a classic Chinese dish, is a way to turn leftover cooked rice into a meal. Our version, however, starts with uncooked rice and simmers it in a blend of chicken broth and water before a simple stir-fry of shiitake mushrooms, chicken and bok choy is stirred in.

Don't use a pot smaller than 6 quarts to cook the rice or the starchy liquid may overflow.

In a small bowl, stir together the chicken, oyster sauce and ¼ teaspoon white pepper. Set aside. In a large Dutch oven over medium-high, combine 4 cups water, the broth, rice and 2 teaspoons salt. Bring to a boil, stirring occasionally. Reduce to low, cover and simmer, stirring once or twice, until the rice is tender, about 8 minutes.

While the rice cooks, in a 12-inch nonstick skillet over medium-high, heat the grapeseed oil until barely smoking. Add the mushrooms and ½ teaspoon salt and cook, stirring, until softened and shrunken in size, 3 to 4 minutes. Add the chicken and cook, stirring, until no longer pink, about 3 minutes. Stir in the ginger. Turn off the heat, stir in the bok choy and set aside until the rice is ready.

When the rice is tender, quickly stir in the bok choy–chicken mixture. Turn off the heat, cover and let stand until the bok choy stems are crisp-tender, about 3 minutes. Taste and season with salt and white pepper. Ladle the rice into bowls. Sprinkle with additional white pepper and scallions, then drizzle with sesame oil.

Lomo Saltado

START TO FINISH:	SERVINGS:
30 minutes	**4**

1½ pounds sirloin tips, trimmed, cut into 3-inch pieces and sliced against the grain into ½-inch strips

1½ teaspoons ground cumin

Kosher salt and ground black pepper

5 tablespoons soy sauce, divided

3 tablespoons grapeseed or other neutral oil, divided

1 large red onion, halved and cut into ½-inch half rings

¼ cup red wine vinegar

2 medium garlic cloves, minced

1 jalapeño chili, stemmed and sliced into thin rounds

1½ cups grape tomatoes, halved

Peru's lomo saltado is fusion cooking at its easiest and most approachable, a quick stir-fry of soy-marinated beef, tomatoes and hot peppers. It's part of the chifa cuisine—Asian-influenced dishes brought to the South American country by indentured Chinese workers in the late 19th century. For our take, we developed flavor by mixing ground cumin into the soy sauce marinade. Tenderloin is often used, but we preferred sirloin tips (also called flap meat) for their meatier flavor as well as lower price. And we seared the meat instead of stir-frying. Readily available jalapeño peppers made a good substitute for the traditional yellow aji peppers. If you prefer little to no spiciness, halve and seed the jalapeño before slicing it into half rings. Classic lomo saltado is frequently served over french fries; your favorite, frozen or otherwise, would be a good choice here. Steamed rice is an equally good, and lighter, accompaniment.

Don't cook the beef without patting it dry. Marinating in soy sauce adds flavor, but also moisture. Drying the beef helps ensure that the slices sear nicely, rather than steam. Also, cook it in two batches; crowding the pan inhibits browning.

In a medium bowl, combine the steak, cumin, 1 teaspoon each salt and pepper, and 2 tablespoons of the soy sauce. Marinate at room temperature for 10 minutes. Drain, pat the meat dry and transfer to a plate.

In a 12-inch skillet over high, heat 1 tablespoon of the oil until barely smoking. Add half of the meat in a single layer and cook, turning once, until well browned on both sides, 2 to 3 minutes total. Transfer to a plate. Repeat with 1 tablespoon of the remaining oil and the remaining meat.

In the same pan over medium-high, heat the remaining 1 tablespoon oil until shimmering. Add the onion and cook until just starting to soften, stirring, for 2 minutes. Stir in the vinegar and remaining 3 tablespoons soy sauce, scraping the bottom of the pan.

Cook for 1 minute, or until the sauce thickens slightly. Stir in the garlic and jalapeño and cook until the garlic is fragrant, about 30 seconds. Add the tomatoes, the meat and any accumulated juices. Cook until the meat is just warmed through, 30 seconds. Taste and season with salt and pepper.

White Balsamic Chicken

with Tarragon

START TO FINISH:	SERVINGS:
30 minutes	**4**

6 bone-in, skin-on chicken thighs (2½ to 3 pounds), trimmed

Kosher salt and ground black pepper

1 tablespoon grapeseed or other neutral oil

3 medium garlic cloves, thinly sliced

1 shallot, minced (about ⅓ cup)

¾ cup white balsamic vinegar

¾ cup low-sodium chicken broth

4 tablespoons minced fresh tarragon, divided

⅓ cup Peppadew peppers, drained and chopped

Sweet-tart white balsamic vinegar and tangy Peppadew peppers bring flavor and color to this weeknight chicken. White balsamic, which isn't concentrated or aged to the extent of regular balsamic vinegar, has a mellow acidity that complements the Peppadews, a variety of small, sweet peppers from South Africa. They add slight heat and additional sweetness, as well as a vivid splash of red. Find them jarred at most grocery stores (and sometimes loose at the olive bar). When reducing the sauce before serving, add water if the liquid is less than 1 cup. Serve with roasted sweet potatoes, boiled baby red potatoes or spinach pasta tossed with butter and poppy seeds.

Don't rush rendering the fat from the skin on the chicken thighs. The skin should be golden brown and feel crisp.

Heat the oven to 450°F with a rack in the middle position. Pat the chicken dry with paper towels, then season with salt and pepper. In a 12-inch oven-safe skillet over medium-high, heat the oil until barely smoking. Add the chicken, skin down, and cook until fat is rendered and the skin is golden brown, about 5 minutes.

Transfer the chicken, skin up, to a plate. Pour off all but 1 tablespoon of fat from the skillet. Stir in the garlic and shallot and cook over medium, stirring occasionally, until light golden brown, about 1 minute. Add the vinegar and broth and bring to a simmer, scraping up any browned bits. Return the chicken to the skillet, skin up. Transfer to the oven and bake until a skewer inserted into the thickest part meets no resistance, 12 to 15 minutes.

Transfer the chicken, skin up, to a deep platter and return the skillet to the stovetop (handle will be hot) over medium-high. Bring the sauce to a boil and cook until reduced to about 1 cup, 2 to 3 minutes. Taste and season with salt and pepper. Off heat, stir in half the tarragon, then spoon the sauce around the chicken. Top with Peppadews and the remaining tarragon.

Mussels with Fennel,

Crème Fraîche and Vermouth

START TO FINISH:	SERVINGS:
35 minutes	**4**

2 tablespoons salted butter

2 large shallots, halved and thinly sliced

1 medium fennel bulb, trimmed, halved, cored and thinly sliced

2 medium Fresno chilies, stemmed and sliced into thin rings

2 teaspoons fennel seeds

Kosher salt

2 cups dry vermouth

6 sprigs fresh thyme

3 pounds mussels, scrubbed and debearded

½ cup crème fraîche

⅓ cup lightly packed fresh tarragon

Fresh mussels cook quickly, making them an ideal weeknight dinner. We steam them in dry vermouth scented with shallots, fresh fennel and fennel seed. Crème fraîche whisked in at the end adds richness and rounds out the other flavors. Serve warm, crusty bread on the side for soaking up the broth.

Don't add the mussels to the pot until the liquid reaches a full boil. A big burst of heat helps the mussels open quickly, keeping them tender and succulent.

In a large Dutch oven over medium, melt the butter. Add the shallots, fennel, chilies, fennel seeds and ½ teaspoon salt. Cook, stirring, until the vegetables have softened, 4 to 6 minutes. Stir in the vermouth and thyme and bring to a simmer. Cover, reduce to low and cook for about 5 minutes.

Bring the liquid to a boil over medium, then add the mussels. Cover and cook until the mussels just begin to open, about 4 minutes. Off heat, let the mussels continue to steam, covered, until fully open, another 3 to 5 minutes, quickly stirring once halfway through.

Using a slotted spoon, transfer the mussels to a serving bowl. Remove and discard the thyme along with any mussels that fail to open. Bring the cooking liquid to a simmer over medium and cook until reduced to about 2 cups, 5 to 6 minutes. Whisk in the crème fraîche and return to a simmer. Pour over the mussels and sprinkle with tarragon.

Sesame Stir-Fried Pork

with Shiitakes

START TO FINISH:
30 minutes

SERVINGS:
6

1-pound pork tenderloin, trimmed of silver skin

2½ cups well-drained napa cabbage kimchi, roughly chopped, plus 2 tablespoons kimchi juice, divided

2½ tablespoons soy sauce, divided

Kosher salt and ground black pepper

3 tablespoons grapeseed or other neutral oil, divided

8 ounces fresh shiitake mushrooms, stems discarded, caps sliced ¼ inch thick

3 medium large garlic cloves, thinly sliced

3 tablespoons mirin

1 tablespoon toasted sesame oil

2 tablespoons sesame seeds, toasted

1 bunch scallions, thinly sliced

Pork tenderloin and kimchi headline this stir-fry, but fresh shiitake mushrooms and a full bunch of scallions add to its umami-rich appeal. For a meatless alternative, substitute a 14-ounce container of extra-firm tofu, drained and cut into 1-inch cubes, for the pork.

Don't finely chop the kimchi. Larger pieces better retain their texture and flavor.

Cut the tenderloin in half lengthwise, then slice each half crosswise about ¼ inch thick. In a medium bowl, stir together the pork, 1 tablespoon of the kimchi juice, 1 tablespoon of the soy sauce and ½ teaspoon pepper.

In a 12-inch skillet over high, heat 1 tablespoon of the grapeseed oil until barely smoking. Swirl to coat the pan, then add the pork and cook, stirring, until no longer pink, about 4 minutes. Transfer to a clean bowl.

In the same pan over medium-high, heat 1 tablespoon of the remaining oil until barely smoking. Add the mushrooms and ½ teaspoon of salt. Cook, stirring occasionally, until the liquid released by the mushrooms has mostly evaporated, about 5 minutes.

Stir in the remaining 1 tablespoon oil and the garlic and cook until fragrant, about 1 minute. Return the pork to the pan with any accumulated juices and cook until the juices evaporate, 30 to 60 seconds.

Add the kimchi, mirin, the remaining 1 tablespoon kimchi juice and the remaining 1½ tablespoons soy sauce. Reduce to medium and cook, stirring and scraping up any browned bits, until the kimchi is heated through, about 3 minutes. Stir in the sesame oil, half of the sesame seeds and half of the scallions. Transfer to a platter and sprinkle with the remaining scallions and sesame seeds.

Peruvian Ceviche

START TO FINISH:
30 minutes

SERVINGS:
4

1½ pounds firm skinless white fish fillets, such as flounder or sea bass, cut into ¼-inch cubes

2 teaspoons kosher salt

½ cup lime juice

½ yellow bell pepper, cored and finely chopped

½ small red onion, minced

1 serrano chili, stemmed and minced

1 medium garlic clove, minced

½ cup chopped fresh cilantro

Ground white pepper

Sweet potato chips, to serve

Peruvian mega-chef Gastón Acurio taught us that a balance of freshness, acidity and spice are what make for a good ceviche, that bracing mix of raw seafood, lime juice, chilies and vegetables. We also learned that the fish is firmed, or "cooked" by the salt, not the lime juice, which is why our acid doesn't go in until the end of the process. For our take on ceviche, sea bass, flounder or any firm white fish will work, but make sure the fish is fresh and from a trusted grocer or fishmonger. Before cutting the fillets into cubes, remove any pin bones; we use tweezers. In Peru, sweet potatoes and corn kernels are traditional ceviche accompaniments; we liked sweet potato chips, which gave us both sweetness and crunch. For a milder ceviche, seed the serrano before mincing.

Don't add the lime juice until just before serving. The acid can soften the protein in the fish.

In a large bowl, gently toss the fish with the salt. Cover and refrigerate for at least 10 minutes and up to 20 minutes.

Meanwhile, in a medium bowl, combine the lime juice, bell pepper, onion, chili and garlic. Cover and refrigerate.

Add the lime juice mixture and the cilantro to the fish and stir to combine. Taste, then season with white pepper. Serve with sweet potato chips.

Ceviche was born from the need to preserve—fishermen would add salt and chili peppers to their catch. The Spanish later introduced lime and onion. And the dish's traditional accompaniments—sweet potatoes and corn—were added by Incan farmers.

Tagliatelle with Portobellos
and Chive Ricotta

START TO FINISH:	SERVINGS:
30 minutes	**4**

1 cup whole-milk ricotta cheese

¼ cup finely chopped fresh chives

Kosher salt and ground black pepper

8 ounces dried tagliatelle

4 tablespoons (½ stick) salted butter, divided

2 pounds portobello mushroom caps, gills removed, quartered and sliced ¼ inch thick

2 medium shallots, halved and thinly sliced

1 cup dry white wine

3 tablespoons red miso

½ cup lightly packed fresh tarragon, finely chopped

Extra-virgin olive oil, to serve

In this hearty vegetarian dish, an umami-rich mushroom sauce combines with tarragon-tossed tagliatelle pasta. Red miso and mild portobellos ground the flavors in an earthy richness that contrasts well with a finishing spoonful of chive-seasoned ricotta cheese. Tagliatelle is an egg noodle similar in shape to fettuccine, but with a finer texture and richer flavor. We used dried tagliatelle, which is sold bundled in nests. Refer to the package directions for cooking times.

***Don't forget to scrape off the gills** from the undersides of the mushroom caps. If left, the gills give the sauce a murky appearance.*

In a small bowl, whisk together the ricotta, chives and ¼ teaspoon each salt and pepper. Set aside. In a large pot, bring 4 quarts of water to a boil. Add the pasta and 2 tablespoons salt and cook until al dente. Reserve 2 cups of the cooking water, drain the pasta and return it to the pot. Add 1 tablespoon of the butter and ½ cup of the reserved cooking water; toss to coat.

Meanwhile, in a 12-inch skillet over medium-high, heat 2 tablespoons of the butter until foaming. Add the mushrooms, shallots and ¼ teaspoon each salt and pepper. Cook, stirring, until the mushrooms have released their moisture and are well browned, about 10 minutes. Add the wine, scrape up any browned bits and simmer until almost evaporated, about 5 minutes.

Add the remaining 1½ cups reserved cooking water to the mushrooms, bring to a simmer and cook over medium-high until the mixture has thickened, about 10 minutes. Off heat, stir in the miso and remaining 1 tablespoon butter. Taste and season with salt and pepper.

Add the tarragon to the pasta and toss, then transfer to a serving bowl. Spoon the mushroom mixture over the pasta. Serve dolloped with the ricotta mixture and drizzled with olive oil.

Chicken Teriyaki Donburi

START TO FINISH:
35 minutes

SERVINGS:
4

4 tablespoons sake, divided

1 tablespoon cornstarch

2 pounds boneless, skinless chicken thighs, trimmed and cut into 1-inch pieces

2 tablespoons grapeseed or other neutral oil, divided

½ cup mirin

¼ cup soy sauce, plus more as needed

1 tablespoon finely grated fresh ginger

½ teaspoon ground black pepper

3 cups cooked Japanese-style short-grain rice

One 3-inch piece cucumber, cut into thin matchsticks (½ cup)

3 scallions, thinly sliced on diagonal

4 teaspoons sesame seeds, toasted

Elizabeth Andoh, an author and expert on Japanese cooking, introduced us to this quick but refined take on chicken teriyaki. A good balance of salty and sweet and a light, glaze-like sauce dresses up, but doesn't overwhelm, chicken thighs. Donburi is a Japanese word that refers to deep, usually ceramic, bowls, as well as to the food served in those bowls—rice with toppings, such as this chicken.

Don't use chicken breasts in place of thighs. Chicken breasts dry out quickly, but thighs remain juicy and flavorful, even when slightly overcooked.

In a medium bowl, whisk together 2 tablespoons of the sake and the cornstarch. Add the chicken and toss to coat. In a 12-inch skillet over medium-high, heat 1 tablespoon of the oil until shimmering. Add half of the chicken in a single layer and cook without stirring until golden brown on the bottom, about 3 minutes. Using a metal spatula, scrape up and flip the chicken, then cook without stirring until golden brown all over, about another 2 minutes. Transfer to a bowl. Return the skillet to medium-high, add the remaining 1 tablespoon oil and repeat with remaining chicken. Discard any fat left in the pan.

Return the skillet to medium and add the mirin, soy sauce, ginger and remaining 2 tablespoons sake. Bring to a simmer and cook, stirring and scraping up any browned bits, until a spoon drawn through leaves a trail, about 5 minutes.

Return the chicken and any accumulated juices to the pan. Add the pepper and cook, stirring, until the chicken is glazed, about 4 minutes. Taste and season with soy sauce. Divide the rice evenly among 4 serving bowls. Spoon the chicken over the rice and top with cucumber, scallions and sesame seeds.

Herbed Bulgur Pilaf

with Fried Chickpeas

START TO FINISH:	SERVINGS:
30 minutes	**4**

2 tablespoons salted butter

3 large shallots, finely chopped

Kosher salt and ground black pepper

1½ cups coarse bulgur

15½-ounce can chickpeas, rinsed, drained and patted dry

2 tablespoons cornstarch

¼ cup extra-virgin olive oil

1 teaspoon ground cumin

1 teaspoon sweet smoked paprika

2 tablespoons lemon juice, plus lemon wedges, to serve

½ cup finely chopped fresh dill, divided

¼ cup finely chopped fresh chives

For this recipe, bulgur—cracked and partially cooked wheat—is cooked pilaf-style with a generous amount of shallots. Lemon, dill and chives, added at the end, brighten the dish and complement the nuttiness of the grain. For textural contrast and a flavor accent, we finish the pilaf with canned chickpeas that are crisped in olive oil and tossed with cumin and smoked paprika.

Don't coat the chickpeas with cornstarch without first drying them thoroughly with paper towels. Excess moisture will cause the oil to splatter and prevent the chickpeas from crisping.

In a large saucepan over medium, melt the butter. Add the shallots and ½ teaspoon salt, then cook, stirring, until beginning to brown, about 5 minutes. Add the bulgur and cook, stirring constantly, until it has a nutty aroma, about 1 minute. Stir in 2¼ cups water and bring to a simmer over medium-high. Cover, reduce to medium-low and cook until the bulgur is tender and has absorbed the liquid, 15 to 17 minutes. Remove from the heat, uncover and drape a kitchen towel over the pan. Replace the cover and let stand for 5 minutes.

While the bulgur cooks, put the chickpeas in a medium bowl, sprinkle with the cornstarch and toss. Transfer to a mesh strainer and shake to remove excess cornstarch. In a 10-inch skillet over medium-high, heat the oil until shimmering. Add the chickpeas and cook, stirring, until golden brown and crisp, about 5 minutes. Remove from the heat and stir in the cumin, paprika, ½ teaspoon salt and ¼ teaspoon pepper.

Using a fork, fluff the bulgur. Stir in the lemon juice, half of the dill and the chives. Taste and season with salt and pepper. Transfer to a serving plate, top with the chickpeas and the remaining dill. Serve with lemon wedges.

This schnitzel makes great sandwiches, particularly paired with a doctored mayo. Mix together 1/2 cup mayonnaise, 1 teaspoon grated lemon zest, 1 teaspoon lemon juice, 1 finely grated garlic clove and 1/2 teaspoon ground black pepper.

Pork Schnitzel

START TO FINISH:
30 minutes

SERVINGS:
4

1¼-pound pork tenderloin, trimmed of silver skin and patted dry

Kosher salt and ground black pepper

⅓ cup all-purpose flour

2 tablespoons cornstarch

¼ teaspoon baking powder

2 large eggs

1¾ cups panko breadcrumbs

10 tablespoons grapeseed or other neutral oil, divided

2 lemons, quartered

Tender, juicy meat with a crisp crust is the hallmark of schnitzel, popular in Germany and Austria. For our schnitzel, we use pork tenderloin, an ultra-tender cut. But instead of cutting the tenderloin crosswise into medallions, we halve it lengthwise, then cut each half crosswise. This creates pieces that are easy to pound into evenly thick cutlets. When pounding, go slow and steady, working from the center outward and using a slight lateral movement rather than a straight up-and-down motion; be careful not to create any holes in the cutlets. The schnitzel are delicious with just a squeeze of lemon, or try them sandwiched, with baby arugula, in warm, crusty rolls slathered with a garlicky mayonnaise.

Don't use a tenderloin larger than 1¼ pounds or the cutlets may be too large to fit two at a time in the skillet. When frying, don't crowd the cutlets in the pan; to brown and crisp properly, they must be in a single layer and not touch or overlap. Don't omit the cornstarch or baking powder; they help create a light, crisp breading.

Cut the tenderloin in half crosswise, making the tail-end half slightly larger, then cut each piece in half lengthwise. Place 2 pieces of pork between 2 large sheets of plastic wrap. Using a meat mallet, gently pound each piece to an even ¼-inch thickness. Repeat with the 2 remaining pieces. Season both sides of each cutlet with salt and pepper.

Set a wire rack in each of 2 rimmed baking sheets and line a large plate with a triple layer of paper towels. In a pie plate or wide, shallow bowl, stir together the flour, cornstarch and baking powder. In a second similar dish, beat the eggs with a fork until well combined. In a third, stir together the panko, ½ teaspoon salt and ¼ teaspoon pepper.

Dredge each cutlet first through the flour, turning to coat and shaking off any excess, then through the egg and finally through the panko. Arrange the cutlets on one of the racks.

In a 12-inch skillet over medium-high, heat 6 tablespoons of the oil until shimmering. Add 2 cutlets and cook, undisturbed, until golden brown, 1 to 2 minutes. Using tongs, flip the cutlets and cook until the second sides are golden brown, about another 1 minute. Remove the skillet from the heat. Transfer the cutlets to the paper towels, flipping to blot excess oil. Transfer to the second prepared wire rack. Repeat with the remaining 4 tablespoons oil and remaining cutlets. Serve immediately with lemon wedges.

Pasta with Seared Cauliflower
and Garlic

START TO FINISH:
30 minutes

SERVINGS:
4

12 ounces campanelle pasta or other short pasta

Kosher salt and ground black pepper

5 tablespoons extra-virgin olive oil, divided

⅓ cup shelled, unsalted pistachios, roughly chopped

1 small cauliflower head (about 2½ pounds), cored and cut into 1-inch florets

8 medium garlic cloves, minced

2 tablespoons minced anchovy fillets, plus 2 tablespoons anchovy oil

2 teaspoons fresh rosemary, minced

½ teaspoon red pepper flakes

4 tablespoons (½ stick) salted butter, divided

1 tablespoon grated lemon zest, plus 2 tablespoons lemon juice

¾ cup lightly packed fresh flat-leaf parsley, roughly chopped

We drew on the flavors of bagna cauda—the sauce-like dip from Italy's Piedmont region that is a harvest ritual—by pairing pasta and skillet-seared cauliflower with garlic and anchovies. The anchovies melt away, leaving behind a salty-savory tang, while butter and some of the pasta cooking water help create a quick pan sauce. Toasted pistachios add crunch; lemon juice and zest brighten the dish. Campanelle is a frilly, trumpet-shaped pasta that catches both cauliflower and sauce; other short pasta shapes, such as farfalle and cavatappi, also worked well.

Don't cook the pasta until entirely al dente. The pasta will soften further when tossed with the sauce.

In a large pot, bring 4 quarts of water to a boil. Add the pasta and 2 tablespoons salt and cook until just shy of al dente. Reserve 1 cup of the cooking water, then drain and set aside. Meanwhile in a 12-inch skillet over medium-high, heat 1 tablespoon of the oil until shimmering. Add the pistachios and cook, stirring, until fragrant and bright green, 30 to 45 seconds. Transfer to a small bowl.

Add 2 tablespoons of oil to the pan and heat over medium until shimmering. Add half of the cauliflower and ¼ teaspoon each salt and pepper. Cook, stirring, until light golden brown and crisp-tender, about 5 minutes. Transfer to a medium bowl. Return the pan to medium heat and repeat with the remaining 2 tablespoons oil, remaining cauliflower and ¼ teaspoon each salt and pepper.

Return all of the cauliflower to the pan. Stir in the garlic, anchovies and oil, rosemary, pepper flakes and 2 tablespoons of butter. Cook, stirring, until the garlic is softened and the anchovies have disintegrated, 4 to 5 minutes. Add the pasta cooking water and bring to a boil over medium-high. Toss in the pasta and remaining 2 tablespoons butter. Cook, tossing, until the sauce has thickened and coats the pasta, about 1 minute.

Off heat, stir in the lemon juice and all but 1 tablespoon of the pistachios. Taste and season with salt and pepper. Transfer to a serving platter and sprinkle with the remaining pistachios, the parsley and lemon zest.

Thai Rice Soup

(Khao Tom)

START TO FINISH: **35 minutes**

SERVINGS: **4**

8 ounces ground pork

3 tablespoons fish sauce, divided, plus more to serve

2 tablespoons chili-garlic sauce, divided, plus more to serve

Kosher salt and ground white pepper

3 tablespoons lard or refined coconut oil

5 large shallots, halved lengthwise and thinly sliced

8 medium garlic cloves, thinly sliced

3 lemon grass stalks, trimmed to bottom 6 inches, dry outer leaves discarded, smashed

2 tablespoons finely grated fresh ginger

2½ quarts low-sodium chicken broth

4 cups cooked jasmine rice

1 cup chopped fresh cilantro

3 tablespoons lime juice, plus lime wedges, to serve

Savory pork meatballs and jasmine rice give this Thai soup heft, but its aromatic broth—made with plenty of shallots, garlic, lemon grass and ginger—has excellent flavor on its own. The soup is a sort of blank canvas for garnishes. Lime wedges and chili-garlic sauce are a start; another option is soft- or hard-cooked eggs, peeled and halved lengthwise.

Don't skip refrigerating the meatballs; chilling helps them hold together in the soup.

In a medium bowl, mix the pork, 1 tablespoon of the fish sauce, 1 tablespoon of the chili-garlic sauce and ¾ teaspoon white pepper. Form into 20 meatballs (about 2 teaspoons each). Place on a large plate and refrigerate for 10 minutes.

In a large Dutch oven over medium-high, heat the lard until shimmering. Add the shallots and ½ teaspoon salt, then cook, stirring, until browned, about 5 minutes. Stir in the garlic and cook until fragrant, about 30 seconds. Stir in the lemon grass and ginger and cook until fragrant, about 30 seconds. Add the broth and bring to a boil, scraping up any browned bits, then reduce to medium and simmer, uncovered, until the flavors blend, about 15 minutes.

Remove and discard the lemon grass. Add the meatballs, stir gently and simmer over medium until just cooked through, 3 to 4 minutes. Stir in the rice and cook until heated through, about 1 minute. Off heat, stir in the remaining 2 tablespoons fish sauce, the remaining 1 tablespoon chili-garlic sauce, the remaining 1 teaspoon white pepper, the cilantro and lime juice. Ladle into bowls and serve with chili-garlic sauce and lime wedges.

Pork Chops in Chipotle Sauce

(Chuletas de Puerco Enchipotladas)

START TO FINISH:
30 minutes

SERVINGS:
4

1 pound plum tomatoes, cored and cut into chunks

1 medium white onion, cut into chunks

4 medium garlic cloves, peeled

4 chipotle chilies in adobo and the sauce clinging to them, plus adobo as needed

1 teaspoon ground cumin

Kosher salt and ground black pepper

4 center-cut bone-in pork chops, about 8 ounces each and about ½-inch thick, patted dry

1 tablespoon grapeseed or other neutral oil

¾ teaspoon dried oregano

1½ ounces cotija cheese, crumbled

Fresh cilantro, to serve

Pan-fried pork chops get a savory-spicy partner in a chipotle-tomato sauce drawn from a Mexican culinary tradition. Four chipotle chilies go into the sauce for substantial, but not incendiary, heat. If you like, add more adobo sauce after simmering to increase the spiciness. To keep things tender and succulent, we browned only one side of ½-inch-thick bone-in pork chops. Simmering the chops in the sauce finished them without overcooking the meat. Slightly thicker chops also work: If using ¾- to 1-inch chops, brown on both sides (about 6 minutes total) before removing them from the pan. Partially cover the skillet during simmering and increase the simmering time to 7 to 9 minutes. Serve with warmed tortillas or roasted potatoes or sweet potatoes.

Don't forget to nick the silver skin on the pork chops. *This prevents them from curling during browning. Also, be sure to let the skillet cool a bit before pouring in the tomato puree. Otherwise the puree will splatter.*

In a blender, puree the tomatoes, onion, garlic, chilies, cumin and 1 teaspoon salt until smooth, about 1 minute. Using a paring knife, make a couple of vertical cuts in the silver skin that encircles each chop; evenly space the cuts and try to cut through the silver skin without cutting into the meat. Season the chops on both sides with salt and pepper.

In a 12-inch skillet over medium-high, heat the oil until barely smoking. Add 2 of the chops in a single layer and cook until well browned, about 3 minutes. Transfer to a large plate, turning the chops browned side up. Repeat with the remaining 2 chops. Let the empty skillet cool for 2 to 3 minutes.

Add the tomato puree and oregano to the skillet. Cook over medium, stirring and scraping up any browned bits, until slightly thickened, 10 to 15 minutes; adjust the heat as needed to maintain a simmer. Return the chops, browned side up, and any accumulated juices to the pan, nestling the chops into the sauce. Spoon the sauce over the chops to submerge. Cook, uncovered, until the meat near the bone reaches 140°F or is just barely pink when cut into, 4 to 5 minutes.

Transfer the chops to a platter. Taste the sauce and season with salt and pepper; for added spiciness, stir in additional adobo. Spoon the sauce over and around the chops, then sprinkle with the cotija and cilantro.

Orecchiette with Sausage
and Chard

START TO FINISH:
35 minutes

SERVINGS:
4

12 ounces orecchiette pasta

Kosher salt and ground black pepper

¼ cup extra-virgin olive oil

10 medium garlic cloves, thinly sliced

1 pound hot or sweet Italian sausage, casings removed

2 teaspoons ground fennel

½ teaspoon red pepper flakes

¾ cup dry white wine

½ cup drained Peppadew peppers, finely chopped

1 pound Swiss or rainbow chard, stems sliced ½ inch thick and leaves roughly chopped, reserved separately

Parmesan cheese, grated, to serve

Orecchiette, or "little ears," are a round pasta from Italy's Puglia region with a cup-like shape that does a great job of catching sauce. We started with the classic pairing of Italian sausage—sweet or hot styles both worked. But instead of the customary broccoli rabe, we used chard, which has an earthier and less bitter taste. Chard leaves wilt quickly, while the stems have a succulent, crisp texture similar to celery. To bring out the best in both, we followed Nancy Silverton's lead from "The Mozza Cookbook," cooking the leaves and stems separately. Can't find orecchiette? Farfalle makes a good substitute. Serve with plenty of grated Parmesan cheese.

Don't discard the chard stems; they add flavor and texture. Make sure to keep the stems and leaves separate after prepping; they go into the skillet at different times.

In a large pot, bring 4 quarts of water to a boil. Add the pasta and 2 tablespoons salt and cook until al dente. Reserve ¾ cup of the cooking water, then drain the pasta and return it to the pot. Set aside.

Meanwhile, in a 12-inch nonstick skillet over medium, heat the oil and garlic, stirring, until the garlic is light golden brown, 2 to 4 minutes. Using a slotted spoon, transfer the garlic to a paper towel–lined plate and set aside. Pour off and reserve the garlic oil.

Add the sausage to the skillet and cook over medium, stirring and breaking it up, until lightly browned, 3 to 4 minutes. Add the fennel and pepper flakes and cook, stirring constantly, until fragrant, about 30 seconds. Stir in the wine and reserved garlic and cook, scraping up any browned bits, until the liquid is reduced and the skillet is nearly dry, 3 to 5 minutes. Stir in the Peppadews, then scrape the mixture into the pot with the pasta. Stir and set the pot over low heat.

Return the skillet to medium-high and heat 2 tablespoons of the reserved garlic oil until shimmering. Stir in the chard stems and ½ teaspoon salt. Cook, stirring, until lightly browned and softened, about 3 minutes. Add the chard leaves and cook, stirring, until wilted and tender, about 3 minutes.

Scrape the chard mixture into the pot with the pasta and stir in up to ½ cup of the reserved pasta water; add only as much as needed to get a creamy consistency. Taste and season with salt and pepper. Transfer to a serving platter then serve with Parmesan and drizzled with the remaining garlic oil.

Hazelnut-Crusted Chicken Cutlets

with Arugula and Fennel Salad

START TO FINISH:
30 minutes

SERVINGS:
4

½ cup hazelnuts, finely chopped

⅓ cup panko breadcrumbs

Kosher salt and ground black pepper

Four 5- to 6-ounce chicken breast cutlets, pounded to an even ¼-inch thickness

½ cup lightly packed fresh tarragon, chopped, divided

⅓ cup grapeseed or other neutral oil

⅓ cup extra-virgin olive oil

¼ cup red wine vinegar

5-ounce container (6 cups) baby arugula

½ medium fennel bulb, trimmed, halved, cored and thinly sliced

1 medium shallot, halved and thinly sliced

1 lemon, cut into wedges

We coated these cutlets with a blend of chopped hazelnuts and panko breadcrumbs, creating a crunchy contrast to the tender chicken. A quickly tossed salad of arugula and fennel dressed with a simple vinaigrette rounds out the meal and provides a refreshingly cool counterpoint to the crispy cutlets. Chicken cutlets are boneless, skinless breasts that have been halved horizontally; look for cutlets that weigh 5 to 6 ounces each. We pounded the cutlets between sheets of plastic wrap to an even ¼-inch thickness before seasoning. This allows them to cook quickly and evenly. If your cutlets are already ¼ inch thick, skip this step.

Don't worry about removing the hazelnut skins; they won't make a difference in the finished dish. And don't pound the cutlets thinner than ¼ inch; they may tear and won't all fit in the skillet.

In a wide, shallow dish, stir together the hazelnuts, panko and 1½ teaspoons salt. Season the cutlets on both sides with salt and pepper, then sprinkle with 3 tablespoons of the tarragon, pressing it into the chicken to adhere. One at a time, add the cutlets to the hazelnut-panko mixture, pressing into the mixture and coating both sides. Place the cutlets on a large plate.

In a 12-inch skillet over medium-high, heat the grapeseed oil until shimmering. Add the cutlets in a single layer and cook until golden brown, about 2 minutes. Flip the cutlets and cook until the second sides are golden, about another 2 minutes. Transfer to a paper towel–lined plate.

In a large bowl, whisk the olive oil, vinegar, remaining tarragon, and ¼ teaspoon each salt and pepper. Add the arugula, fennel and shallot, then toss. Serve the cutlets with the salad and lemon wedges on the side.

The recipe calls for discarding the chunk of pecorino after it boils with the pasta. But most of us couldn't resist popping it in our mouths.

Pasta all'Amatriciana

START TO FINISH:
30 minutes

SERVINGS:
4

3 tablespoons extra-virgin olive oil, divided

3 ounces thinly sliced pancetta, finely chopped

10 medium garlic cloves, thinly sliced

½ teaspoon red pepper flakes

¾ cup dry white wine

14½-ounce can whole peeled tomatoes, drained, juices reserved, tomatoes crushed by hand into small pieces

1-ounce chunk pecorino Romano cheese, plus more finely grated, to serve

Kosher salt and ground black pepper

12 ounces spaghetti

This classic pasta dish traditionally is prepared with guanciale (cured pork cheek), but more widely available pancetta is a good substitute. Be sure to purchase thinly sliced pancetta and chop it finely to ensure the pieces crisp with cooking. Simmering a chunk of pecorino Romano with the pasta is an unconventional technique, but we found that it allowed the cheese to season the pasta throughout, resulting in a fuller-flavored finished dish. We also boiled the pasta in only 2 quarts of water to concentrate the starch and cheese flavor. If the sauced pasta thickens before you serve it, toss in a little more reserved cooking water to loosen its consistency.

Don't boil the pasta until al dente. Drain it when it's a minute or two shy of al dente; it will continue to cook when added to the sauce in the skillet.

In a 12-inch skillet over medium, heat 1 tablespoon of the oil until shimmering. Add the pancetta and cook, stirring, until well-browned and crisp, 5 to 7 minutes. Using a slotted spoon, transfer to a paper towel–lined plate and set aside.

Return the skillet to medium and add the garlic; cook, stirring, until light golden brown, about 2 minutes. Stir in the pepper flakes and cook until fragrant, about 30 seconds. Add the wine, increase to medium-high and cook, stirring, until most of the liquid has evaporated, 5 to 7 minutes. Add the drained tomatoes and cook, stirring, until heated, about 2 minutes. Stir in 3 tablespoons of the reserved tomato juice, then remove from the heat.

Meanwhile, in a large pot, bring 2 quarts of water and the pecorino chunk to a boil, stirring occasionally to prevent the cheese from sticking to the pot. Stir in the pasta and 2 teaspoons salt. Cook, stirring often, until the pasta is just shy of al dente. Remove and discard the pecorino, then drain the pasta in a colander set in a large heat-safe bowl; reserve the cooking water.

Set the skillet over medium-high, stir in 1½ cups of the reserved pasta water and bring to a simmer. Add the drained pasta, tossing with tongs. Cook, stirring occasionally, until most of the liquid has been absorbed, 3 to 6 minutes.

Off heat, stir in the remaining 2 tablespoons oil, the pancetta and 2 teaspoons black pepper. Transfer to a serving bowl and serve with grated pecorino on the side.

Vietnamese Shaking Beef

(Bò Lúc Lắc)

START TO FINISH:
30 minutes

SERVINGS:
4

1½ pounds beef sirloin tips or tri-tip, trimmed, patted dry, cut into 1½-inch pieces

3 tablespoons soy sauce, divided

Kosher salt and ground black pepper

5 tablespoons lime juice, divided, plus lime wedges, to serve

3 tablespoons fish sauce

2 tablespoons white sugar

2 tablespoons grapeseed or other neutral oil, divided

8 medium garlic cloves, finely chopped

1 small red onion, sliced ¼ inch thick

1 bunch watercress, stemmed

The name of this Vietnamese dish refers to the way cooks shake the pan while the beef cooks. Though we were inspired by the flavors of the traditional dish, we preferred to minimize the meat's movement so the pieces achieve a nice dark, flavor-building sear. Sirloin tips (also called flap meat) or tri-tip are excellent cuts for this recipe—both are meaty, tender and reasonably priced (many recipes for shaking beef call for pricier beef tenderloin). If you can find baby watercress, use a 4-ounce container in place of the regular watercress; baby cress has a particularly peppery bite that pairs well with the beef. Serve with steamed jasmine rice.

Don't cut the beef into pieces smaller than 1½ inches or they may overcook. And don't forget the lime wedges for serving. A squeeze of fresh lime juice brightens the other flavors.

In a medium bowl, combine the beef, 2 tablespoons soy sauce and ½ teaspoon pepper. Toss and set aside. In a small bowl, stir together 4 tablespoons of the lime juice, the fish sauce, sugar and remaining 1 tablespoon soy sauce.

In a 12-inch skillet over medium-high, heat 1 tablespoon of the oil until barely smoking. Swirl to coat the pan, then add the beef in a single layer. Cook without stirring until well browned, about 1½ minutes. Flip each piece and cook until the second sides are well browned, about another 1½ minutes. Transfer to a medium bowl.

To the same skillet, add the remaining 1 tablespoon oil, the garlic and 1 teaspoon pepper. Cook over low, stirring constantly, until fragrant and the garlic is no longer raw, about 30 seconds. Pour in the lime juice mixture and any accumulated meat juices, increase to medium-high and cook, stirring constantly, until the liquid is syrupy and a spoon leaves a trail when dragged across the skillet, 2 to 4 minutes.

Add the beef and cook, stirring and scraping up any browned bits, until the sauce clings lightly to the meat, about 2 minutes. Add the onion and stir until slightly softened, about 1 minute. Remove from the heat.

In a medium bowl, toss the watercress with the remaining 1 tablespoon lime juice and ½ teaspoon salt. Make a bed of the watercress on a serving platter. Top with the beef mixture and its juices. Serve with lime wedges.

Risi e Bisi

START TO FINISH:
35 minutes

SERVINGS:
4

6 cups low-sodium chicken broth

2 sprigs fresh thyme

2-ounce piece Parmesan cheese rind

Kosher salt and ground black pepper

2 tablespoons salted butter, divided

3 ounces pancetta, cut into 1-inch pieces (½ cup)

¾ cup finely chopped shallots

2 medium garlic cloves, thinly sliced

1½ cups Arborio rice

2 cups (10 ounces) frozen baby peas

3 ounces finely grated Parmesan cheese, (1½ cups) plus extra to serve

2 tablespoons lemon juice, or to taste

This traditional Venetian dish, usually made in spring when fresh peas are at their best, is similar to risotto but is slightly soupier and not quite as creamy. Medium-grain Arborio rice worked best; it has the necessary starch to thicken the cooking liquid. We used frozen baby peas to give this year-round ease. High-quality Parmesan cheese is key to the dish's savoriness.

Don't forget to simmer the Parmesan rind in the broth. It's an easy way to add deep savory flavors.

In a medium saucepan over medium-high, combine the broth, thyme, Parmesan rind and ½ teaspoon salt. Bring to a boil, then reduce to low and keep at a bare simmer.

In another medium saucepan over medium, melt 1 tablespoon of the butter. Add the pancetta and cook, stirring, until golden and crisp, about 6 minutes. Use a slotted spoon to transfer to a paper towel–lined plate. Pour off and discard all but 2 tablespoons of the fat.

Return the pan to medium heat and add the shallot and garlic. Cook, stirring, until softened but not browned, about 5 minutes. Stir in the rice and cook until the edges begin to appear translucent, about 3 minutes. Remove and discard the thyme and rind from the broth. Add 2 cups of the broth and 1½ teaspoons salt to the rice and cook, stirring and adjusting the heat to maintain a gentle simmer, until mostly absorbed, about 6 minutes. Add the remaining broth 2 cups at a time, letting it be absorbed before adding more, and simmer until the rice is just tender and quite soupy (a little runny around the edges), 20 to 25 minutes total.

Off heat, stir in the peas and ½ teaspoon pepper. Cover and let sit until heated through, 1 to 2 minutes. Stir in the cheese, the remaining 1 tablespoon butter and the lemon juice. If too thick, add more broth. Taste and season with salt and pepper. Divide among 4 shallow bowls and top with the pancetta and extra Parmesan.

Persian Barley-Vegetable Soup

START TO FINISH: **35 minutes**

SERVINGS: **4**

⅔ cup quick-cooking barley

1 tablespoon extra-virgin olive oil

3 medium carrots, peeled and finely shredded

1 medium leek, dark green top discarded, white and light green parts finely chopped

Kosher salt and ground black pepper

1 teaspoon ground turmeric

1 quart low-sodium chicken broth

5 tablespoons chopped dried cranberries, divided

¼ cup sour cream, plus more to serve

1 tablespoon lemon juice

Chopped fresh dill, flat-leaf parsley or mint, to serve

Toasting the barley may not be traditional to this Persian comfort food, but we found it was an easy way to subtly enhance the soup's flavor and aroma. Shredded carrots lend an earthy sweetness, ground turmeric creates a golden hue and sour cream adds a rich and tangy touch. Be sure to use the small holes of a box grater to finely shred the carrots. For this soup, we used quick-cooking barley rather than pearled barley. Quick-cooking barley, which resembles rolled oats, allows the dish to be on the table in under 45 minutes. The dried cranberries may seem a curious addition, but they lend welcome tartness and color and are a good stand-in for hard-to-find barberries, widely used in Persian cooking.

Don't stir the sour cream directly into the soup. Tempering it first with a bit of the hot liquid ensures it won't curdle. Also, don't use reduced-fat sour cream or Greek yogurt in place of regular sour cream. Greek yogurt separated when stirred in and reduced-fat sour cream lacks the proper richness.

In a large saucepan over medium-high, toast the barley, stirring occasionally, until lightly browned, 4 to 5 minutes. Transfer to a small bowl. Set the pan over medium and add the oil, carrots, leek and ¼ teaspoon salt. Cover and cook, stirring occasionally, until the vegetables have softened, about 10 minutes.

Stir in the turmeric and cook until fragrant, about 30 seconds. Stir in the broth and barley. Bring to a boil over medium-high, then reduce to medium-low, cover and cook, stirring occasionally and adjusting the heat to maintain a simmer, until the barley is tender, 10 to 12 minutes. Off heat, stir in 3 tablespoons of the cranberries.

In a small bowl, whisk together the sour cream and ⅓ cup of the soup, then slowly whisk this mixture back into the soup. Let stand for 5 minutes, then stir in the lemon juice. Taste and season with salt and pepper. Ladle into bowls and serve, with additional sour cream, the dill and remaining cranberries on the side.

Spiced Turkey Cutlets

with Apricot-Shallot Chutney

START TO FINISH:	SERVINGS:
35 minutes	**4**

1 teaspoon ground cinnamon

½ teaspoon ground cloves

¼ teaspoon cayenne pepper

Kosher salt and ground black pepper

3 tablespoons lemon juice, divided, plus 1 tablespoon grated lemon zest

⅓ cup plus 2 tablespoons grapeseed or other neutral oil, divided

Four 4- to 6-ounce turkey breast cutlets, pounded to ¼ inch thick

4 medium shallots, each peeled and cut into 8 wedges

¼ cup chopped dried apricots

2 teaspoons honey

2 teaspoons yellow mustard seeds

½ cup whole-wheat flour

2 tablespoons chopped fresh cilantro, divided

Quick-cooking turkey cutlets are the perfect foil for a fruity and savory chutney inspired by Morocco's tradition of pairing sweet, spiced relishes with meats. We pound the cutlets to a ¼-inch thickness so they cook evenly. We then dredge the cutlets in whole-wheat flour, which takes on a nutty flavor during cooking. The chutney, with its balance of apricots, shallots and warm spices, adds punchy, sweet-tart flavor. If you prefer, substitute dried sour cherries for the apricots.

Don't pound the turkey cutlets *if they come out of the package already ¼ inch thick. Use them as they are.*

In a medium bowl, stir together the cinnamon, cloves, cayenne, 2 teaspoons salt and 1½ teaspoons black pepper. Set aside 2 teaspoons of the mix. Whisk 2 tablespoons of the lemon juice and 1 tablespoon of the oil into the remaining spice mix. Add the turkey cutlets and coat on both sides. Set aside.

In a 10-inch skillet over medium, heat 1 tablespoon of the oil until shimmering. Add the shallots and cook, stirring, until lightly golden, about 4 minutes. Stir in 1 teaspoon of the reserved spice mix and cook until fragrant, about 20 seconds. Stir in ⅔ cup water, the apricots, honey and mustard seeds. Cover and cook over medium-low, stirring once or twice, until the shallots have softened and the liquid is syrupy, about 15 minutes. Remove from the heat and set aside.

Pat the cutlets dry with paper towels. In a wide, shallow dish, stir together the flour and remaining 1 teaspoon spice mix, then distribute in an even layer. Line a large plate with paper towels.

In a 12-inch skillet over medium-high, heat the remaining ⅓ cup oil until shimmering. Transfer each cutlet to the flour mixture and turn to coat both sides, then gently shake off the excess and place in the skillet. Cook until golden brown on the bottom, about 2 minutes. Flip and cook until the second sides are golden, about another 2 minutes. Transfer to the prepared plate to drain, then place on a serving plate.

Stir the remaining 1 tablespoon lemon juice and the zest into the chutney, then taste and season with salt and pepper. Transfer to a serving bowl and sprinkle with the cilantro. Serve with the cutlets.

The combination of creamy yogurt, tangy sumac and tomato paste creates an amazing sauce that had us coming back for seconds.

Pasta with Browned Butter,
Yogurt and Herbs

START TO FINISH:	SERVINGS:
30 minutes	**4**

6 tablespoons plain whole-milk yogurt

1 teaspoon grated lemon zest

3 tablespoons minced fresh oregano, divided

2 teaspoons sumac, divided

Kosher salt and ground black pepper

12 ounces campanelle or other short pasta

8 tablespoons (1 stick) salted butter, cut into 4 pieces

¼ cup tomato paste

4 medium garlic cloves, minced

½ cup lightly packed fresh mint, chopped

½ cup lightly packed fresh flat-leaf parsley, chopped

This dish was inspired by a sauce traditionally spooned over manti, Turkish boiled dumplings typically filled with meat. For rich, full flavor, make sure to cook the butter until the milk solids are deeply browned. Any short, sauce-catching pasta shape works well here, even filled pastas, such as ravioli or tortellini.

Don't use tomato paste from a tube for this recipe. Tomato paste sold in tubes usually is double concentrated and will give the dish an overwhelming tomato flavor.

In a large bowl, stir together the yogurt, lemon zest, 2 tablespoons of the oregano, 1 teaspoon of the sumac and 1½ teaspoons salt. Set aside. In a large pot, bring 4 quarts of water to a boil. Add the pasta and 2 tablespoons salt and cook until the pasta is al dente. Reserve ½ cup of the cooking water, then drain the pasta. Add the pasta and reserved cooking water to the yogurt mixture and toss to coat.

Meanwhile, in a 10-inch skillet over medium, melt the butter. Continue to cook, swirling the pan, until the milk solids at the bottom are deep golden brown and the butter has the aroma of toasted nuts, 4 to 5 minutes. Remove from the heat and whisk in the tomato paste, garlic, ½ teaspoon each salt and pepper, the remaining 1 tablespoon oregano and remaining 1 teaspoon sumac. The mixture will appear slightly broken.

Add the mint, parsley and all but 2 tablespoons of the butter mixture to the pasta and toss. Taste and season with salt and pepper. Transfer to a serving bowl and drizzle with the remaining butter mixture and sprinkle with additional pepper.

Toasted Pearl Couscous

with Fried Eggs

START TO FINISH:
30 minutes

SERVINGS:
4

½ teaspoon ground sumac

½ teaspoon za'atar seasoning

5 tablespoons extra-virgin olive oil, divided

1 cup pearl couscous

1 medium shallot, minced

2½ cups hot water

4 medium garlic cloves, 2 minced and 2 smashed and peeled

Kosher salt

4 teaspoons lemon juice

2 tablespoons salted butter

2 scallions, thinly sliced on diagonal

4 large eggs

For this vegetarian main, we browned pearl couscous (also called Israeli couscous) to give it a toasted-wheat flavor, then cooked it risotto-style for a rich, creamy consistency. The couscous is an ideal base for runny-yolked fried eggs sprinkled with mix of za'atar and sumac. If you like, finish with harissa or hot sauce for a hit of heat and spice to perk up the other flavors. A simple parsley or arugula salad on the side makes a good counterpoint to the creaminess of the couscous.

Don't use regular couscous in place of pearl couscous. Regular couscous is much finer, requires different hydration and doesn't have the right chewiness. Also, don't over-toast the couscous. Aim for a light golden brown; toasting beyond that produces a flavor that overwhelms the other ingredients.

In a small bowl, combine the sumac and za'atar. Set aside. In a medium saucepan over medium, heat 1 tablespoon of the oil until shimmering. Add the couscous and cook, stirring constantly, until lightly browned, 3 to 4 minutes. Transfer to a paper towel-lined plate and set aside.

To the same pan, add 1 tablespoon of the remaining oil, the shallot and minced garlic. Set over medium heat and cook, stirring constantly, until the shallot has softened, about 1 minute. Return the couscous to the pan, then stir in ½ teaspoon salt. Pour in ½ cup of the hot water and cook, stirring, until most of the water is absorbed, about 2 minutes. Repeat this 4 more times, cooking until the couscous is tender, 10 to 15 minutes. Off heat, stir in the lemon juice, butter and scallions. Taste and season with salt, then cover and set aside.

In a 12-inch nonstick skillet over medium, heat the remaining 3 tablespoons oil and the smashed garlic. Cook, stirring and flipping the garlic, until golden, 1 to 2 minutes. Remove and discard the garlic, then reduce to medium-low. Crack an egg into each quadrant of the pan and use a silicone spatula to gently push the edges of the egg whites toward the yolks to keep the eggs separate. Cover and cook until the whites are set but the yolks are runny, about 1½ minutes. Remove the pan from the heat.

Serve the couscous in individual bowls, topped with a fried egg and a generous pinch of the sumac mixture.

Vietnamese Meatball

Lettuce Wraps

START TO FINISH:
35 minutes

SERVINGS:
4

3 teaspoons grapeseed or other neutral oil, divided

1 pound ground pork

⅓ cup chopped fresh cilantro, plus sprigs, to serve

½ teaspoon ground black pepper

6 scallions, white and light green parts minced, dark green parts thinly sliced

5 tablespoons fish sauce, divided

2 tablespoons plus 2 teaspoons white sugar, divided

½ cup lime juice

1 or 2 serrano chilies, stemmed, seeded and thinly sliced

2 medium carrots, peeled and shredded (1 cup)

Lettuce leaves, to serve

In Vietnam, meatballs are often skewered and grilled. But for a quick weeknight meal, a skillet does a fine job. You could serve these over steamed rice or rice vermicelli, but we liked them with herbs and lettuce leaves for wrapping, along with a lime juice and fish sauce mixture for drizzling. They're also a great filling for our Vietnamese skirt steak sandwiches (see page 305).

Don't be timid when mixing the pork; you want to vigorously stir it to compact it. This creates a pleasantly springy texture in the meatballs.

Coat a large plate with 1 teaspoon of the oil; set aside. In a medium bowl, combine the pork, 3 tablespoons water, cilantro, pepper, minced scallions, 2 tablespoons of fish sauce and 2 teaspoons sugar. Mix vigorously with a silicone spatula until combined, 20 to 30 seconds. The mixture will be soft and sticky. With lightly moistened hands, form into 20 balls and place on the prepared plate. Cover and refrigerate for 15 minutes.

Meanwhile, in a small bowl, stir together the lime juice, the 3 remaining tablespoons fish sauce, the remaining 2 tablespoons sugar and the chilies until the sugar dissolves. Set aside.

Line another plate with paper towels. In a 12-inch nonstick skillet over medium-high, heat the remaining 2 teaspoons oil until barely smoking. Add the meatballs and cook undisturbed until the bottoms are golden brown, 1 to 2 minutes. Using a spatula, turn each meatball and continue to cook, adjusting the heat as needed and occasionally turning the meatballs, until golden brown all over, 4 to 5 minutes. Transfer to the prepared plate, tent with foil and let rest 5 minutes.

In a small bowl, toss the carrots with 2 tablespoons of the lime juice sauce. Serve the meatballs with the carrots, cilantro sprigs, sliced scallions and lettuce leaves for wrapping. Spoon the remaining sauce onto the wraps.

Roast Cod

with Tahini-Herb Butter

START TO FINISH:	SERVINGS:
30 minutes	**4**

Four 6-ounce cod fillets, about 1 inch thick, patted dry

2 tablespoons extra-virgin olive oil

Kosher salt and ground black pepper

4 tablespoons (½ stick) salted butter, softened

3 tablespoons tahini

2 teaspoons grated lemon zest, plus lemon wedges, to serve

⅛ teaspoon cayenne pepper

3 tablespoons minced fresh flat-leaf parsley

3 tablespoons minced fresh cilantro

1 tablespoon sesame seeds, toasted

A compound butter made with nutty-tasting tahini and fresh herbs lends richness to simple roasted cod fillets. We used 1-inch-thick fillets when developing this recipe, but they can vary in thickness, so assess yours before cooking and adjust the time as needed. If your fillets vary in thickness, check the thinner ones for doneness before the thicker ones and remove them from the oven as they finish.

Don't forget to take the butter out of the refrigerator and allow it to soften before beginning this recipe. If the butter is cold, it won't mix well with the other ingredients.

Heat the oven to 450°F with a rack in the middle position. Brush the fillets on both sides with the oil, then season with salt and pepper. Place the fillets skin side down in a 13-by-9-inch baking pan. Roast until the center of each reaches 120°F or the flesh flakes easily, 12 to 15 minutes.

Meanwhile, in a small bowl, stir together the butter, tahini, lemon zest, cayenne, and 2 tablespoons each of the parsley and cilantro. Taste and season with salt and pepper; set aside.

When the fish is done, leave the fillets in the pan and dollop the butter mixture over them. Tent with foil, then let rest for 5 minutes. Transfer the fillets to a serving platter. Sprinkle with sesame seeds and the remaining herbs. Squeeze 1 lemon wedge over the fillets and serve with additional lemon wedges.

Black-Eyed Pea Stew

with Tomato (Red-Red)

START TO FINISH:
30 minutes

SERVINGS:
4

¼ cup refined coconut oil

1 large yellow onion, quartered lengthwise and thinly sliced

2 jalapeño chilies, stemmed, halved, seeded and thinly sliced

3-ounce piece fresh ginger, cut into 4 to 6 chunks

1 tablespoon tomato paste

1 tablespoon curry powder

1 teaspoon chipotle chili powder

Four 15½-ounce cans black-eyed peas, drained and rinsed

2 tablespoons soy sauce

1 pint cherry or grape tomatoes, halved

Kosher salt and ground black pepper

Lime wedges, to serve

Plantain chips, to serve

Heady with ginger and chilies, Ghana's "red-red" stew gets its namesake color from a combination of red palm oil and tomatoes. We found the more widely available refined coconut oil was a good substitute for red palm oil. For the legumes, we preferred Whole Foods' 365 Everyday Value canned black-eyed peas for their soft, creamy texture. Goya brand, sold in slightly larger cans, also yielded good results, but the texture was a bit firmer. Red-red typically is paired with thick slabs of fried plantain; we opted for the simplicity and crunch of store-bought plantain chips. If you like, garnish the stew with cilantro leaves and, for added spice, offer hot sauce on the side.

Don't use unrefined coconut oil, which will give the dish a distinct coconut flavor.

In a large Dutch oven over medium-high, heat the coconut oil until shimmering. Add the onion and cook, stirring occasionally, until beginning to brown, about 5 minutes. Stir in the jalapeños, ginger, tomato paste, curry powder and chipotle powder. Cook until fragrant, about 1 minute.

Add the black-eyed peas and stir well. Stir in 1½ cups water, the soy sauce and tomatoes, then bring to a simmer. Reduce to medium-low and cook, uncovered, stirring occasionally and adjusting the heat to maintain a gentle but steady simmer, until slightly thickened, about 20 minutes.

Remove and discard the ginger chunks, then taste and season with salt and pepper. Let cool for 5 minutes. Serve with lime wedges and plantain chips.

When we teach this dish at Milk Street's cooking school, we skip the skewers and arrange the strips of chicken on a wire rack set in a rimmed baking sheet. Not as pretty. Just as delicious. And easier!

Moroccan Chicken Skewers

START TO FINISH:
30 minutes

SERVINGS:
4

3 lemons

¼ cup extra-virgin olive oil, plus extra to serve

2 medium garlic cloves, finely grated

1 tablespoon finely grated fresh ginger

1 tablespoon ground cumin

1 tablespoon ground coriander

Kosher salt and ground black pepper

3 tablespoons honey, divided

1½ pounds boneless, skinless chicken thighs, trimmed and cut crosswise into thirds

¼ cup minced fresh cilantro, flat-leaf parsley or mint

Charred lemon halves topped with a drizzle of honey provide a sweet-tart counterpoint to chicken in this robustly flavored dish. The chicken gets a spice rub inspired by a recipe for chermoula in Mourad Lahlou's "New Moroccan." Minced fresh cilantro, parsley or mint brings bright color and herbal freshness to the dish. Use whichever you prefer, or a combination.

Don't marinate the chicken longer than 30 minutes or the lemon juice and ginger will make it mushy.

With a wand-style grater, use 1 lemon to grate 1 tablespoon zest and squeeze 2 tablespoons juice into a large bowl. Stir in the oil, garlic, ginger, cumin, coriander, 2 teaspoons salt, 1 teaspoon pepper and 2 tablespoons of honey. Add the chicken, toss and set aside for 15 to 30 minutes. Set a wire rack in a rimmed baking sheet. Heat the broiler with a rack about 4 inches from the element.

Thread the chicken onto four 12-inch metal skewers, scrunching multiple pieces onto each skewer; set the skewers on the prepared rack. Cut the remaining 2 lemons in half and arrange cut side up next to the chicken.

Broil until the chicken is well charred all over, 10 to 15 minutes, turning halfway through; the lemon halves should be charred on the cut sides.

Transfer the skewers and lemon halves to a platter. Drizzle the remaining 1 tablespoon honey over the cut sides of the lemons. Squeeze the juice from 1 lemon half over the chicken, drizzle with olive oil and sprinkle with the herbs. Serve with the remaining lemon halves on the side.

Minchi, like any hash, begs to be topped with a fried egg and a squeeze of Sriracha.

Macanese Meat-and-Potato
Hash (Minchi)

START TO FINISH:	SERVINGS:
35 minutes	**4**

1¾ pounds Yukon Gold potatoes, peeled and cut into ½-inch cubes

Kosher salt and ground black pepper

12 ounces ground pork

3 tablespoons finely grated fresh ginger

2 tablespoons packed dark brown sugar

2 tablespoons tomato paste

6 scallions, thinly sliced, white and green parts reserved separately

3 tablespoons grapeseed or other neutral oil, divided

2 tablespoons soy sauce

2 tablespoons Worcestershire sauce

2 tablespoons unseasoned rice vinegar

½ cup lightly packed fresh cilantro, chopped

This classic Macanese hash can be served for dinner, lunch or breakfast. Variations abound, but minchi usually consists of minced meat and fried potatoes seasoned with soy and Worcestershire sauces. Fresh ginger, not a usual player, brightens up the mix.

Don't microwave the potatoes until fully cooked; they should be only almost tender so they don't turn to mush in the skillet.

In a large microwafe-safe bowl, combine the potatoes, ¾ teaspoon salt and ¼ cup water. Cover with plastic wrap and microwave on high until almost tender, about 5 minutes, stirring halfway through. Drain the potatoes.

In a medium bowl, stir together the pork, ginger, sugar, tomato paste, scallion whites and ¾ teaspoon pepper. In a 12-inch nonstick skillet over medium, heat 1 tablespoon of oil until shimmering. Add the pork mixture and cook, breaking it into small pieces and stirring once or twice, until lightly browned, 5 minutes. Transfer to a clean bowl and wipe out the skillet

Set the skillet over medium-high, add the remaining 2 tablespoons oil and heat until shimmering. Add the potatoes and cook, stirring and adjusting heat as needed, until browned and crisped, about 15 minutes. Return the pork to the skillet and add the soy and Worcestershire sauces and vinegar. Toss, then stir in half each of the scallion greens and cilantro. Taste, season with salt and pepper, then transfer to a serving dish and sprinkle with the remaining scallions and cilantro.

Chickpea and Yogurt Soup

START TO FINISH:
30 minutes

SERVINGS:
4

1 large yellow onion, chopped

2 tablespoons salted butter

Kosher salt and ground black pepper

½ cup Arborio rice

4 medium garlic cloves, finely grated

¾ teaspoon red pepper flakes

1 quart low-sodium chicken broth

15½-ounce can chickpeas, drained

1 cup whole-milk yogurt

½ cup chopped fresh parsley

¼ cup chopped fresh dill

Regular whole-milk yogurt—not Greek-style—brought rich, tangy flavor to this soup inspired by a weeknight meal from Yasmin Khan, author of "The Saffron Tales: Recipes from the Persian Kitchen." Be sure to whisk the yogurt into the soup off heat; it will break and curdle if the liquid is too hot. We liked the balanced heat from ¾ teaspoon of red pepper flakes, but for a milder dish, decrease to ½ teaspoon. For a heartier soup, stir in a few handfuls of baby arugula before removing the pot from the heat. Khan prefers this soup seasoned with dried mint and chives, but we found dill and parsley added plenty of flavor.

Don't substitute long-grain white rice for the Arborio. The soup won't develop its silky texture.

In a 2-quart saucepan over medium, combine the onion, butter and 1 teaspoon salt. Cook, stirring occasionally, until the onion is softened and browned around the edges, 6 to 8 minutes. Stir in the rice, garlic and pepper flakes, then cook, stirring, until the garlic is fragrant, about 30 seconds. Add the broth and 1 cup water, then bring to a boil. Reduce to medium-low and simmer for 15 minutes.

Add the chickpeas, then cook, stirring occasionally, until the rice is very soft and the soup has thickened, about 5 minutes. Off heat, whisk in the yogurt, parsley and dill. Taste and season with salt and pepper.

Paprika-Rubbed Pork Tenderloin

START TO FINISH:
30 minutes

SERVINGS:
4

1 tablespoon sweet paprika

2 teaspoons hot smoked paprika

2 teaspoons fresh thyme, minced

Kosher salt and ground black pepper

Two 1¼-pound pork tenderloins, trimmed of silver skin and halved crosswise

2 tablespoons grapeseed or other neutral oil

6 medium garlic cloves, thinly sliced

2 teaspoons honey

¾ cup low-sodium chicken broth

2 tablespoons sherry vinegar

6 tablespoons (¾ stick) salted butter, chilled and cut into 10 pieces

2 tablespoons chopped fresh flat-leaf parsley

Earthy, hot smoked paprika, otherwise known as pimenton de la Vera, is a defining flavor of Basque cooking. We combine it with regular sweet paprika, thyme and garlic to give smoky-spicy flavor to pan-roasted pork tenderloins. If you can't find hot smoked paprika, use sweet smoked paprika but add ¼ teaspoon cayenne pepper for a bit of heat. The tenderloins are seared on the stovetop then finished in the oven, so you'll need an oven-safe 12-inch skillet. Remove the pork from the oven when it hits 135°F; it will continue to cook with residual heat as you make the sauce. Serve this with roasted fennel and rosemary (page 235) or egg noodles tossed with browned butter and poppy seeds.

Don't add the butter all at once to the pan sauce. Swirling it in 1 tablespoon at a time creates an emulsified sauce that's glossy and full-bodied. If the sauce breaks and the butter separates, drizzle in a few drops of water while swirling the pan until the sauce once again becomes shiny and emulsified.

Heat the oven to 450°F with a rack in the middle position. In a large bowl, mix together both paprikas, the thyme and 2 teaspoons salt. Add the pork, turn to coat and massage into the meat. Let stand at room temperature for 15 minutes.

In an oven-safe 12-inch skillet over medium-high, heat the oil until shimmering. Add the pork and cook, turning occasionally, until browned on all sides, about 4 minutes. Transfer the skillet to the oven and roast until the center of the thickest piece reaches 135°F, or just slightly pink when cut into, 9 to 12 minutes.

Using an oven mitt, transfer the skillet from the oven to the stovetop. Transfer the pork to a large plate, tent with foil, and let rest 10 minutes. Meanwhile, add the garlic to the skillet and cook over medium-high, stirring constantly, until toasted and fragrant, about 1 minute. Add the honey and stir until it slightly darkens, about 30 seconds. Pour in the broth and simmer until reduced and thickened slightly, about 2 minutes.

Add the vinegar and simmer for 30 seconds. Add the butter 1 piece at a time, swirling the pan to emulsify the sauce before adding more butter. Remove from the heat and stir in the parsley. Taste and season with salt and pepper. Cut the tenderloins crosswise into thin slices and arrange on a platter. Spoon the sauce over the pork.

Three-Cup Chicken

START TO FINISH:
35 minutes (15 minutes active)

SERVINGS:
4

2 teaspoons cornstarch

3 tablespoons soy sauce

¾ cup sake

2 tablespoons packed brown sugar

1 tablespoon grapeseed or other neutral oil

2 pounds boneless, skinless chicken thighs, trimmed, patted dry and cut into 1-inch-wide strips

12 medium garlic cloves, halved lengthwise

1 bunch scallions, cut into 1-inch lengths

1 serrano chili, stemmed and sliced into thin rounds

¼ cup minced fresh ginger

2 tablespoons toasted sesame oil

3 cups lightly packed fresh basil leaves, torn if large

Taiwanese three-cup chicken is named for the formula once used to prepare the dish: 1 cup each of sesame oil, soy sauce and rice wine. Not surprisingly, recipes no longer adhere to that ratio, but the name has stuck. Bone-in chicken legs that have been hacked into pieces are traditional for this one-pan dish; we opted for boneless, skinless chicken thighs for easier prep and eating. Though we prefer to use a wok, this recipe also works in a 12-inch skillet. Serve with rice , steamed or stir-fried vegetables, and sesame seeds, if desired.

Don't begin cooking *until all ingredients are prepared; the dish comes together quickly. Don't stir the chicken for about 5 minutes after adding it to the skillet. This helps the chicken brown and develop flavor.*

In a small bowl, stir together the cornstarch and soy sauce, then stir in the sake and sugar. Set aside. Heat a wok over medium-high for 3 minutes, or until a drop of water evaporates within 1 to 2 seconds. Add the oil and swirl to coat the wok. Add the chicken in an even layer and cook without stirring until browned, about 5 minutes.

Add the garlic and cook, stirring occasionally, until the garlic is well-browned and softened, about 4 minutes. Add the scallions, serrano, ginger and sesame oil, then cook, stirring constantly, until the scallions begin to wilt, about 1 minute.

Stir the sake-cornstarch mixture to recombine, then add to the wok. Cook, stirring constantly, until the sauce is thickened, about 3 minutes. Off heat, add the basil and stir until it begins to wilt, about 30 seconds.

Peruvian Quinoa and Corn Chowder

(Chupe de Quinoa)

START TO FINISH:	SERVINGS:
30 minutes	**4**

1 tablespoon extra-virgin olive oil

1 medium red onion, finely chopped

¼ cup ají amarillo paste (see note)

3 tablespoons fresh oregano, chopped

Kosher salt and ground black pepper

8 ounces sweet potato, peeled and cut into ½-inch pieces (1½ cups)

1½ cups corn kernels

¾ cup quinoa, preferably red, rinsed and drained

1¼ quarts (5 cups) low-sodium chicken broth

⅓ cup heavy cream

⅓ cup lightly packed fresh mint, chopped

Lime wedges, to serve

Ají amarillo, an orange-yellow chili with a fruity yet earthy flavor, is ubiquitous in Peruvian cuisine. The fresh chilies are difficult to find in the U.S., but ají amarillo paste, sold in jars, is available at well-stocked markets and specialty stores. The paste is key to the deep, spicy flavor of this quinoa chowder. If you can't find it, use 1 or 2 minced jalapeños instead (if you like, seed the jalapeños for milder heat). The soup is especially good made with fresh in-season corn but, in a pinch, substitute frozen corn kernels. Serve with a simple salad of shredded cabbage, sliced avocado and crumbled queso fresco.

Don't forget to rinse the quinoa to remove the naturally occurring saponin that gives quinoa a bitter flavor. But check the packaging first, as some quinoa is sold prewashed; if so, there's no need to rinse.

In a large Dutch oven over medium, heat the oil until shimmering. Add the onion and cook, stirring, until light golden brown, about 4 minutes. Add the ají amarillo paste, oregano, 1 teaspoon salt and ½ teaspoon pepper. Cook, stirring constantly, until fragrant, about 30 seconds.

Stir in the sweet potato, corn, quinoa and broth. Bring to a boil, then cover and reduce to medium-low. Cook, stirring occasionally, until the potatoes and quinoa are tender, 16 to 19 minutes. Taste and season with salt and pepper. Off heat, stir in the cream. Ladle into bowls, sprinkle with mint and serve with lime wedges.

Miso-Marinated Skirt Steak

START TO FINISH:
35 minutes

SERVINGS:
4

3 tablespoons red miso

1 tablespoon soy sauce

1 tablespoon chili-garlic sauce

1 tablespoon white sugar

2 teaspoons toasted sesame oil

2 teaspoon finely grated fresh ginger

2 medium garlic cloves, finely grated

1½ pounds skirt steak, trimmed and cut crosswise into 5- to 6-inch pieces, patted dry

2 tablespoons unseasoned rice vinegar

5 teaspoons grapeseed or other neutral oil, divided

For this recipe, we preferred red miso for its deep, rich, savory flavor. It's used in both the marinade and the sauce. When slicing the steak, be sure to cut against the grain. This results in shorter muscle fibers, which translates to more tender meat. Serve over steamed rice and, if you like, sprinkle with sesame seeds and sliced scallions.

Don't force the pieces of steak to release from the skillet; when they're nicely seared and ready to be flipped, they will release easily from the pan

In a medium bowl, whisk together the miso, soy sauce, chili-garlic sauce, sugar, sesame oil, ginger and garlic. Measure 2 teaspoons of the mixture into a small bowl and set aside. Add the steak to the remaining mixture, turn to coat and marinate at room temperature for 15 minutes. Meanwhile, to the reserved 2 teaspoons, stir in the vinegar and 3 teaspoons of the grapeseed oil, then set aside.

Remove the steak from the bowl and pat dry with paper towels. In a 12-inch skillet over medium-high, heat the remaining 2 teaspoons grapeseed oil until barely smoking. Add half the steak in a single layer and cook without disturbing until well browned, 2 to 3 minutes. Flip and cook until the second sides are well browned and the center of the thickest piece reaches 125°F for medium-rare, another 2 to 3 minutes. Transfer to a platter, then repeat with the remaining steak, using the fat in the pan. Tent with foil and let rest for 10 minutes.

Stir any accumulated juices on the platter into the reserved miso mixture. Cut the steak against the grain on the bias into thin slices and return to the platter. Serve with the miso sauce.

For deeper flavor with any pasta dish, borrow a trick from our recipe for pasta all'Amatriciana and add an extra 1-ounce chunk of cheese to the pasta boiling water. It effortlessly infuses the pasta with extra flavor.

Rigatoni with Roman
Broccoli Sauce

START TO FINISH:	SERVINGS:
35 minutes	**4**

Kosher salt and ground black pepper

1 pound broccoli, stems and florets separated

1½ cups packed baby spinach

2 medium garlic cloves, chopped

4 tablespoons (½ stick) salted butter, cut into 4 pieces

1 tablespoon drained capers

½ teaspoon red pepper flakes

2 tablespoons grated lemon zest, divided

12 ounces rigatoni pasta

1 ounce pecorino Romano or Parmesan cheese, finely grated (½ cup), plus more to serve

Romans use the leaves that grow around heads of broccoli to make a flavorful sauce for pasta. In the U.S., most of the leaves are stripped off before broccoli is sold. Our recipe instead uses the stems, which are equally flavorful and produce a silky sauce. Baby spinach maintains the color of the original recipe.

Don't undercook the broccoli stems. We're accustomed to cooking vegetables until crisp-tender, but the stems here should be cooked until fully tender.

In a large pot, bring 4 quarts water and 2 tablespoons salt to a boil. Peel the broccoli stems, reserving any leaves, and cut crosswise into ½-inch rounds. Add the stems and leaves to the boiling water and cook until fully tender, about 10 minutes. Stir in the spinach and cook until wilted, about 20 seconds. Using a slotted spoon, transfer the vegetables to a blender; reserve ½ cup of the cooking water. Keep the water at a boil.

Cut the broccoli florets into 1- to 1½-inch pieces. Add the florets to the boiling water and cook until crisp-tender, about 3 minutes. Using the slotted spoon, transfer to a colander and rinse under cold water until cooled. Again, keep the water at a boil.

To the blender, add the garlic, butter, capers, pepper flakes, ¾ teaspoon salt, 1 tablespoon of the lemon zest and the reserved broccoli cooking water. Puree until smooth and bright green, about 30 seconds. Taste and season with salt and pepper.

Stir the rigatoni into the boiling water and cook until al dente. Reserve ½ cup of the cooking water, then drain. Return the pasta to the pot and add the broccoli florets, the broccoli puree, ¼ cup of the reserved cooking water, the remaining 1 tablespoon lemon zest and the cheese.

Cook over medium, stirring constantly, until the sauce thickens slightly and the pasta is well coated, 1 to 2 minutes. Remove from the heat. Taste and season with salt and pepper.

Done in under 30 minutes

Seared Salmon with Avocado Sauce
and Tomato-Cilantro Salsa / 175

Gruyère and Chive Omelet / 177

Kale and White Bean Soup / 179

Peanut-Sesame Noodles / 181

Singapore Chili Shrimp / 183

Cilantro-Tomato Omelet with Turmeric Butter / 184

Salmon Chraimeh / 187

Soba with Edamame and Watercress / 189

Cacio e Pepe / 191

Garlic and Cilantro Soup with Chickpeas
(Açorda a Alentejana) / 193

Onion Frittata with Sherry Vinegar Sauce / 194

Spaghetti with Pancetta (Pasta alla Gricia) / 197

Spaghetti al Limone / 199

Lemon Grass–Coconut Tofu / 201

Turkish Scrambled Eggs with Spicy Tomato
and Capers (Menemen) / 203

Roman Spaghetti Carbonara / 205

Spicy Garlic Soba with Greens / 207

Palestinian Crispy Herb Omelet / 209

Sopa Seca with Butternut Squash / 210

Fastest

Seared Salmon

with Avocado Sauce and Tomato-Cilantro Salsa

START TO FINISH:	SERVINGS:
20 minutes	**4**

1½ cups cherry or grape tomatoes, roughly chopped

5 tablespoons lime juice, divided, plus lime wedges, to serve

Kosher salt

2 scallions, cut into 1-inch lengths

1 Anaheim chili, stemmed, seeded, cut into rough 1-inch pieces

1 habanero chili, stemmed and seeded

2 tablespoons white vinegar

1½ cups lightly packed fresh cilantro, divided

1 ripe avocado, halved, pitted, peeled and chopped

Four 6-ounce center-cut salmon fillets (each 1 to 1¼ inches thick), patted dry

1 tablespoon grapeseed or other neutral oil

2 tablespoons salted butter

We borrow from Colombia's take on guacamole—spiked with both lime juice and vinegar, as well as fresh chilies—to create an easy, no-cook sauce for salmon fillets. A fresh tomato-cilantro salsa finishes the dish, adding a bright, acidic note to balance the rich, savory fish.

Don't shy away from using the habanero chili. Its fruity flavor pairs perfectly with the avocado. It does give bold spiciness to the sauce, but the richness of the salmon keeps the heat in check.

In a medium bowl, toss the tomatoes with 1 tablespoon of the lime juice and ¼ teaspoon salt. Set aside. In a blender, combine the scallions, both chilies, vinegar, 2 tablespoons of the remaining lime juice and ¾ teaspoon salt. Blend until smooth, about 30 seconds. Add ¾ cup of the cilantro and the avocado. With the blender running, stream in 3 tablespoons water and blend until smooth and creamy, about 1 minute, scraping the blender jar. If needed, add up to 1 tablespoon more water to achieve the correct consistency. Set aside.

Season the salmon on both sides with salt. In a 12-inch nonstick skillet over medium-high, heat the oil until shimmering. Add the fillets flesh side down, reduce to medium and cook until golden, about 4 minutes. Using a wide metal spatula, flip the fillets, add the butter and increase to medium-high. Once the butter stops foaming, spoon it over the fillets, adjusting the heat to prevent the butter from burning. Cook and baste the fish until the thickest parts reach 115°F to 120°F, or are nearly opaque when cut into, 2 to 3 minutes. Pour the remaining 2 tablespoons lime juice into the pan and baste the fillets once or twice more.

With a wide metal spatula, transfer the fillets to individual plates. Spoon about 2 tablespoons avocado sauce over each fillet. Add the remaining ¾ cup cilantro to the tomatoes and toss, then spoon over the salmon. Serve the remaining avocado sauce on the side, along with lime wedges.

We are fans of the late Judy Rodger's San Francisco Zuni Café and its eponymous cookbook. Its timeless recipes and terrific tips make it an essential cookbook.

Gruyère and Chive Omelet

START TO FINISH:
15 minutes

SERVINGS:
4

8 large eggs

4 tablespoons finely chopped fresh chives, divided

Kosher salt and ground black pepper

6 tablespoons (¾ stick) salted butter, divided

⅓ cup dry white wine

¼ cup whole-grain mustard

2 ounces crusty white bread, torn into rough ½-inch pieces (2 cups)

4 ounces shredded Gruyère cheese (1 cup)

This unusual Gruyère and chive omelet—our adaptation of a recipe from "The Zuni Café Cookbook" by Judy Rodgers—pairs crisp, buttery croutons with soft, creamy eggs. The Gruyère adds a touch of funkiness, while the mustard and chives brighten the dish. Offer a green salad to complete the meal.

Don't let the butter brown *before pouring in the eggs. This means that the skillet is too hot, which will cause the omelet to overbrown on the bottom. The goal is a pale golden exterior.*

In a medium bowl, whisk the eggs, 2 tablespoons of the chives, and ½ teaspoon each salt and pepper.

In a 12-inch nonstick skillet over medium, melt 4 tablespoons of the butter. Add the wine and mustard and stir to combine. Bring to a simmer and cook until the liquid has evaporated and the mixture begins to sizzle, about 3 minutes. Transfer to a medium bowl, add the bread and toss to coat. Set the skillet over medium, add the seasoned bread and cook, stirring, until golden brown and crisp, 3 to 4 minutes. Transfer to a plate and set aside. Wipe out the skillet.

Set the skillet over medium-high and add the remaining 2 tablespoons butter. When the butter has melted, swirl the pan to coat. Pour in the egg mixture and, using a silicone spatula, draw the edges toward the center and gently stir, working your way around the perimeter of the pan. Cook the eggs this way until they form soft, creamy curds on top and the bottom has set but not browned, about 1 minute. Off heat, scatter the cheese over the omelet, cover and let stand until the cheese has melted and the surface of the omelet is set, about 3 minutes.

Run the spatula around the edge and underneath the omelet to loosen, then slide onto a cutting board. Scatter the toasted bread over half of the omelet and, using the spatula, fold the omelet in half to enclose the bread. Cut the omelet into 4 wedges and sprinkle with the remaining 2 tablespoons chives.

Kale and White Bean Soup

START TO FINISH:	SERVINGS:
25 minutes	**6**

¼ cup extra-virgin olive oil, plus extra to serve

1 medium yellow onion, finely chopped

8 medium garlic cloves, thinly sliced

4 oil-packed anchovy fillets, patted dry and minced

½ teaspoon red pepper flakes

2 quarts low-sodium chicken broth

2 sprigs fresh rosemary

2 ounces Parmesan cheese rind, plus finely grated Parmesan, to serve

Two 15½-ounce cans cannellini beans, drained and rinsed, divided

1 bunch lacinato kale (1 pound), stemmed and torn into bite-size pieces

Kosher salt and ground black pepper

Lemon wedges, to serve

Canned cannellini beans transform this otherwise long-simmering soup into an easy weeknight meal. The Parmesan rind added a deep savoriness; some grocery stores sell just the rinds, or if you have a chunk of Parmesan in your refrigerator, trim off its rind for use in the soup. If you reheat leftovers, you may need to add additional broth, as the soup becomes thicker as it stands. Crusty bread is the perfect accompaniment.

Don't fear the anchovies, even if you are not an anchovy fan. They help build rich, meaty flavor in the soup but don't leave any trace of fishiness. And don't simmer the soup for longer than directed; overcooking causes the beans to break down and make the soup overly thick.

In a large Dutch oven over medium, heat the oil until shimmering. Add the onion and cook, stirring occasionally, until softened, 5 to 7 minutes. Stir in the garlic, anchovies and pepper flakes, then cook, stirring, until fragrant, about 30 seconds.

Add the broth, rosemary, Parmesan rind and 1 cup of the beans. Bring to a boil over medium-high, then reduce the heat to medium, cover and simmer for 15 minutes. Remove and discard the rosemary sprigs and Parmesan rind.

Stir in the remaining beans and kale. Return to a simmer and cook, uncovered, until the kale is tender, 5 to 7 minutes. Taste and season with salt and pepper. Drizzle with olive oil, sprinkle generously with grated Parmesan and serve with lemon wedges on the side

Peanut-Sesame Noodles

START TO FINISH:
25 minutes

SERVINGS:
4

For the sauce:

¼ cup natural peanut butter

2½ tablespoons unseasoned
rice vinegar

2 tablespoons toasted
sesame oil

4 teaspoons white miso

4 teaspoons soy sauce

1 tablespoon white sugar

2 teaspoons finely grated
fresh ginger

½ teaspoon finely grated garlic

¼ teaspoon cayenne pepper

For the noodles:

12 ounces dried udon noodles

3 scallions, thinly sliced
on diagonal

Thick, quick-cooking udon—Japanese wheat noodles—make easy work of supper. We infuse ours with robust flavor with a peanut-sesame sauce seasoned with ginger, soy sauce and miso. Traditionally, this dish calls for Chinese sesame paste, which has a dark color and rich flavor, but can be difficult to find. Instead, we use natural peanut butter, which turned out to be a fine substitute. The sauce can be made ahead and refrigerated for up to a week; bring it to room temperature before using. Check the packaging of your noodles for their cooking time. To round out the dish, add cooked shredded chicken, poached shrimp, cubes of sautéed tofu or edamame.

Don't forget to rinse the noodles in cold water after cooking; they will become gummy otherwise.

To make the sauce, in a large bowl whisk together all ingredients until smooth; set aside.

In a large pot, bring 4 quarts of water to a boil. Add the noodles and cook until tender, according to package directions. Reserve ¼ cup of the cooking water, then drain the noodles. Rinse under cold water and drain again.

Add the noodles and 2 tablespoons of the reserved cooking water to the sauce and toss until coated. Sprinkle with the scallions.

Singapore Chili Shrimp

START TO FINISH:
20 minutes

SERVINGS:
4

4 large shallots, peeled
and quartered

2-inch piece fresh ginger,
peeled and sliced ½-inch thick

1 stalk lemon grass, trimmed
to the lower 6 inches,
dry outer layers discarded,
chopped

6 medium garlic cloves

6 tablespoons ketchup

3 tablespoons fish sauce

3 tablespoons chili-garlic
sauce

6 tablespoons unseasoned
rice vinegar

1¾ pounds jumbo shrimp,
peeled, deveined, tails
removed and patted dry

3 tablespoons grapeseed
or other neutral oil, divided

3 scallions, thinly sliced
on diagonal

This shrimp supper features a balance of sweet, savory and spicy. Don't be surprised by the ketchup—it's a standard ingredient in Singapore chili crab, which was our inspiration. To achieve a shrimp flavor that suffuses the dish, we puree a few raw shrimp into the sauce. This also gives the sauce a rich, full-bodied consistency. Serve with steamed rice.

Don't overcook the shrimp. Remove them from skillet as soon as they turn opaque. We liked the dish made with extra-jumbo shrimp; if you use smaller, they'll require a shorter cooking time.

In a food processor, finely chop the shallots, ginger, lemon grass and garlic, about 15 seconds, scraping the sides as needed. Set aside in a small bowl. Rinse out and dry the work bowl, then add the ketchup, fish sauce, chili-garlic sauce, vinegar, 6 tablespoons water and 6 of the shrimp (4 ounces). Process until smooth, about 20 seconds, then set aside.

In a 12-inch nonstick skillet over medium-high, heat 1 tablespoon of the oil until barely smoking. Add half the remaining shrimp in an even layer and cook without disturbing until deep golden brown on the bottoms, 1 to 2 minutes. Stir and cook until opaque on both sides, another 20 to 30 seconds. Transfer to a medium bowl. Repeat with 1 tablespoon of the remaining oil and the remaining shrimp, adding them to the first batch.

In the same skillet over medium-high, heat the remaining 1 tablespoon oil until shimmering. Add the pureed shallot mixture and cook, stirring constantly, until fragrant, about 2 minutes. Pour in the ketchup mixture and cook, stirring and scraping up any browned bits, until slightly reduced, 2 to 3 minutes. Pour through a fine mesh strainer over a medium bowl, pressing on the solids; you should have about 1¼ cups liquid. Discard the solids

Return the liquid to the skillet, pour in any accumulated shrimp juices (do not add the shrimp) and set the pan over medium-high. Cook, stirring, until slightly thickened, about 1 minute. Remove from heat, add the shrimp and stir until heated through, 30 to 60 seconds. Transfer to a platter and sprinkle with scallions.

Cilantro-Tomato Omelet

with Turmeric Butter

START TO FINISH:
25 minutes

SERVINGS:
4

1 pint grape or cherry
tomatoes, halved

8 large eggs

1 cup finely chopped
fresh cilantro

Kosher salt and ground
white pepper

3 tablespoons salted butter

1 tablespoon ground turmeric

4 medium shallots, halved
and thinly sliced

1 tablespoon extra-virgin
olive oil

2 tablespoons lime juice

2 teaspoons fish sauce

A simple, herbed tomato omelet shines in this recipe inspired by the flavors of Southeast Asian egg dishes. To keep the flavors and texture distinct, the tomatoes and eggs are cooked separately. Well-browned shallots make up the other half of the filling and cilantro, a full cup of it, is whisked directly into the eggs. We use turmeric butter, made by briefly heating ground turmeric in melted butter, to cook both the eggs and shallots, infusing the dish with earthy flavor. Fish sauce may not be the first thing you think of as an accompaniment to eggs, but it's common in Asian cooking. In this case, it finishes the omelet with a satisfyingly salty tang. For a heartier meal, try this with steamed rice and a plentiful sprinkling of hot sauce.

Don't use a conventional skillet for this recipe; nonstick is essential for the omelet to slide easily out of the pan.

Line a large plate with several layers of paper towels. Place the tomatoes cut side down on the paper towels; set aside. In a medium bowl, whisk together the eggs, cilantro, and 1 teaspoon each salt and white pepper.

In a 12-inch nonstick skillet over medium, melt the butter. When the foaming subsides, stir in the turmeric and cook until fragrant, about 30 seconds. Set aside 1 tablespoon of the turmeric butter.

Return the skillet and remaining butter to medium-high. Pour in the egg mixture and, using a silicone spatula, draw the edges toward the center and gently stir, working your way around the perimeter of the pan. Cook until they form soft, creamy curds on top and the bottom has set, about 1 minute. Slide the omelet onto a serving plate and tent with foil.

Return the skillet to medium-high. Add the remaining turmeric butter, the shallots and ½ teaspoon salt. Cover and cook, stirring occasionally, until the shallots are well browned, about 4 minutes. Transfer to a small bowl.

Add the oil to the skillet and heat over medium-high until barely smoking. Add the tomatoes in an even layer and cook without stirring until they begin to blister, about 1 minute. Return the shallots to the skillet and stir to combine. Off heat, stir in the lime juice and fish sauce.

Scatter the tomato mixture over half of the omelet and, using the spatula, fold the omelet over itself to enclose the filling. Cut the omelet into 4 wedges.

We initially called for removing the skin from the fillet before cooking, a finicky task. Then we realized it would be infinitely easier to peel the skin off the cooked fish. It lifts right off. Problem. Solved.

Salmon Chraimeh

START TO FINISH:
20 minutes

SERVINGS:
4

Four skin-on 6-ounce center-cut salmon fillets, 1 to 1½ inches thick

Kosher salt and ground black pepper

1 tablespoon extra-virgin olive oil, plus more to serve

4 scallions, thinly sliced, dark green parts reserved

3 medium garlic cloves, thinly sliced

1 jalapeño chili, stemmed, halved, seeded and thinly sliced

1 teaspoon coriander seeds

1 teaspoon cumin seeds

¾ teaspoon smoked paprika

14½-ounce can diced tomatoes

2 tablespoons finely chopped fresh mint

¼ cup lightly packed fresh cilantro, chopped

Lemon wedges, to serve

Center-cut salmon fillets deliver weeknight ease with vibrant flavor in this recipe inspired by the Sephardic dish chraimeh, fish braised in a mildly spicy tomato sauce. The name comes from the word for thief and refers to the way the spice comes at the end of the sauce, sneaking up on the diner. We tailored ours to work with pantry staples and scaled down the amount of garlic typically used. Look for salmon pieces that are evenly thick, about 1 to 1½ inches. We liked our salmon cooked between 115°F and 120°F, which leaves the thickest part with some translucency. If you like it more thoroughly cooked, after simmering remove the skillet from the heat and leave the fillets in the covered pan until cooked to desired doneness.

Don't use fillets of widely varying thicknesses; *they will require different cooking times. If unavoidable, begin checking the thinner fillets ahead of the thicker ones.*

Season the salmon fillets on both sides with salt and pepper. In a 10-inch skillet over medium-high, heat the oil until shimmering. Add the white and light green scallion parts, garlic and jalapeño. Cook, stirring occasionally, until lightly browned, about 2 minutes. Stir in the coriander, cumin and paprika, then cook until fragrant, about 30 seconds.

Stir in the tomatoes, ½ teaspoon salt and ¼ teaspoon pepper. Bring to a simmer, then nestle the fillets, skin side up, in the sauce. Reduce to medium, cover and simmer for 6 to 8 minutes, or until the thickest parts reach 115°F to 120°F.

Using tongs, carefully peel off and discard the skin from each fillet, then use a spatula to transfer to serving plates flesh side up. If the sauce is watery, continue to simmer over medium-high until slightly thickened, 1 to 2 minutes. Off heat, stir in the mint and cilantro. Taste and season with salt and pepper. Spoon the sauce over the salmon, sprinkle with the scallion greens, drizzle with olive oil and serve with lemon wedges.

Soba with Edamame
and Watercress

START TO FINISH:	SERVINGS:
25 minutes	**4**

6 tablespoons low-sodium soy sauce

2 tablespoons plus 2 teaspoons chili-garlic sauce

1 teaspoon toasted sesame oil

12 ounces dried soba noodles

10-ounce bag frozen shelled edamame (2 cups)

2 or 3 bunches watercress (see note), stemmed (about 5 cups)

1 tablespoon plus 1 teaspoon grapeseed or other neutral oil

1 tablespoon sesame seeds, toasted

Nutty-flavored soba noodles, peppery watercress and no-fuss frozen, shelled edamame combine for this refreshing yet hearty vegetarian dish. This is one-pot cooking at its simplest; the edamame go in a few minutes before the soba are done cooking—the noodles and legumes finish together. Toasted sesame seeds add a finishing crunch. Watercress is sold bunched like mature spinach, as well as "live" with roots attached; either type works well in this recipe. Grab two bunches if the stems are wispy, or three if the stems are thick. Thin, delicate stems are perfectly edible, but you'll want to pluck off any that are tough and fibrous.

Don't thaw the edamame before using; *they cook fine from frozen.*

In a small bowl, stir together the soy sauce, chili-garlic sauce and sesame oil. In a large pot, bring 4 quarts water to a boil. Add the soba and cook until tender; add the edamame during the last 3 minutes of cooking. Drain and set aside.

Add the watercress to the hot pot, then return the noodles and edamame to the pot. Drizzle with the grapeseed oil and toss. Add the soy mixture and toss again. Transfer to a serving bowl and sprinkle with sesame seeds.

Cacio e Pepe

START TO FINISH:	SERVINGS:
20 minutes	**4**

2 teaspoons cornstarch

6 ounces pecorino Romano cheese, finely grated (3 cups), plus more to serve

12 ounces linguini or spaghetti

Kosher salt and ground black pepper

Made of just pasta, cheese and plenty of freshly ground black pepper, cacio e pepe is a study in the power of letting a few ingredients shine. The origins of the dish are debated—one theory is cheese and black pepper were the only ingredients shepherds could carry into the mountains. But it's widely accepted as the mother of classic Roman pastas. Add pancetta and you have pasta alla gricia (recipe page 197). Add eggs and it becomes carbonara (recipe page 205). The pepper in cacio e pepe (literally, cheese and pepper) is key, cutting through the richness of the cheese and bringing balance to the dish. Pecorino Romano, a salty, hard sheep's milk cheese, is traditional. We recommend looking for imported pecorino for the best flavor. The addition of cornstarch allowed us to overcome the tendency of lower-quality cheese to clump, but for best flavor, we recommend using pecorino imported from Italy.

Don't use pre-shredded cheese, even if it's true pecorino Romano. And grate it on a wand-style grater; larger shreds won't melt. Don't pour the pecorino mixture onto the piping-hot, just-drained pasta; letting the pasta cool for a minute or so ensures the mixture won't break from overheating.

In a large pot, bring 4 quarts of water to a boil. Meanwhile, in a large saucepan, whisk 1½ cups cold water and the cornstarch until smooth. Add the pecorino and stir until evenly moistened. Set the pan over medium-low and cook, whisking constantly, until the cheese melts and the mixture comes to a gentle simmer and thickens slightly, about 5 minutes. Remove from the heat and set aside.

Stir the pasta and 2 tablespoons salt into the boiling water and cook until al dente. Reserve about ½ cup of the cooking water, then drain the pasta very well. Return the pasta to the pot and let cool for about 1 minute.

Pour the pecorino mixture over the pasta and toss with tongs until combined, then toss in 2 teaspoons pepper. Let stand, tossing two or three times, until most of the liquid has been absorbed, about 3 minutes. The pasta should be creamy, but not loose. If needed, toss in reserved pasta water 1 tablespoon at a time to adjust the consistency. Transfer to a warmed serving bowl and serve, passing more pecorino and pepper on the side.

Garlic and Cilantro Soup

with Chickpeas (Açorda a Alentejana)

START TO FINISH:
20 minutes

SERVINGS:
4

2 cups lightly packed fresh cilantro, roughly chopped

½ ounce Parmesan cheese, finely grated (¼ cup), plus more to serve

1 jalapeño chili, stemmed and roughly chopped

1 tablespoon grated lemon zest, plus 1 tablespoon lemon juice

1 teaspoon sweet smoked paprika, divided, plus more to serve

Kosher salt and ground black pepper

¾ cup extra-virgin olive oil, divided

5 ounces rustic bread (such as ciabatta), sliced ½ inch thick and torn into bite-size pieces (about 2 cups)

8 medium garlic cloves, roughly chopped

1½ quarts low-sodium chicken broth

Two 15½-ounce cans chickpeas, rinsed and drained

4 soft-cooked eggs, peeled (optional)

This soup, with its fragrant, herb-flecked broth, is our take on Portuguese açorda a alentejana. Soft-cooked eggs are a perfect garnish that also turn the soup into a complete meal. To soft-cook eggs, bring 2 cups water to a simmer in a large saucepan fitted with a steamer basket. Add the eggs, cover and steam over medium for 7 minutes. Immediately transfer to ice water to stop the cooking.

Don't skimp on the olive oil in this soup. The croutons absorb oil as they toast and the broth takes on a rich, creamy texture when the pesto is stirred in.

In a food processor, combine the cilantro, Parmesan, jalapeño, lemon zest and juice, ½ teaspoon of the paprika, 1 teaspoon salt and ½ teaspoon pepper. Process until finely chopped, about 20 seconds, scraping the sides as needed. With the machine running, add ½ cup of the oil and process to a pesto-like consistency, 30 to 45 seconds. Set aside.

In a small bowl, toss the bread with the remaining ¼ cup oil and the remaining ½ teaspoon paprika. Toast in a large Dutch oven over medium, stirring occasionally, until golden brown and crisp, 6 to 8 minutes. Using a slotted spoon, return the bread to the bowl, leaving excess oil in the pot; set the croutons aside.

Set the Dutch oven over medium and add the garlic. Cook, stirring constantly, until fragrant, about 1 minute. Add the broth and chickpeas and bring to a simmer over medium-high. Cook, stirring, until heated through, about 3 minutes. Off heat, stir in the pureed cilantro mixture, then taste and season with salt and pepper.

Divide the croutons among 4 serving bowls. Ladle in the soup and top each with 1 egg, if using. Sprinkle with additional paprika and Parmesan.

Onion Frittata
with Sherry Vinegar Sauce

START TO FINISH:	SERVINGS:
25 minutes	**4**

8 large eggs

Kosher salt and ground black pepper

4 tablespoons (½ stick) salted butter, cut into 4 pieces, divided

1 medium yellow onion, chopped (about 1 cup)

1 medium garlic clove, finely grated

¼ cup plus 1 teaspoon sherry vinegar

1 ounce grated Parmesan cheese (½ cup)

4 tablespoons minced fresh chives, divided

1 tablespoon whole-grain mustard

Cookbook author Deborah Madison's unhurried and unfussy approach to cooking inspired this recipe for turning basic eggs into a rich and satisfying meal. The sautéed onion gives the frittata a sweet succulence that is complemented by a butter-vinegar sauce and fresh chives. If you like, use red wine vinegar in place of the sherry vinegar and 2 ounces (1/2 cup) shredded Gruyère cheese instead of Parmesan. A pile of simply dressed greens and a crusty baguette make a great accompaniment.

Don't use a conventional skillet; *nonstick is essential for helping the frittata slide out of the pan with ease.*

Heat the oven to 325°F with a rack in the upper-middle position. In a large bowl, beat the eggs with ¾ teaspoon salt and ½ teaspoon pepper.

In a 10-inch oven-safe nonstick skillet over medium-low, melt 1 tablespoon of the butter. Add the onion and ½ teaspoon salt, cover and cook, stirring occasionally, until softened and moisture is released, about 5 minutes. Uncover, increase heat to medium-high and cook, stirring, until well browned, about 10 minutes. Stir in the garlic and 1 teaspoon of sherry vinegar. Cook until the vinegar has evaporated, 30 to 60 seconds.

Pour the eggs into the skillet and cook, using a silicone spatula to push and stir from the edges to the center, until the eggs begin to set, about 1 minute. Transfer the skillet to the oven and bake until just set, 3 to 5 minutes. Remove from the oven and sprinkle with the Parmesan. Return to the oven and bake until the cheese melts, about 1 minute.

Run the spatula around the edge and under the frittata to loosen, then slide onto a serving plate. Sprinkle with 2 tablespoons of the chives. Set the empty skillet over medium-high, add the remaining ¼ cup vinegar and simmer until reduced to 2 tablespoons, 2 to 4 minutes. Off heat, stir in the mustard and remaining 3 tablespoons butter a piece at a time until melted. Stir in the remaining 2 tablespoons chives, then taste and season with salt and pepper. Cut the frittata into wedges and serve with the sauce on the side.

Spaghetti with Pancetta

(Pasta alla Gricia)

START TO FINISH:	SERVINGS:
20 minutes	**4**

3 ounces pancetta, finely chopped

2 teaspoons cornstarch

6 ounces pecorino Romano cheese, finely grated (3 cups), plus more to serve

12 ounces linguini or spaghetti

Kosher salt and ground black pepper

Gricia is one of the core Roman pasta dishes, built off the base of cacio e pepe (recipe page 191). Guanciale (cured pork cheek) is traditional for gricia, but we used more widely available pancetta. Bacon was too smoky.

Don't use pre-shredded cheese. *Likewise, grate the cheese on a wand-style grater and let the pasta cool before pouring the pecorino mixture on.*

In a large pot, bring 4 quarts of water to a boil. Meanwhile, in a 10-inch skillet over medium, cook the pancetta until crisp, about 5 minutes. Using a slotted spoon, transfer the pancetta to a paper towel–lined plate; reserve 2 tablespoons of the rendered fat.

In a large saucepan, whisk 1½ cups cold water and the cornstarch until smooth. Add the pecorino and stir until evenly moistened. Set the pan over medium-low and cook, whisking constantly, until the cheese melts and the mixture comes to a gentle simmer and thickens slightly, about 5 minutes. Remove from the heat, whisk in reserved pancetta fat and set aside.

Stir the pasta and 2 tablespoons salt into the boiling water and cook until al dente. Reserve about ½ cup of the cooking water, then drain the pasta very well. Return the pasta to the pot and let cool for about 1 minute.

Pour the pecorino mixture over the pasta and toss with tongs until combined, then toss in 2 teaspoons pepper and crisped pancetta. Let stand, tossing two or three times, until most of the liquid has been absorbed, about 3 minutes. The pasta should be creamy, but not loose. If needed, toss in reserved pasta water 1 tablespoon at a time to adjust the consistency. Transfer to a warmed serving bowl and serve with more pecorino and pepper on the side.

This intensely lemony pasta, inspired by a dish we ate in Rome, is made almost entirely from pantry staples. It's one of our simplest—and most flavorful—pasta recipes.

Spaghetti al Limone

START TO FINISH:
15 minutes

SERVINGS:
4

5 tablespoons salted butter, divided

8 medium garlic cloves, minced

1 teaspoon red pepper flakes

¾ cup dry white wine

12 ounces spaghetti

Kosher salt and ground black pepper

2 tablespoons grated lemon zest, plus 3 tablespoons lemon juice

¾ cup finely chopped fresh flat-leaf parsley or basil

Grated Parmesan cheese, to serve

This simple dish may have few ingredients, but it boasts bold, bright flavors. Many versions include cream, but we preferred to use a little butter and some of the starchy spaghetti cooking water; this gave the pasta a saucy consistency and light creaminess that didn't mute the freshness of the lemon. Feel free to switch in linguine for the spaghetti and adjust the lemon zest and juice to your taste.

Don't cook the pasta *until al dente. Drain it when it's a minute or two shy of al dente; it will continue to cook in the skillet.*

In a 12-inch skillet over medium, melt 3 tablespoons of the butter. Add the garlic and cook, stirring constantly, until fragrant, about 30 seconds. Add the pepper flakes and cook, stirring constantly, until the garlic begins to turn golden, about 1 minute. Pour in the wine and cook until reduced to about ½ cup, about 3 minutes. Remove from the heat and set aside.

In a large pot, bring 2 quarts of water to a boil. Stir in 1 tablespoon salt and the pasta; cook until just shy of al dente. Reserve 2 cups of the cooking water, then drain and set aside.

Set the skillet with the garlic mixture over medium-high, stir in 1½ cups of the reserved pasta water and bring to a simmer. Add the drained pasta and toss. Cook, stirring, until most of the liquid has been absorbed, 2 to 3 minutes.

Off heat, stir in the remaining 2 tablespoons butter, 1 teaspoon black pepper, the lemon juice and zest, and the parsley. Taste and season with salt and, if needed, adjust the consistency by adding more pasta water a few tablespoons at a time. Transfer to a serving bowl and serve with grated Parmesan.

Lemon Grass–Coconut Tofu

START TO FINISH:	SERVINGS:
25 minutes	**4**

1 teaspoon ground turmeric

Kosher salt and ground black pepper

Two 14-ounce containers extra-firm tofu, cut into 1-inch cubes and patted dry

4 medium plum tomatoes (2 quartered, 2 diced)

1 medium shallot, cut into eighths

1 bunch fresh cilantro, stems thinly sliced and reserved separately from leaves

1 tablespoon fish sauce

1 tablespoon chili-garlic sauce

3 stalks lemon grass, trimmed to the lower 6 inches, dry outer layers discarded, thinly sliced

¼ cup grapeseed or other neutral oil

14-ounce can coconut milk, well stirred

1 tablespoon lime juice

Tofu and turmeric team up in this one-pan meal bursting with Southeast Asian flavors. We start by cubing tofu, coating it in spices, then frying it to a crisp brown. The blender quickly pulls together an aromatic tomato–lemon grass paste which blends with coconut milk for a rich sauce. Cilantro, both stems and leaves, adds herbal contrast while fish sauce and chili-garlic sauce contribute savory notes and heat. We found that extra-firm tofu had the best texture, but firm tofu worked well, too. To make the dish vegetarian, substitute an equal amount of soy sauce for the fish sauce. Serve with steamed jasmine rice.

Don't stir the tofu immediately after adding it to the skillet; the pieces stick to the surface until they develop a crust on the bottom. Once that happens, after about 3 minutes, the pieces will release easily. And be sure to use a nonstick pan.

In a medium bowl, stir together the turmeric, 2 teaspoons salt and ½ teaspoon pepper. Add the tofu and toss to coat. Set aside.

In a blender, combine the quartered tomatoes, shallot, cilantro stems, fish sauce and chili-garlic sauce. Blend until finely chopped, about 30 seconds. Add the lemon grass and blend, scraping the blender frequently, until a smooth, thick paste forms, about 90 seconds. Set aside.

In a 12-inch nonstick skillet over medium-high, heat the oil until shimmering. Add the tofu in an even layer and cook without stirring until well browned on the bottoms and the pieces release easily from the pan, about 3 minutes. Using a spatula, turn the pieces and cook until browned on all sides, another 7 to 9 minutes. Transfer to a large paper towel-lined plate.

Return the skillet to medium-high. Add the tomato–lemon grass paste and cook, stirring, until slightly darkened and thickened, 2 to 3 minutes. Stir in the coconut milk, 1 teaspoon salt, ½ teaspoon pepper and the diced tomatoes. Bring to a simmer then cover, reduce to low and cook until the tomatoes soften, about 5 minutes.

Add the tofu and stir to coat. Cover and simmer, stirring occasionally, until the tofu has absorbed some of the sauce, about 10 minutes. Taste and season with salt and pepper. Stir in the lime juice and sprinkle with the cilantro leaves.

Menemen is one of Istanbul's brunch staples, served as part of an elaborate spread that includes fresh cheese, bread, rose petal preserves, spiced cucumbers, olives and more.

Turkish Scrambled Eggs

with Spicy Tomato and Capers (Menemen)

START TO FINISH:	SERVINGS:
20 minutes	**4**

4 tablespoons extra-virgin olive oil, divided, plus more to serve

2 poblano chilies, stemmed, seeded and finely chopped

1 bunch scallions, thinly sliced

3 medium garlic cloves, minced

1 tablespoon Aleppo pepper or 1 teaspoon red pepper flakes

Kosher salt and ground white pepper

1 plum tomato, cored and finely chopped

2 tablespoons drained capers

8 large eggs

⅓ cup crumbled feta cheese

3 tablespoons chopped fresh dill

Poblano chilies are Mexican in heritage, but their earthy flavor and mild heat make them ideal for this version of Turkish-style scrambled eggs. Using Aleppo pepper nudges the dish even closer to traditional Turkish flavors, but if you don't have any, regular red pepper flakes work, too. Serve on warmed plates to prevent the eggs from cooling too quickly. Round out the meal with crisp slices of toast.

Don't wait until the eggs are firm and fully set before removing the pan from the heat; the eggs will continue to cook in the time it takes to portion and serve.

In a 12-inch nonstick skillet over medium, heat 2 tablespoons of the oil until shimmering. Add the poblanos, scallions, garlic, Aleppo pepper, and ½ teaspoon each salt and white pepper. Cover and cook, stirring, until the chilies are softened but not browned, 6 to 8 minutes. Transfer to a medium bowl and stir in the tomato and capers; set aside. Wipe out the skillet.

In a medium bowl, whisk the eggs and ¾ teaspoon salt. Return the skillet to medium and heat the remaining 2 tablespoons oil until shimmering. Pour the eggs into the center of the pan. Using a silicone spatula, continuously stir the eggs, pushing them toward the middle as they set at the edges and folding the cooked egg over on itself. Cook until just set, about 1½ minutes. The curds should be shiny, wet and soft. Taste and season with salt and pepper, then divide among warmed serving plates.

Top each serving with a portion of the poblano mixture. Sprinkle with feta and dill, then drizzle with oil.

We'd never seen a whisk used to make carbonara. But we were shocked by how light and bright the resulting sauce is.

Roman Spaghetti Carbonara

START TO FINISH:
25 minutes

SERVINGS:
4

3 ounces thinly sliced pancetta, chopped

6 large egg yolks

2 teaspoons cornstarch

6 ounces pecorino Romano cheese, finely grated (3 cups), plus more to serve

12 ounces spaghetti

Kosher salt and ground black pepper

Some say spaghetti carbonara emerged after World War II, thanks in part to American soldiers and their packets of eggs. Others say the name is drawn from "carbone," or charcoal—a reference to the dish's complexion thanks to a copious amount of black pepper. Whatever the roots, this brighter take on carbonara came from Pipero Roma, a white-tablecloth restaurant in Rome. Their secret: The egg yolks are whisked until cooked and slightly foamy, creating a sauce that is much lighter in texture than most carbonara recipes. Mixing the yolks with water and cornstarch ensures the cheese won't clump when tossed with the pasta.

Don't substitute bacon for the pancetta. *The smokiness of the bacon will overwhelm the cleaner flavors of the egg-based sauce.*

In a 10-inch skillet over medium, cook the pancetta, stirring, until crisp, about 5 minutes. Using a slotted spoon, transfer to a paper towel-lined plate. Measure out and reserve 3 tablespoons of the rendered fat; if needed, supplement with olive oil. Set the pancetta and fat aside.

In a large pot, bring 4 quarts water to a boil. Meanwhile, in a large saucepan, whisk 1¾ cups cold water, the egg yolks and cornstarch until smooth. Add the cheese and stir until evenly moistened. Set the pan over medium-low and cook, whisking constantly, until the mixture comes to a gentle simmer and is airy and thickened, 5 to 7 minutes; use a silicone spatula to occasionally get into the corners of the pan. Off heat, whisk in the reserved pancetta fat. Set aside.

Stir the pasta and 2 tablespoons salt into the boiling water and cook until al dente. Reserve about ½ cup of the cooking water, then drain the pasta very well. Return the pasta to the pot and let cool for about 1 minute.

Pour the pecorino-egg mixture over the pasta and toss with tongs until well combined, then toss in 2 teaspoons pepper. Let stand, tossing the pasta several times, until most of the liquid has been absorbed, about 3 minutes. Crumble in the pancetta, then toss again. The pasta should be creamy, but not loose. If needed, toss in up to 2 tablespoons reserved pasta water to adjust the consistency. Transfer to a warmed serving bowl and serve with more pecorino and pepper on the side.

Spicy Garlic Soba

with Greens

START TO FINISH:	SERVINGS:
20 minutes	**4**

8.8-ounce package dried soba noodles

1 tablespoon packed light brown sugar

⅓ cup low-sodium soy sauce

2 tablespoons salted butter

2 medium leeks, white and light green parts only, halved lengthwise and thinly sliced (2 cups)

8 medium garlic cloves, minced

5 teaspoons gochujang

1 tablespoon finely grated fresh ginger

2 pounds lacinato kale, stemmed and cut crosswise into ½-inch ribbons

Kosher salt and ground black pepper

Spicy, garlicky soba noodles and dark green kale yield a hearty and quick vegetarian meal. Leeks add a delicate, onion flavor. We liked using a buckwheat-wheat blended soba noodle, but any variety will work. The dish is fine as is, though a sunny-side up egg would be a nice complement. Gochujang, a chili paste common in Korean cooking, adds savory-salty heat to the noodles. It can be found in Asian markets and most larger supermarkets.

Don't forget to rinse the soba noodles with cold water right after they finish cooking. They'll turn gummy and lose their texture if they sit in warm water. And don't use regular soy sauce; it will make the dish too salty.

In a large pot, bring 4 quarts water to a boil. Add the soba and cook until al dente, about 5 minutes. Reserve ½ cup of the cooking water, then drain and rinse the noodles under cold water. Drain well, then set aside.

In a small bowl, whisk the reserved soba cooking water, the brown sugar and soy sauce until the sugar dissolves. Set aside.

Return the pot to medium-high and melt the butter. Once foaming has subsided, add the leeks and cook until lightly browned, stirring occasionally, 2 to 3 minutes. Reserve 3 tablespoons of the leeks for garnish. Add the garlic, gochujang and ginger. Cook, stirring constantly, until fragrant, about 30 seconds. Stir in the kale and reserved soy sauce mixture. Cover and cook on medium until the greens are wilted and tender, 5 to 7 minutes.

Add the noodles, using tongs to gently loosen them as they go into the pot. Stir to combine and continue to cook until most of the liquid has been absorbed, about 2 minutes. Taste and season with salt and pepper. Transfer to serving bowls and top with the reserved leeks.

Palestinian Crispy Herb Omelet

START TO FINISH:
25 minutes

SERVINGS:
4

1 cup plain Greek yogurt

Kosher salt

1¼ cups lightly packed
flat-leaf parsley, finely
chopped, divided

1 cup lightly packed fresh mint,
finely chopped, divided

1 cup lightly packed fresh dill,
finely chopped, divided

4 tablespoons plus 1 teaspoon
extra-virgin olive oil, divided

½ teaspoon lemon juice,
plus lemon wedges, to serve

8 large eggs

8 scallions, thinly sliced

3 serrano chilies, stemmed,
seeded and minced

1 tablespoon cornstarch

Sliced tomatoes, to serve

Warmed pita bread, to serve

Middle Eastern ijee inspired these herb-packed, crisp-crusted omelets. Most of the work is in the herb prep; once you're at the stove, the cooking is done in a matter of minutes. These omelets are meant to be thin, so we developed the recipe to make two 12-inch omelets that are folded in half. Sliced tomatoes and pita bread complete the meal.

Don't reduce the amount of olive oil. Two tablespoons per batch may seem excessive, but that much is needed for the omelets to crisp on the bottom.

In a small bowl, stir together the yogurt, ½ teaspoon salt, ¼ cup of the parsley, 2 tablespoons of the mint, 2 tablespoons of the dill, 1 teaspoon olive oil and the lemon juice. In a medium bowl, whisk the eggs, scallions, chilies, cornstarch, 1 teaspoon salt and all remaining herbs.

In a 12-inch nonstick skillet over medium-high, heat 2 tablespoons of the oil until barely smoking. Pour in half the egg mixture and, using a silicone spatula, gently spread to cover the surface of the skillet. Cook until the bottom is browned and crisp and the top is no longer runny, 2 to 3 minutes.

Remove the pan from the heat, cover and let stand until the eggs are set on top, 30 to 60 seconds. Slide the omelet onto a platter, folding it in half with the spatula. Loosely tent with foil to keep warm.

Pour the remaining 2 tablespoons oil into the pan and heat over medium-high until barely smoking. Cook the remaining egg mixture in the same way to make a second omelet. Transfer to the platter, folding in half. Cut the omelets into wedges. Serve with the herbed yogurt, lemon wedges, tomatoes and pita bread.

Sopa Seca with Butternut Squash

START TO FINISH:
25 minutes

SERVINGS:
4

4 tablespoons extra-virgin olive oil, divided

12 ounces angel hair pasta, broken into 1-inch pieces

2 pounds butternut squash, peeled, seeded, cut into ½-inch pieces (4 cups)

Kosher salt and ground black pepper

1 medium yellow onion, finely chopped

1 bunch cilantro, tender stems finely chopped, leaves roughly chopped and kept separate

4 medium garlic cloves, minced

1½ teaspoons ground cumin

1½ teaspoons sweet paprika

¼ teaspoon cinnamon

1¼ quarts low-sodium chicken broth

3 tablespoons lime juice

4 ounces queso fresco cheese, crumbled, to serve

1 avocado, pitted, peeled and diced, to serve

5 scallions, thinly sliced, to serve

Sopa seca, which translates to "dry soup" from the Spanish, is a Mexican dish that typically features toasted pasta cooked with broth and tomatoes. The toasted pasta absorbs the liquid, yielding noodles that are "dry," but rich with the flavors of soup. Toasting the pasta, which first is broken into pieces, creates a rich, nutty flavor foundation and an interesting texture for the finished dish. For our version, we opted to use butternut squash instead of tomatoes. The squash added a pleasing sweetness and paired nicely with the seasonings, transforming the dish into a hearty meal for fall or winter.

Don't forget to stir the pasta as it toasts; this helps it brown evenly.

In a large Dutch oven over medium, heat 2 tablespoons of oil until shimmering. Add the pasta and cook, stirring, until golden, about 5 minutes. Transfer to a paper towel-lined plate and set aside. Wipe out the pot.

In the Dutch oven, toss the squash with the remaining 2 tablespoons oil, 2 teaspoons salt and ½ teaspoon pepper. Return to medium-high heat and cook, stirring occasionally, until the squash begins to brown and is almost tender, about 4 minutes. Add the onion and 1 teaspoon each salt and pepper, then cook, stirring occasionally, until the onion has softened, about 5 minutes.

Add the cilantro stems, garlic, cumin, paprika and cinnamon. Cook, stirring, until fragrant, about 1 minute. Add the toasted pasta and broth, then bring to a simmer. Cover, reduce heat to medium and cook until the pasta is al dente and has absorbed most of the liquid, about 7 minutes.

Stir in the lime juice and half of the cilantro leaves. Taste and season with salt and pepper. Ladle into bowls and serve topped with the remaining cilantro leaves, avocado, queso fresco and scallions.

Our first attempts at this dish, using the traditional tomato base, were flops, always coming out dry or dull. Then we found a Rick Bayless recipe that swapped in butternut squash for the tomato. The sweet, earthy squash transformed the dish.

Quick sides to round out a meal

Easy Additions

Bulgur-Tomato Salad
with Herbs and Pomegranate Molasses (Eetch)

START TO FINISH:	SERVINGS:
30 minutes	**4**

3 tablespoons tomato paste

2 tablespoons extra-virgin olive oil

1 medium red bell pepper, stemmed, seeded and finely chopped

6 scallions (4 finely chopped, 2 thinly sliced, reserved separately)

Kosher salt and ground black pepper

3 medium garlic cloves, finely chopped

1½ teaspoons ground cumin

1 teaspoon Aleppo pepper or ¼ teaspoon red pepper flakes

1 cup coarse bulgur

1 tablespoon pomegranate molasses, plus more if needed

1 pint grape tomatoes, halved

¾ cup chopped fresh mint or flat-leaf parsley

This Armenian salad, known as eetch, is heartier and more substantial than tabbouleh. Instead of soaking the bulgur in water—as is done for tabbouleh—the bulgur is hydrated in a mixture of tomato paste and water, so the grains take on a red-orange hue. If you want to make the salad more tart and tangy, mix in a splash of lemon juice. For a more substantial meal, add blanched green beans and crumbled feta cheese.

Don't use fine or medium bulgur. These varieties have different liquid-absorption rates than coarse bulgur, the type called for in this recipe. They also don't have the same hearty chew.

In a small bowl, whisk together 1⅓ cups water and the tomato paste. Set aside. In a 10-inch skillet over medium, heat the oil until shimmering. Add the bell pepper, chopped scallions and ½ teaspoon salt. Cover and cook, stirring occasionally, until the bell pepper is tender, about 5 minutes. Stir in the garlic, cumin and Aleppo pepper, then cook until fragrant, about 1 minute.

Stir in the bulgur, tomato paste mixture and 1¼ teaspoons salt. Bring to a boil over medium-high. Cover, reduce to low and simmer until the bulgur has absorbed the liquid, 12 to 15 minutes. Remove from the heat and let stand, covered, for 5 minutes.

Transfer to a wide, shallow bowl and let cool until just warm, about 5 minutes. Drizzle the pomegranate molasses over the bulgur, then fold until combined. Fold in the tomatoes, mint and the sliced scallions. Taste and season with salt, black pepper and additional molasses.

Shaved Zucchini Salad
with Parmesan and Herbs

START TO FINISH:	SERVINGS:
10 minutes	**4**

1 teaspoon grated lemon zest, plus 3 tablespoons juice

3 tablespoons extra-virgin olive oil

¼ teaspoon honey

Kosher salt and ground black pepper

1 pound zucchini (2 medium)

1 ounce Parmesan cheese, finely grated (about ½ cup), plus more shaved, to serve

½ cup lightly packed fresh mint, torn

½ cup lightly packed fresh basil, torn

¼ cup hazelnuts, toasted, skinned and coarsely chopped

We adopt the Italian technique of slicing raw zucchini into thin ribbons for this vibrant salad. The zucchini really shines, balanced with the clean, sharp flavors of a lemony dressing along with Parmesan and hazelnuts. A Y-style peeler makes it easy to shave zucchini, or you can use a mandoline. Don't worry if the ribbons vary in width; this adds to the visual appeal of the dish. Toasted sliced, slivered or chopped whole almonds can be used in place of the hazelnuts.

Don't dress the salad until you are ready to serve. The zucchini and herbs are delicate and quickly wilt.

In a large bowl, whisk together the lemon zest and juice, oil, honey, ½ teaspoon salt and ¼ teaspoon pepper. Set aside. Use a Y-style peeler or mandoline to shave the zucchini from top to bottom, rotating as you go. Stop shaving when you reach the seedy core. Discard the cores.

To the dressing, add the shaved zucchini, cheese, mint and basil, then toss until evenly coated. Transfer to a serving plate and sprinkle with shaved Parmesan and hazelnuts.

Charred Brussels Sprouts

with Garlic Chips

START TO FINISH:	SERVINGS:
30 minutes	**8**

20 medium garlic cloves, peeled and thinly sliced (about ½ cup)

½ cup plus 1 tablespoon grapeseed or other neutral oil, divided

Kosher salt and ground white pepper

2 pounds medium Brussels sprouts, trimmed and halved

¼ cup slivered almonds

2 lemon grass stalks, trimmed to bottom 6 inches, dry outer layers discarded, thinly sliced (about ¾ cup)

1 tablespoon plus 1 teaspoon grated lemon zest, divided, plus 3 tablespoons lemon juice

1 teaspoon white sugar

To keep our roasted sprouts fresh and bright we reversed the seasoning process, doing it at the end, instead of the beginning. The cooked sprouts were tossed with ground almonds, lemon grass and lemon juice and zest, a combination inspired by a dish we enjoyed at Angus An's Maenam Restaurant in Vancouver. Garlic balanced the brightness; to keep it from burning we cooked it separately from the sprouts, thinly slicing and frying 20 cloves. The crispy fried garlic chips added a savory note. Leftover oil from frying the chips can be used for salad dressings or drizzled on pasta. The sprouts were best served on a platter; in a bowl, the sprouts on the bottom tended to soften as they sat.

Don't undercook the almond–lemon grass mixture. *Browning it well helps tenderize the lemon grass and develop toasty flavor.*

Heat the oven to 500°F with a rack in the middle position. In a small saucepan over medium, combine the garlic and ½ cup oil. Cook, stirring, until uniformly light golden brown, 4 to 5 minutes. Set a fine mesh strainer over a small heatproof bowl. Strain the mixture, then transfer the garlic chips to a paper towel-lined plate and season with ¼ teaspoon salt. Reserve the oil.

In a large bowl, toss the Brussels sprouts with ¼ cup of the reserved garlic oil. Arrange the sprouts cut side down on a rimmed baking sheet. Roast until tender when pierced with a knife and well browned on the cut sides, 15 to 20 minutes.

Meanwhile, in a food processor, combine the almonds, lemon grass, 1 tablespoon lemon zest, 2 teaspoons salt, 1 teaspoon white pepper, the sugar and 1 tablespoon of the garlic oil. Process until finely chopped, about 45 seconds. Set aside.

In a 12-inch heavy-bottomed skillet over high, heat the remaining 1 tablespoon grapeseed oil until beginning to smoke. Add the almond mixture, immediately reduce heat to medium-high and cook, stirring constantly, until fragrant and deep golden brown, about 3 minutes. Transfer to a large heatproof bowl.

When the sprouts are done, immediately add them to the almond mixture along with the lemon juice and remaining 1 teaspoon lemon zest. Toss, then taste and season with salt and white pepper. Transfer to a platter, then sprinkle with the garlic chips and drizzle with garlic oil.

Asparagus with Sauce Gribiche
and Fried Capers

START TO FINISH:
25 minutes

SERVINGS:
4

6 tablespoons grapeseed or other neutral oil

¼ cup drained capers, patted dry, plus 2 tablespoons caper brine

3 tablespoons white balsamic vinegar

1 small shallot, minced

4 hard-cooked large eggs, peeled

2 tablespoons Dijon mustard

2 tablespoons prepared horseradish

Kosher salt

½ cup packed fresh flat-leaf parsley, chopped

⅓ cup packed fresh tarragon, chopped

2 pounds asparagus, trimmed

The classic French sauce gribiche is similar to mayonnaise, but made with cooked, not raw, egg yolks, and seasoned with capers and herbs. For this dish, we used white balsamic vinegar instead of conventional wine vinegar because we preferred balsamic's mild sweetness. And instead of adding capers to the sauce, we used caper brine; the capers themselves we fried to create a crisp garnish for the asparagus. Finally, a dose of horseradish gave the sauce a welcome piquancy. When buying asparagus, choose spears that are similar in size; we preferred pencil-sized spears. The cooking time will vary based on the thickness.

Don't be timid when patting the capers dry. Lay them out on paper towels, then press on them with additional towels. Removing the moisture minimizes splattering as they fry. Also, don't allow the oil to smoke during frying; it also is used in the dressing and to cook the asparagus, but will taste bitter if it gets too hot.

In a 12-inch skillet over medium-high, heat the oil until shimmering. Add the capers and cook, stirring, until most of the bubbling has subsided and the capers are crisp, 2 to 3 minutes. Using a slotted spoon, transfer the capers to a small paper towel-lined plate. Reserve the skillet, leaving the oil in it.

In a medium bowl, combine the vinegar and shallot. Set aside for about 10 minutes. Halve the hard-cooked eggs. Add the yolks to the shallots; finely chop the whites. To the yolks, add the mustard, horseradish, caper brine and ½ teaspoon salt. Mash with a fork until smooth and creamy. Stir in the chopped egg whites, parsley, tarragon and 3 tablespoons of the oil from the skillet.

Return the skillet to high until the oil shimmers. Add the asparagus and ½ teaspoon salt and cook, tossing once or twice, until bright green with lightly charred spots, 2 to 4 minutes. Add 2 tablespoons water, then cover and reduce to medium. Cook until the asparagus is crisp-tender, 1 to 2 minutes. Using tongs, transfer to a serving platter. Spoon the sauce over the asparagus and sprinkle with the fried capers.

Stir-Fried Broccoli

with Sichuan Peppercorns

START TO FINISH:	SERVINGS:
30 minutes	**4**

3 tablespoons unseasoned rice vinegar, divided

1½ tablespoons soy sauce

1 teaspoon white sugar

¼ teaspoon kosher salt

3 medium garlic cloves, finely grated

1½ teaspoons finely grated fresh ginger

¼ to ½ teaspoon red pepper flakes

2 scallions, white and pale green parts minced, dark green parts thinly sliced on diagonal

1¼ pounds broccoli, florets cut into 1-inch pieces, stems peeled and sliced ¼ inch thick

3 tablespoons peanut oil, divided

2 teaspoons toasted sesame oil

½ to 1 teaspoon Sichuan peppercorns, toasted and finely ground

Restaurants and even some homes in China use super-charged wok burners to get the high heat that quickly renders raw vegetables tender on the outside, crisp on the inside. We mix oil and water for a skillet-friendly method. The water begins the cooking as it steams off, leaving the oil behind to finish—and lightly brown—the broccoli. We season the dish with Sichuan peppercorns, which don't provide heat so much as a pleasant resinous flavor and an intriguing tingling sensation on your lips and tongue. To enhance their flavor and aroma, we toasted the peppercorns over medium heat for about 2 minutes, let them cool, then ground them to a fine powder in a spice grinder.

Don't overtoast *the Sichuan peppercorns. It's better to err on the side of lightly toasted, as the peppercorns become unpleasantly bitter if overdone.*

In a small bowl, stir together ⅓ cup water, 2 tablespoons of vinegar, the soy sauce and sugar. In another small bowl, stir together 2 tablespoons water and the salt. In a third, combine the garlic, ginger, pepper flakes and minced scallions.

In a 12-inch skillet over medium-high, combine the broccoli, salt water and 2 tablespoons of peanut oil. Cover and cook for 1 minute; the water should reach a simmer. Uncover and cook, stirring occasionally, until crisp-tender and browned in spots, 8 to 10 minutes. Transfer to a large plate.

Return the skillet to medium-high, add the remaining 1 tablespoon peanut oil and the garlic-ginger mixture. Cook, stirring, until fragrant, 10 to 15 seconds. Add the soy sauce mixture and simmer, stirring and scraping up any browned bits, until slightly reduced, 2 to 3 minutes. Return the broccoli to the skillet and stir to coat.

Off heat, stir in the sesame oil, remaining 1 tablespoon of vinegar and ½ teaspoon of ground Sichuan peppercorns. Taste and season with more peppercorns, if desired. Serve sprinkled with the sliced scallion greens.

Chickpea and Cucumber Salad
(Chana Chaat)

START TO FINISH:	SERVINGS:
25 minutes	**6**

Two 15½-ounce cans chickpeas, drained, rinsed and patted dry

1 small red onion, finely chopped

2 teaspoons curry powder, toasted (see note)

Kosher salt and ground black pepper

⅓ cup tamarind chutney

1½ tablespoons hot sauce, plus more as needed

3 tablespoons lime juice, plus lime wedges, to serve

2 tablespoons packed light brown sugar

3 cups (4 ounces) fried wonton strips

1 English cucumber, quartered lengthwise and cut crosswise into ¼-inch pieces

1 cup lightly packed fresh cilantro, finely chopped

Chaat is a style of savory South Asian street snack with dozens of variations. All feature a mix of contrasting flavors and textures—sweet, tart and spicy, as well as creamy and crunchy. This is our version of chickpea (chana) chaat; it's a good appetizer or side to grilled meats or seafood. To mimic the crunch of fried samosa wrappers that are sometimes added, we used the fried wonton strips sold near the croutons at the supermarket. For convenience, we used store-bought tamarind chutney (look in the international aisle) and spiked it with brown sugar, lime juice and hot sauce. For the latter, we preferred the acidic heat of Tabasco or Frank's Red Hot sauce. Feel free to substitute chopped tomato and/or mango for all or some of the cucumber. And if you like, drizzle with whole-milk plain yogurt.

Don't use the curry powder without toasting it in a dry a skillet over medium for 1 minute, stirring constantly. This deepens its flavors and cooks out any raw notes.

In a large bowl, toss the chickpeas, onion, curry powder, 2 teaspoons salt and 1 teaspoon pepper. Set aside.

In a small bowl, whisk together the chutney, hot sauce, lime juice and sugar. Taste and season with more hot sauce, if desired. Pour ¼ cup of this mixture over the chickpeas and toss. Cover and let stand for 15 minutes.

To the chickpea mixture, mix in the wonton strips, cucumber and half the cilantro. Taste and season with salt and pepper. Drizzle with half the remaining chutney mixture and sprinkle with the remaining cilantro. Serve with the extra chutney mixture and lime wedges.

Tomato-Herb Salad with Sumac

START TO FINISH:
35 minutes

SERVINGS:
4

1 small red onion, halved and thinly sliced

6 tablespoons lemon juice, divided

4 medium garlic cloves, peeled

¼ cup extra-virgin olive oil

4 teaspoons ground sumac, divided

Kosher salt

2 pounds plum tomatoes, cored and cut into 4 or 6 wedges

½ cup lightly packed fresh flat-leaf parsley

⅓ cup roughly chopped fresh dill

⅓ cup lightly packed fresh mint, torn

Tart and vibrant, sumac is a common seasoning in Middle Eastern cooking. We use it here to balance the sweetness of tomatoes, mixing it into an oniony vinaigrette. The tomatoes, along with an abundance of herbs, get gently tossed in the vinaigrette and a final spoonful of sumac adds a finishing sprinkle of flavor. Note that this salad is best made with perfectly ripe, in-season tomatoes. For added color and flavor contrast, add diced or coarsely crumbled feta cheese.

Don't use the onion *without first soaking it in lemon juice. This tames its bite. Likewise, don't use the garlic raw—blanching the cloves mellows their pungency.*

In a small bowl, stir together the onion and 2 tablespoons of the lemon juice. Let stand for 20 minutes. Meanwhile, bring a small saucepan of water to a boil. Add the garlic, cook for 1 minute, then drain. Finely chop the garlic, then use the flat side of a chef's knife to mash it to a coarse paste. Transfer to a small bowl and whisk in the remaining 4 tablespoons lemon juice, the oil, 3 teaspoons of sumac and ¾ teaspoon salt.

Add the tomatoes to a large bowl and sprinkle with ¼ teaspoon salt. Drain the onion, pat dry and add to the tomatoes, along with the parsley, dill and mint. Drizzle the garlic mixture over the herbs and gently toss. Transfer to a platter and sprinkle with the remaining 1 teaspoon sumac.

Cilantro Rice

START TO FINISH:
30 minutes

SERVINGS:
4

1½ cups long-grain white rice, rinsed and drained

Kosher salt

2 cups lightly packed fresh cilantro, roughly chopped

1 jalapeño chili, stemmed, seeded and roughly chopped

3 scallions, roughly chopped

3 medium garlic cloves, peeled

2 tablespoons extra-virgin olive oil

1 teaspoon lime juice, plus lime wedges, to serve

This colorful side dish can be turned into a light main by topping it with fried eggs. To keep the flavor and color of cilantro fresh and bright, we blend the herb with a few aromatics until smooth, then mix the puree into the rice after the grains are cooked.

Don't fluff the rice immediately after cooking. *Covering the pan with a towel and allowing the rice to rest for 5 minutes prevents the grains from turning mushy when the cilantro puree is folded in.*

In a medium saucepan over high, stir together the rice, 2 cups water and 1 teaspoon salt. Bring to a simmer, then cover, reduce to low and cook until the liquid is absorbed, 15 to 20 minutes.

Meanwhile, in a blender puree until smooth ¼ cup water, 1 teaspoon salt, the cilantro, jalapeño, scallions, garlic and oil, about 1 minute. If necessary, add additional water 1 teaspoon at a time to reach a smooth consistency.

When the rice is done, remove the pan from the heat, lift the cover, then drape a kitchen towel over the pan. Replace the cover and let stand for 5 minutes.

Using a fork, gently fluff the rice. Add the cilantro puree and lime juice, then gently fold in. Serve with lime wedges.

Scotch Bonnet Slaw

(Haitian Pikliz)

START TO FINISH:	SERVINGS:
15 minutes	**4 Cups**

½ cup white vinegar

2 tablespoons lime juice

2 tablespoons white sugar

2 habanero or Scotch bonnet chilies, stemmed and seeded

1 medium garlic clove, peeled

1 teaspoon fresh thyme leaves

¾ teaspoon kosher salt

2 cups thinly sliced green cabbage (6 to 8 ounces)

1 large carrot, peeled and shredded

1 medium shallot, halved and thinly sliced

Serve this crunchy, spicy Haitian slaw alongside braised meats or fried foods, as a garnish for tacos or atop a bowl of black beans. For a spicier version, leave some or all of the seeds in the chilies. Shred the carrot using the large holes of a box grater. Leftovers can be refrigerated in an airtight container for up to two days.

Don't touch your eyes or face after handling the chilies with bare hands, as the capsaicin (the heat-containing compound) is easily transferred. If you can, wear rubber gloves to prep the chilies.

In a blender, puree the vinegar, lime juice, sugar, chilies, garlic, thyme and salt until smooth, about 30 seconds. Transfer to a large bowl, then add the cabbage, carrot and shallot. Toss well. Cover and refrigerate for at least 2 hours before serving.

Thai Stir-Fried Spinach

START TO FINISH:
20 minutes

SERVINGS:
4

1 tablespoon fish sauce

1 tablespoon oyster sauce

2 teaspoons white sugar

¾ teaspoon red pepper flakes

3 tablespoons grapeseed or other neutral oil, divided

3 tablespoons coarsely chopped garlic

1½ pounds bunch spinach, trimmed of bottom 1½ inches, washed and dried well

This simple, bold stir-fry uses regular bunch spinach rather than the water spinach common in Thai cooking. The wilted leaves and crisp-tender stems combine for a pleasing contrast of textures. Be sure to dry the spinach well after washing (a salad spinner works best); excess water will cause splattering and popping when the spinach is added to the hot oil. We liked to serve this with steamed jasmine rice to soak up the sauce.

Don't use baby spinach, which can't handle high-heat cooking and doesn't have stems to offer textural contrast. And don't allow the spinach leaves to fully wilt in the pan; some leaves should still look fairly fresh, but will continue to cook after being transferred to the bowl.

In a small bowl, whisk together the fish sauce, oyster sauce, sugar and pepper flakes until the sugar dissolves. Set aside.

In a wok over medium-high, heat 2 tablespoons of the oil until just barely smoking. Remove the wok from the heat, add the garlic and cook, stirring, until just beginning to color, 20 to 30 seconds. Return the wok to high and immediately add ½ of the spinach. Using tongs, turn the spinach to coat with the oil and garlic. When the spinach is nearly wilted and the garlic has turned golden brown, 30 seconds or less, transfer to a large bowl. The leaves will continue to wilt but the stems should remain crisp-tender.

Return the wok to high heat. Add the remaining 1 tablespoon oil, swirl to coat the wok and heat until just barely smoking. Add the remaining spinach and cook, as before, for 20 to 30 seconds. Transfer to the bowl with the first batch of spinach.

Pour the fish sauce mixture over the spinach and toss. Transfer to a platter and drizzle with any accumulated liquid.

Roasted Fennel with Rosemary

START TO FINISH:
40 minutes

SERVINGS:
4

4 medium fennel bulbs (about 2¾ pounds), trimmed, halved, cored and cut lengthwise into 1-inch wedges

3 tablespoons extra-virgin olive oil

½ teaspoon ground fennel seeds

Kosher salt and ground black pepper

¼ cup dry white wine

1 tablespoon minced fresh rosemary

¼ teaspoon red pepper flakes

Roasting brings out the natural sweetness of fresh fennel, but it also mellows its characteristic flavor. To keep the flavor bold and true, we season it with ground fennel seed. A splash of white wine and a pinch of red pepper flakes enhance the dish. Pair with roasted meats or poultry, seared steaks or chops, or sautéed chicken breast.

Don't forget to remove the cores *of the fennel bulb halves. The cores are often tough and fibrous.*

Heat the oven to 475°F with a rack in the middle position. In a large bowl, toss together the fennel wedges, oil, ground fennel, 1 teaspoon salt and ¼ teaspoon pepper. Transfer in an even layer to a stovetop-safe large roasting pan. Roast until browned and a knife inserted into the largest piece meets no resistance, 30 to 35 minutes, stirring once halfway through.

Remove the pan from the oven and set over low on the stovetop. Pour in the wine and cook, scraping up any browned bits, until the wine has almost evaporated, about 2 minutes. Stir in the rosemary and pepper flakes. Taste and season with salt and pepper.

Gochujang-Glazed Potatoes
(Gamja Jorim)

START TO FINISH:	SERVINGS:
30 minutes	**4**

3 tablespoons plus
2 teaspoons soy sauce

¼ cup mirin

1 tablespoon gochujang

1 tablespoon white sugar

2 medium garlic cloves,
finely grated

Kosher salt and ground
black pepper

1 tablespoon grapeseed or
other neutral oil

2 pounds small Yukon Gold
potatoes (1½ to 2 inches in
diameter), quartered

2 teaspoons toasted
sesame oil

2 teaspoons unseasoned rice
vinegar

2 teaspoons sesame seeds,
toasted

2 scallions, thinly sliced

Gamja jorim, or salty-sweet soy-simmered potatoes, are a common banchan (small plate) on the Korean table. For our version, we added gochujang (Korean fermented chili paste) for a little heat and extra umami. Yukon Gold potatoes 1½ to 2 inches in diameter worked best. If your potatoes are very small (about 1 inch in diameter), cut them in half; if larger than 2 inches, cut them into eighths. Depending on the sugar content of your potatoes, they may or may not brown lightly as they cook before the soy mixture is added. This is a great side dish to grilled meats and seafood.

Don't stir vigorously *once the potatoes are nearly glazed. Doing so may cause the pieces to break apart.*

In a small bowl, whisk together ½ cup water, 3 tablespoons of the soy sauce, the mirin, gochujang, sugar, garlic, 1 teaspoon salt and ½ teaspoon pepper.

In a 12-inch nonstick skillet over medium, heat the oil until shimmering. Add the potatoes and stir to coat. Cover and cook, stirring occasionally, until the edges of the potatoes are translucent, 10 to 12 minutes.

Stir in the soy sauce mixture. Bring to a simmer over medium-high, then reduce to medium, cover and cook, stirring occasionally, until the tip of a knife inserted into the largest piece meets no resistance, about 10 minutes.

Uncover and cook over medium-high, stirring gently but frequently, until the liquid completely evaporates and the potatoes are glazed, about 5 minutes.

Off heat, stir in the remaining 2 teaspoons soy sauce, the sesame oil, vinegar and sesame seeds. Taste and season with salt and pepper. Transfer to a platter and sprinkle with the scallions.

Lemon and Herb Pilaf

with Hazelnuts

START TO FINISH:
30 minutes

SERVINGS:
4

3 tablespoons salted butter

1½ cups basmati rice, rinsed and drained

2 medium shallots, minced

2 teaspoons ground coriander

Kosher salt and ground black pepper

¼ cup lemon juice, plus 1 tablespoon grated lemon zest

1 cup roughly chopped fresh flat-leaf parsley

½ cup finely chopped fresh tarragon

1 cup hazelnuts, toasted, skinned and finely chopped

Tender rice and rich, crunchy hazelnuts partner in this fresh take on rice pilaf inspired by a recipe in "Yashim Cooks Istanbul" by crime writer and historian Jason Goodwin. We add flavor from heaps of fresh parsley and tarragon, along with a good measure of lemon juice and zest. We liked basmati rice best because the grains retain their shape well, but jasmine rice works, too. Rinsing the rice removes excess starch and helps ensure that the grains cook up light and fluffy; rinse the rice in a mesh strainer until the water runs almost clear, then drain well to remove excess moisture. This recipe can easily be doubled and prepared in a Dutch oven.

Don't forget to remove the hazelnuts' papery skins after toasting but before chopping. The best way to do this is by enclosing the nuts in a kitchen towel and rubbing vigorously; don't worry if they're not completely skin-free.

In a large saucepan over medium, melt the butter. Add the rice, shallots, coriander and 2 teaspoons salt. Cook, stirring, until the rice is just beginning to brown, 2 to 3 minutes. Stir in 2 cups water and bring to a boil over medium-high, then reduce to low, cover and cook until tender and the water is absorbed, 10 to 12 minutes.

Off heat, stir in the lemon juice. Drape a kitchen towel over the pot, cover and let sit for 5 minutes. Fluff the rice with a fork, then stir in the parsley, tarragon, lemon zest and hazelnuts. Taste and season with salt and pepper.

Yogurt Flatbreads

with Flavored Butters

START TO FINISH:	MAKES:
40 minutes	**6 flatbreads**

206 grams (1½ cups) bread flour, plus more for dusting

35 grams (¼ cup) whole-wheat flour

2 teaspoons kosher salt

1 teaspoon baking powder

¾ cup plain whole-milk yogurt

2 teaspoons honey

3 tablespoons salted butter, melted, or flavored butter (see facing page)

Made throughout the Middle East, non-yeasted flatbreads are the definition of quick bread, taking relatively little time to prepare. We added yogurt to a whole wheat- and honey-flavored dough for both its tangy bite and tenderizing qualities. Bread flour gives these flatbreads pleasant chew, but you can substitute an equal amount of all-purpose flour. If you do use all-purpose, you will likely have to add a couple extra tablespoons of flour during kneading because the dough will be slightly wetter. You'll need a 12-inch cast-iron skillet; a 10-inch cast-iron skillet will work, too, but there will be a little less room for maneuvering the rounds when flipping. We liked serving these with flavored butters.

Don't leave any floury bits in the bowl during mixing. All the flour must be incorporated so the dough isn't too sticky to work with. Don't overflour the counter when rolling out the rounds; excess flour will scorch in the skillet.

In a large bowl, stir together both flours, the salt and baking powder. Add the yogurt and honey and stir until a shaggy dough forms. Using your hands, knead in the bowl until the dough forms a cohesive ball, incorporating any dry bits; the dough will be slightly sticky.

Turn the dough out onto a counter dusted with bread flour and continue kneading until the dough is tacky instead of sticky, about 1 minute. The finished dough may appear slightly lumpy; this is fine. Divide into 6 pieces and shape each into a ball. Loosely cover with plastic wrap and let rest for 10 minutes. Meanwhile, heat a 12-inch cast-iron skillet over medium-high.

On a lightly floured counter, roll each ball to an 8-inch circle. Place one dough round in the heated skillet and cook until the bottom is dark spotty brown, 1 to 1½ minutes. Using tongs, flip the round and cook the second side until dark spotty brown, about 1 minute. Transfer to a wire rack, flipping so the first side to cook faces down, then brush with butter. Repeat with the remaining dough rounds. Serve immediately.

GARLIC-HERB BUTTER

Combine 3 tablespoons salted butter and 1 finely grated garlic clove in a small saucepan over medium. Cook, stirring, until the garlic is just beginning to color, about 30 seconds. Off heat, add 2 tablespoons finely chopped fresh flat-leaf parsley, 1 tablespoon finely chopped fresh dill, 1 tablespoon finely chopped fresh cilantro, tarragon or basil, and a pinch of salt.

ZA'ATAR BUTTER

Combine 3 tablespoons salted butter and 1 tablespoon za'atar in a small saucepan over medium. Cook until the butter is bubbling and the seeds are just beginning to color, about 30 seconds.

HARISSA BUTTER

Melt 3 tablespoons salted butter in a small saucepan over medium. Off heat, stir in 1 tablespoon harissa.

Bold, bright salads for supper

Ginger Beef and Rice Noodle Salad / 245

Indonesian Fried Tofu Salad (Rujak) / 247

Greens with Walnuts, Parmesan
and Pancetta Vinaigrette / 249

Jasmine Rice and Herb Salad with Shrimp / 251

Korean Chicken Salad (Dak Naengchae) / 253

Kale-Miso Salad with Roasted Sweet Potatoes / 255

Fattoush / 256

Herbed Egg Salad with Pickled Red Onion / 259

Chili-Rubbed Pork with
Cucumber-Melon Salad / 261

Chicken Salad with Apple, Celery Root
and Fennel / 263

Potato Salad and Smoked Trout
with Horseradish and Chives / 265

Shrimp, Fennel and Radish Salad / 267

Sugar Snap and Radish Salad
with Olive-Oil Tuna / 269

Miso-Ginger Chicken Salad / 271

Bread Salad with Kale, Beets
and Blue Cheese / 272

Thai Grapefruit Salad with Shrimp (Som Tom O) / 275

**Supper
Salads**

Ginger Beef
and Rice Noodle Salad

START TO FINISH:	SERVINGS:
40 minutes	**4**

¼ cup plus 1 tablespoon fish sauce, divided

2 tablespoons finely grated fresh ginger, divided

3 tablespoons plus 2 teaspoons packed light brown sugar, divided

Kosher salt and ground black pepper

1 pound sirloin tips, patted dry

12 ounces thin rice noodles

¼ cup lime juice

1 teaspoon chili-garlic sauce

1 tablespoon peanut oil

1 cup lightly packed fresh mint, torn

1 cup lightly packed fresh cilantro

½ cup dry roasted peanuts, roughly chopped

For this Vietnamese-inspired beef and rice noodle salad, we liked the rich, meaty flavor of sirloin tips, a cut sometimes sold as flap meat or faux hanger steak. It's fine if the tips are in two or three pieces, as the meat will be sliced for serving. If you can't find sirloin tips, flank steak is a good substitute. If the flank is of an even ½-inch thickness, it does not need to be pounded. We used Thai Kitchen thin rice noodles (sometimes called rice vermicelli). And if the noodles are in very long strands, snip them a few times with scissors after draining to make them easier to eat. If the taste of the fish sauce is too strong in the dressing, thin it with a few teaspoons of water.

Don't skip pounding the sirloin tips. This allows the marinade to penetrate the muscle fibers and helps the meat cook evenly. Don't slice the meat immediately after cooking. A short rest allows the juices to redistribute.

In a medium bowl, combine 1 tablespoon of fish sauce, 1 tablespoon of the ginger, 2 teaspoons brown sugar, 1 teaspoon salt and ¼ teaspoon pepper. Set aside. Place the sirloin tips between 2 sheets of plastic wrap and, using a meat mallet, gently pound to an even ½-inch thickness. Add the beef to the fish sauce mixture and turn to coat. Marinate at room temperature for 15 minutes.

Bring a large pot of water to a boil. Add the noodles and immediately remove the pot from the heat. Let stand, stirring 2 or 3 times, until tender, 3 to 5 minutes. Drain in a colander, rinse under cold water and drain again. Transfer to a large bowl and set aside.

In a small bowl, whisk together the remaining ¼ cup fish sauce, the remaining 1 tablespoon ginger, the remaining 3 tablespoons brown sugar, the lime juice, 2 tablespoons water and the chili-garlic sauce until the sugar dissolves.

In a 12-inch nonstick skillet over medium-high, heat the oil until barely smoking. Add the beef and cook until browned on both sides, turning once, about 6 minutes. Transfer to a plate and let rest for 5 minutes. Meanwhile, to the noodles add ½ cup of the fish sauce-lime juice mixture, the mint, cilantro and peanuts; toss to combine. Transfer to a serving platter or individual bowls.

Cut each piece of meat into thirds with the grain, then slice as thinly as possible against the grain. Place the slices on top of the noodles and drizzle with the accumulated juices. Serve with the remaining fish sauce-lime juice mixture on the side.

We tried mango, papaya, sour apples, melon, cherry tomatoes, jicama and more in this Southeast Asian dish. The game-changer? Red grapes. Along with pineapple and lime, they give the salad sweetness and tang.

Indonesian Fried Tofu Salad

(Rujak)

START TO FINISH:	SERVINGS:
45 minutes	**4**

14-ounce container extra-firm tofu, drained, cut into 1-inch cubes

2 teaspoons fish sauce

1 tablespoon hoisin sauce

3 tablespoons chili-garlic sauce, divided

1 teaspoon grated lime zest, plus ¼ cup lime juice, divided

3 tablespoons peanut oil, divided

1 medium ripe pineapple (18 ounces) peeled, cored and cut into ½-inch chunks (5½ cups)

10 ounces red seedless grapes, halved

1 English cucumber, quartered lengthwise and thinly sliced on diagonal

Kosher salt

½ cup salted dry-roasted peanuts, finely chopped

Rujak is a fruit and vegetable salad with countless variations across Indonesia, Malaysia and Singapore. The ingredient list can be lengthy, but we streamlined by using only easy-to-find ingredients that offer big flavor, texture and visual impact. Fried tofu turns the sweet, savory and spicy salad into a light main course.

Don't use silken tofu. *Its soft, custard-like texture won't hold up to pressing and frying. Extra-firm tofu is best for this recipe.*

Line a rimmed baking sheet with a triple layer of paper towels. Lay the tofu in single layer over them and cover with additional paper towels. Place another baking sheet over the tofu, then place a heavy skillet or other weight on top to press. Let stand for 20 minutes.

Meanwhile, in a large bowl, whisk together the fish sauce, hoisin, 1 table-spoon of the chili-garlic sauce, the lime zest and 1 tablespoon of the lime juice. Gradually whisk in 1 tablespoon of the oil. Set aside.

In another large bowl, combine the pineapple, grapes and cucumber. Stir in the remaining 2 tablespoons chili-garlic sauce, the remaining 3 tablespoons lime juice and 1¼ teaspoons salt. Transfer to shallow serving bowl and set aside.

Remove the weight, baking sheet and paper towels from the tofu and season on all sides with salt. Line a plate with paper towels. In a 12-inch nonstick skillet over medium, heat the remaining 2 tablespoons oil until shimmering. Add the tofu in a single layer and cook, turning occasionally, until most surfaces are crisped and browned, about 10 minutes. Transfer to the prepared plate and turn the pieces once to blot off excess oil. Immediately add the tofu to the dressing and toss. Let stand to allow the tofu to soak in the dressing, about 5 minutes.

Add about half the peanuts to the tofu mixture, then toss. Taste and season with salt. Transfer to the serving bowl, on top of the fruit mixture. Sprinkle with the remaining peanuts.

Greens with Walnuts, Parmesan
and Pancetta Vinaigrette

START TO FINISH:	SERVINGS:
15 minutes	**6**

12 ounces mixed bitter greens (12 cups), torn

2 tablespoons sherry vinegar

1 tablespoon Dijon mustard

Kosher salt and ground black pepper

6 ounces thinly sliced pancetta, chopped

1 medium shallot, finely chopped

3 tablespoons extra-virgin olive oil

1 cup walnuts, toasted and roughly chopped

1 ounce Parmesan cheese, shaved (½ cup)

Bitter greens pair with a rich dressing for this take on salade frisée au lardons. The dish typically is made with frisée lettuce, a poached egg and meaty salt pork for the lardons. We take our lead from Paul Bertolli, who refurbished the classic in his 2003 "Cooking by Hand," using a mix of greens, toasted walnuts, pancetta and Parmesan. To make this salad, use any combination of bitter greens such as frisée, endive, radicchio, escarole or arugula. To toast the walnuts, spread them evenly on a rimmed baking sheet and bake at 350°F until lightly browned and fragrant, 5 to 7 minutes. A sharp Y-shaped vegetable peeler is the perfect tool for shaving the Parmesan cheese. For a heartier meal, and one that harkens back to this salad's bistro roots, top with a fried egg.

Don't allow the dressing to cool before adding it to the greens. Its consistency is best when warm, and its heat slightly softens the sturdy greens. By the same token, make sure the greens are not cold when dressed so the warm dressing doesn't firm up on contact.

Place the greens in a large bowl and set aside. In a separate bowl, whisk together the vinegar, mustard and ½ teaspoon salt.

In a medium skillet over medium, cook the pancetta, stirring occasionally, until crisp, about 7 minutes. Using a slotted spoon, transfer the pancetta to a paper towel–lined plate. Pour off all but 1 tablespoon fat from the skillet, then return it to medium heat. Add the shallot and cook, stirring, until light golden brown, about 2 minutes. Add the oil and the vinegar mixture, then remove from the heat and whisk until combined. Let sit for 30 seconds to warm through.

Add the warm dressing, walnuts and 1 teaspoon pepper to the greens and toss well. Taste and season with salt. Divide the salad among plates and top each portion with pancetta and Parmesan.

Jasmine Rice and Herb Salad

with Shrimp

START TO FINISH:
35 minutes

SERVINGS:
4

1½ cups jasmine rice, rinsed and drained

½ cup coconut milk

¼ cup lime juice

2 tablespoons fish sauce

3 tablespoons finely grated fresh ginger

8 scallions, thinly sliced, white and green parts reserved separately

Kosher salt

1 pound cooked medium shrimp, tails removed, cut into bite-size pieces

1 cup lightly packed fresh basil, finely chopped

1 cup lightly packed fresh cilantro, finely chopped

½ cup unsweetened shredded coconut, toasted

Malaysian nasi ulam, a rice dish suffused with a variety of Southeast Asian herbs, inspired this recipe. We use readily available herbs and add shrimp to make a light main dish out of the salad. If you find Thai basil, use it in place of Italian basil. You can buy cooked shrimp in the seafood department of most supermarkets or poach your own peeled and deveined shrimp in barely simmering water seasoned with a handful of cilantro stems. Cook just until the shrimp turn opaque, then transfer to ice water to stop the cooking. Dry the shrimp well before using.

Don't use sweetened shredded coconut flakes; their sweetness will alter the flavor of the dish.

In a large saucepan over medium-high, bring the rice and 2 cups water to a simmer, then reduce to low, cover and cook until tender and the water is absorbed, about 12 minutes. Turn off the heat and let the rice sit, covered, for 10 minutes.

Meanwhile, line a rimmed baking sheet with kitchen parchment. When the rice is done, fluff with a fork, then spread in an even layer on the baking sheet. Let cool for 15 minutes.

In a large bowl, whisk together the coconut milk, lime juice, fish sauce, ginger, scallion whites and 1 teaspoon salt. Add the shrimp, toss and let stand for 5 minutes. Add the rice, scallion greens, basil, cilantro and coconut and toss. Taste and season with salt.

Korean Chicken Salad

(Dak Naengchae)

START TO FINISH:	SERVINGS:
15 minutes	**4**

8 ounces green beans, trimmed

¾ cup pine nuts, toasted, divided

2 tablespoons yellow mustard

1 tablespoon gochujang

3 tablespoons lemon juice, divided

Kosher salt

3 cups sliced or shredded cooked chicken

8 ounces red cabbage, shredded (3 cups)

1 cup cherry tomatoes, halved

½ English cucumber, halved lengthwise and thinly sliced crosswise

2 scallions, thinly sliced on diagonal

Pine nuts blended with water and a few seasonings create a rich, creamy dressing for this easy chicken salad. The Korean mustard called gyeoja would be the authentic choice here, but we use regular yellow mustard and add a hit of spice with gochujang, a widely available Korean fermented chili paste. Use whatever vegetables suit your taste. Good choices include sliced radishes, shredded iceberg lettuce, grated carrots and thinly sliced bell peppers.

Don't use the pine nuts without first toasting them. *Toasting produces a richer, fuller-flavored dressing.*

Bring a medium saucepan of salted water to a boil. Fill a medium bowl with ice water. Add the green beans to the boiling water and cook until bright green and crisp-tender, about 3 minutes. Drain, then immediately add to the ice water. Let stand just until cool, about 1 minute, then drain again. Pat the beans dry, cut in half and set aside.

Set aside 3 tablespoons of the pine nuts for garnish. In a blender, process the remaining pine nuts to a coarse paste, scraping the sides as needed, about 20 seconds. Add ¼ cup water, the mustard, gochujang, 2 tablespoons of the lemon juice and ¾ teaspoon salt. Blend until smooth and pourable, about 30 seconds.

In a medium bowl, toss the chicken with about ½ cup of the dressing and the remaining tablespoon of lemon juice, then taste and season with salt. In another medium bowl, toss together the green beans, cabbage, tomatoes, cucumber, the remaining dressing and ¾ teaspoon salt. Transfer the vegetables to a serving platter. Spoon the chicken over the center and sprinkle with the reserved pine nuts and scallions.

Kale-Miso Salad

with Roasted Sweet Potatoes

START TO FINISH:	SERVINGS:
45 minutes	**4**

4 medium orange-fleshed sweet potatoes (about 2¼ pounds), peeled, halved crosswise and cut into 1-inch wedges

6 tablespoons extra-virgin olive oil, divided

¼ teaspoon sweet paprika

Kosher salt and ground black pepper

1 medium garlic clove, finely grated

4 teaspoons sherry vinegar

1½ teaspoons white miso

5 ounces baby kale

3 scallions, thinly sliced on diagonal

½ cup roughly chopped fresh cilantro

½ cup chopped walnuts, toasted

Sweet potatoes roasted until deeply browned and tossed with a touch of paprika are a great foil for the savory, minerally notes of a miso-dressed kale salad. The char on the potatoes provides a note of bitterness that balances the richness of the miso. Scallions and cilantro add fresh herbal notes and toasted walnuts add crunch.

Don't dress the salad *until just before serving. If left to stand, the kale will turn limp and soggy.*

Heat the oven to 425°F with a rack in the middle position. Line a rimmed baking sheet with kitchen parchment. In a large bowl, toss the sweet potatoes with 4 tablespoons of the oil. Spread the potatoes in an even layer on the baking sheet and roast until tender and the edges begin to darken, about 30 minutes.

Stir the potatoes, return to the oven and increase to 500°F. Roast until dark spotty brown and slightly crisped, about another 10 minutes. Transfer to a large bowl. Sprinkle with the paprika, ½ teaspoon each salt and pepper, then toss.

While the potatoes roast, in a small bowl, stir together the garlic and vinegar. Let stand for 10 minutes to mellow the garlic. Whisk in the remaining 2 table-spoons oil, the miso and ¼ teaspoon pepper. Set aside.

When the potatoes are done, in another large bowl, toss together the kale, scallions, cilantro and half the walnuts. Pour in the dressing and toss. Divide the sweet potatoes among serving plates and top with the salad. Sprinkle with the remaining walnuts.

Fattoush

START TO FINISH:
30 minutes

SERVINGS:
6

1 pound seedless red grapes, halved

¼ cup cider vinegar

Kosher salt and ground black pepper

½ cup extra-virgin olive oil, divided

3 medium garlic cloves, finely grated

2 teaspoons ground cumin

½ to ¾ teaspoon red pepper flakes

Two 8-inch pita bread rounds, each split into 2 rounds

½ cup plain whole-milk yogurt

½ cup finely chopped fresh dill

1 tablespoon pomegranate molasses (optional)

2 teaspoons ground sumac (optional)

1 English cucumber, quartered lengthwise, thinly sliced

6- to 7-ounce romaine heart, chopped into bite-size pieces

1 cup lightly packed fresh mint, finely chopped

This take on a Middle Eastern bread salad gets crunch and texture from pita bread split into rounds and brushed generously with seasoned olive oil before toasting to produce thin, crisp pieces packed with flavor. Pickled grapes are not a common fattoush ingredient, but we loved their sweet-tart flavor and succulent texture, an idea we borrowed from chef Ana Sortun of Oleana in Cambridge, Massachusetts. Both the pita and the grapes can be prepared a day in advance; store the pita in an airtight container to keep it fresh. Sumac, a fruity, lemony Levantine spice, has earthy, citrusy notes, and pomegranate molasses is tangy and lightly fruity. Both ingredients are optional, but they give the fattoush complexity and a distinct Middle Eastern character.

Don't combine the salad ingredients *until just before serving or the pita chips will get soggy.*

Heat the oven to 400°F with a rack in the middle position. In a medium bowl, stir together the grapes, vinegar and ½ teaspoon salt. Cover and refrigerate.

In a small bowl, stir together ¼ cup of the oil, the garlic, cumin and pepper flakes. Arrange the pita rounds rough side up on a rimmed baking sheet, then brush each with the flavored oil, using all of it. Sprinkle with salt and black pepper. Bake until browned and crisp, 10 to 12 minutes. Set aside to cool. When cool enough to handle, break into bite-size pieces.

Drain the grapes, reserving the pickling liquid. In a large bowl, combine the remaining ¼ cup oil, the yogurt, dill, molasses and sumac, if using, and 1 teaspoon each salt and black pepper. Add the reserved pickling liquid and whisk well. Add the cucumber, romaine, mint, pickled grapes and pita pieces. Toss until evenly coated.

Quick pickled onions are an easy way to add crunch and tangy flavor. We use them to balance the richness of the eggs, but they also are good tucked into sandwiches, grilled cheese or tacos, and sprinkled over roasted or blanched broccoli or kale.

Herbed Egg Salad

with Pickled Red Onion

START TO FINISH:	SERVINGS:
30 minutes	**4**

3 tablespoons finely chopped red onion

2 tablespoons Champagne or white wine vinegar

Kosher salt and ground black pepper

12 large eggs

¼ teaspoon ground turmeric

¼ cup finely chopped fresh tarragon

3 tablespoons finely chopped fresh chives

3 tablespoons finely chopped fresh flat-leaf parsley

Lemon wedges, to serve

Flaky salt (such as Maldon Sea Salt Flakes)

This egg salad, inspired by a recipe from "In My Kitchen" by Deborah Madison, is made without mayonnaise. Instead, three of the 12 cooked egg yolks are mashed to a paste with onion-infused vinegar, then mixed into coarsely chopped eggs to lightly bind the salad. The flavors are fresh and bright, and the salad is especially delicious served with rustic dark bread.

Don't steam the eggs for longer than 9 minutes. The eggs should be just shy of hard cooked. If cooked past that point, the yolks will be too firm to form a smooth sauce when mashed with the vinegar. Don't finely chop the eggs; we liked the salad with eggs that were in coarse, uneven bits.

In a small bowl, stir together the onion, vinegar and ½ teaspoon salt; set aside. Fill a large Dutch oven with about 1 inch of water. Place a folding steamer basket in the pot, cover and bring to a boil over medium-high. Add the eggs, cover and steam for 9 minutes. Meanwhile, fill a medium bowl with ice water.

Immediately transfer the eggs to the ice water and let stand until cooled. Crack and peel the eggs. Cut 9 of the eggs lengthwise into quarters, then cut the quarters crosswise into thirds. Transfer to a medium bowl. Add ¾ teaspoon salt and ½ teaspoon pepper and gently toss. Halve the remaining 3 eggs and transfer the yolks to a small bowl; roughly chop the whites and add them to the bowl with the chopped eggs.

Set a fine mesh strainer over the bowl containing the yolks and pour the onion mixture into the strainer; set the drained onions aside. Using a fork, mash the yolk-vinegar mixture until smooth, then whisk in the turmeric.

Sprinkle the tarragon, chives and parsley over the chopped eggs and add the yolk mixture. Fold until just combined; do not overmix. Taste and season with salt and pepper. Transfer to a serving bowl and sprinkle with the reserved onions. Serve with lemon wedges and flaky salt.

Chili-Rubbed Pork

with Cucumber-Melon Salad

START TO FINISH:	SERVINGS:
35 minutes	**4**

5 teaspoons ancho chili powder, divided

2 teaspoons ground cumin

Kosher salt and ground black pepper

1¼ pound pork tenderloin, trimmed of silver skin and cut crosswise into 3 pieces

2 teaspoons grated lime zest, divided, plus 3 tablespoons lime juice

3 tablespoons light agave syrup, divided

2 cups cubed seedless red watermelon (about 8 ounces)

2 cups cubed cantaloupe (about 8 ounces)

½ English cucumber, halved lengthwise, seeded and cut into bite-size pieces

5 tablespoons roughly chopped fresh mint, divided

2 tablespoons grapeseed or other neutral oil

This colorful dish is a study in contrasting flavors and temperatures. We draw on the fresh and chili-spiked fruit salads of Mexico to create a dish of seared and spiced pork paired with cool, crunchy melon and cucumber. For an optional salty, tangy accent, offer crumbled queso fresco on the side. The pork starts stovetop and finishes in the oven so you'll need a 10-inch oven-safe skillet.

Don't cut the cooked pork without first letting it rest. Resting allows the juices to redistribute throughout the muscle fibers, thereby keeping the pork juicy.

Heat the oven to 450°F with a rack in the middle position. In a medium bowl, mix 2 teaspoons of the chili powder, the cumin, 2 teaspoons salt and ½ teaspoon pepper. Add the pork and toss to coat, massaging the seasonings into the meat. Let stand at room temperature for 15 minutes.

Meanwhile, in a 10-inch oven-safe skillet over medium, toast the remaining 3 teaspoons chili powder, stirring constantly, until fragrant, 1 to 2 minutes. Transfer to a large bowl and add 1 teaspoon of the lime zest, 2 tablespoons of the lime juice, 2 tablespoons of the agave and 1 teaspoon salt. Stir to dissolve the salt, then add the watermelon, cantaloupe, cucumber and 4 tablespoons of the mint. Toss, then cover and refrigerate until ready to use.

In the same skillet over medium-high, heat the oil until barely smoking. Add the pork and cook, turning occasionally, until golden brown on all sides, 3 to 4 minutes total. Move the skillet to the oven and roast until the center of the thickest piece reaches 135°F or is just slightly pink when cut into, 9 to 12 minutes. Transfer the pork to a plate and let rest for 10 minutes.

In a medium bowl, stir together the remaining 1 teaspoon lime zest, the remaining 1 tablespoon lime juice, the remaining 1 tablespoon agave and the remaining 1 tablespoon mint. Cut each piece of pork in half lengthwise, then crosswise into bite-size pieces. Add the pork and any accumulated juices to the bowl and toss to coat.

Using a slotted spoon, transfer the melon salad to a serving platter, then top with the pork. Pour the liquid from the melon salad into a small bowl and serve with the melon and pork.

Chicken Salad

with Apple, Celery Root and Fennel

START TO FINISH:
20 minutes

SERVINGS:
4

½ cup mayonnaise

¼ cup whole-grain mustard

¼ cup drained capers, roughly chopped, plus 1 tablespoon caper brine

2 tablespoons lemon juice

Kosher salt and ground black pepper

3 cups shredded cooked chicken

5 ounces peeled celery root, half cut into 1-inch matchsticks, half shredded on the large holes of a box grater

1 Granny Smith apple, cored and cut into 1-inch-long matchsticks

1 small fennel bulb, trimmed, halved, cored and thinly sliced

½ cup packed fresh flat-leaf parsley, roughly chopped

¾ cup walnuts or hazelnuts, toasted and chopped

Céléri rémoulade is a classic French slaw-like salad made with celery root and mayonnaise. We built on that and turned it into this bright, fresh chicken salad. The celery root is prepared two ways: Half is cut into matchsticks, half is shredded on the large holes of a box grater. The combination heightens the salad's textural and visual appeal. You could poach and shred chicken breasts for this recipe, or you can simply shred the meat of a store-bought rotisserie chicken. Serve the salad on a bed of arugula.

Don't peel the apple; *the skin adds a touch of color. Also, don't use a sweet apple; the tartness of a Granny Smith perks up the other flavors.*

In a large bowl, stir together the mayonnaise, mustard, capers and brine, lemon juice and ½ teaspoon pepper. Add the chicken, all of the celery root, apple, fennel, parsley and nuts. Fold with a rubber spatula until well combined. Taste and season with salt and pepper.

Potato Salad and Smoked Trout

with Horseradish and Chives

START TO FINISH:
50 minutes

SERVINGS:
6

2 pounds red potatoes,
cut into 1-inch pieces

Kosher salt and ground
black pepper

6 medium radishes, halved
and thinly sliced

5 tablespoons white wine
vinegar, divided

½ cup sour cream

3 tablespoons prepared
horseradish

2 tablespoons extra-virgin
olive oil

8 ounces smoked trout, skin
discarded, flesh broken into
small flakes

2 tablespoons finely chopped
fresh dill

6 tablespoons finely chopped
fresh chives, divided

Scandinavians frequently combine potent smoked fish and mild, creamy potatoes. For this dish, we find a modest amount of sour cream both binds the salad and adds a tanginess that, along with the pungency of the horseradish, works well with the salty richness of smoked trout. Up the horseradish if you like. Tossing the potatoes with vinegar, salt and pepper immediately after draining them allows them to soak up the seasonings as they cool. Serve the salad on a bed of watercress, lettuce or your favorite greens. Leftovers can be refrigerated for a couple days; bring to room temperature before serving.

Don't dress the potatoes until they've cooled to the point of barely warm to the touch. If the potatoes are hot, they'll cause the dressing to break.

In a large saucepan, combine the potatoes and 2 tablespoons salt, then add enough water to cover by 1 inch. Bring to a boil over high, then reduce to medium-low and simmer until a knife inserted into the largest piece meets no resistance, about 20 minutes.

Meanwhile, in a small bowl, combine the radishes, 2 tablespoons of the vinegar and ¼ teaspoon salt. Toss and set aside. In a large bowl, whisk together 1 tablespoon of the remaining vinegar, the sour cream, horseradish, oil and ¼ teaspoon each salt and pepper. Refrigerate until needed.

When the potatoes are done, drain in a colander, then spread in an even layer in a large baking dish. Sprinkle with the remaining 2 tablespoons vinegar and ½ teaspoon each salt and pepper. Refrigerate, uncovered, until barely warm to the touch, about 20 minutes.

Add the cooled potatoes to the sour cream mixture and fold with a rubber spatula until evenly coated. Drain the radishes, discarding the liquid. Fold in the radishes, smoked trout, dill and 4 tablespoons of the chives. Taste and season with salt and pepper. Transfer to a serving bowl and sprinkle with the remaining 2 tablespoons chives.

Shrimp, Fennel and Radish Salad

START TO FINISH:
15 minutes

SERVINGS:
4

⅓ cup mayonnaise

1 tablespoon extra-virgin olive oil

¼ cup minced fresh dill

1 teaspoon Dijon mustard

1 teaspoon lemon juice

Kosher salt and ground black pepper

1 pound large cooked shrimp, cut into ½-inch pieces

1 small fennel bulb, trimmed, halved, cored and shaved

4 radishes, trimmed and shaved

8 large Bibb lettuce leaves, washed and dried

San Francisco's Tartine Bakery & Café is known for its rustic breads, as well as the casual charm of its pastries. They also make a mean sandwich. Case in point: a bay shrimp salad served on a toasted croissant. The sweet, tiny shrimp pair perfectly with trout roe and fresh fennel. We ditched the roe and paired the fennel with radish and a zippy mustard-mayonnaise dressing. Use a mandoline to make quick work of shaving the fennel and radishes. You can buy cooked shrimp in the seafood department of most grocers, or poach your own peeled and deveined shrimp in barely simmering water seasoned with 1 tablespoon black peppercorns and two bay leaves. Cook the shrimp until pink and opaque, then transfer to ice water to stop the cooking. Dry the shrimp well before using.

Don't forget to cut away the core from the fennel bulb halves before shaving them. The core is often dense and fibrous.

In a medium bowl, whisk together the mayonnaise, oil, dill, mustard, lemon juice and ¼ teaspoon each salt and pepper. Stir in the shrimp. In a separate bowl, combine the fennel, radishes and ½ teaspoon each salt and pepper.

Arrange the lettuce on individual plates. Arrange the fennel mixture over the lettuce, then top with the shrimp mixture.

We found plenty of extra uses for the tuna-mayonnaise sauce in this recipe. Try it on sliced tomatoes or as a dip for cucumbers, endive or carrots. Swap it out for regular mayonnaise in egg or shrimp salad, or spoon it on grilled salmon.

Sugar Snap and Radish Salad
with Olive-Oil Tuna

START TO FINISH:	SERVINGS:
30 minutes	**4**

Kosher salt and ground white pepper

1 pound sugar snap peas, trimmed and strings removed

Two 5-ounce cans olive oil–packed tuna, drained and flaked into bite-size pieces

7 tablespoons extra-virgin olive oil, divided

2 tablespoons grated lemon zest, divided, plus 4 tablespoons lemon juice, divided

2 teaspoons fish sauce

¼ cup mayonnaise

1 bunch radishes, halved and thinly sliced

1 cup lightly packed fresh basil, torn if large

2 tablespoons poppy seeds

This recipe, inspired by chef Joshua McFadden of Ava Gene's in Portland, Oregon, plays fast and loose with convention. Northern Italian tonnato—a silky, savory sauce made with tuna—typically is served with veal. But we like to balance the puree's rich, meaty flavor with sweet snap peas and peppery radishes. Flaked tuna tops off the salad. Asian fish sauce may be a surprise ingredient, but just a couple teaspoons of it bolsters the flavor of the tuna.

Don't use tuna packed in water. *It lacks the flavor and richness of oil-packed tuna and has a drier, mealier texture.*

Fill a large bowl with ice water. In a large saucepan, bring 2 quarts water to a boil. Stir in 2 tablespoons salt and the snap peas. Cook until bright green and crisp-tender, about 2 minutes. Drain, then immediately transfer to the ice water. Let stand until completely cooled, about 2 minutes, then drain again. Slice half the peas in half on the diagonal, then set aside.

In a small bowl, toss half (about ¾ cup) of the tuna with 2 tablespoons of oil, 1 tablespoon of lemon zest, 1 tablespoon of lemon juice, and ¼ teaspoon each salt and white pepper. Set aside.

In a blender, combine the remaining tuna, the remaining 1 tablespoon lemon zest, 1 tablespoon of the remaining lemon juice, ¼ teaspoon white pepper, the fish sauce and mayonnaise. Blend until a smooth paste forms, about 45 seconds, scraping the blender jar as needed. With the machine running, drizzle in 3 tablespoons of the remaining oil and blend until creamy and thick, about another 45 seconds. If needed, drizzle in up to 1 tablespoon water to achieve the proper consistency. Taste and season with salt and pepper, then set aside.

In a large bowl, toss together the peas, radishes, basil and poppy seeds. Add the remaining 2 tablespoons lemon juice, the remaining 2 tablespoons olive oil, and ¼ teaspoon each salt and white pepper. Toss well. On a serving platter, spread about ⅔ cup of the tuna sauce in an even layer. Top with the vegetables, then sprinkle with the flaked tuna. Serve with the remaining sauce on the side.

Miso-Ginger Chicken Salad

START TO FINISH:
30 minutes

SERVINGS:
4

⅓ cup white miso

2-inch piece fresh ginger, peeled and thinly sliced

⅔ cup slivered almonds, toasted, divided

⅓ cup lime juice

1 teaspoon Dijon mustard

1 teaspoon honey

Kosher salt and ground white pepper

½ cup grapeseed or other neutral oil

3 cups shredded cooked chicken (see note)

6 medium scallions, thinly sliced (½ cup)

½ cup lightly packed fresh cilantro, finely chopped

½ English cucumber, halved lengthwise, seeded and thinly sliced (1 cup)

For this quick, flavor-packed salad, we dressed the shredded meat from a rotisserie chicken with a tangy, gingery miso dressing. Sliced cucumber and a generous dose of herbs add freshness, and slivered almonds bring a pleasing crunch. One 3-pound rotisserie chicken will yield about 3 cups of shredded meat. The dressing can be made ahead and refrigerated up to four days.

Don't use the dressing immediately after blending. *Allowing it to stand for at least 30 minutes lets the flavors meld.*

In a blender, combine ⅓ cup water, the miso, ginger, ⅓ cup of the almonds, the lime juice, mustard, honey and ½ teaspoon white pepper. Blend until smooth, about 1 minute. Add the oil and blend until thick, about 1 minute. Transfer to a jar, cover and refrigerate for at least 30 minutes or up to 4 days.

In a large bowl, combine the chicken, scallions, cilantro, cucumber and remaining ⅓ cup almonds. Add 1 cup of the dressing and toss. Taste and season with salt and pepper. Serve with the remaining dressing on the side.

Bread Salad with Kale,

Beets and Blue Cheese

START TO FINISH:
45 minutes (25 minutes active)

SERVINGS:
4

1 medium shallot, minced

2 tablespoons sherry vinegar

4 slices bacon, chopped

4 tablespoons extra-virgin olive oil, divided

5 ounces rustic bread, such as ciabatta, cut into 1-inch pieces (about 4 cups)

1 small bunch lacinato kale (about 6 ounces), stemmed and thinly sliced crosswise

Kosher salt and ground black pepper

8-ounce package cooked baby beets, each beet cut into 6 or 8 wedges

1 tablespoon honey

4 ounces blue cheese, coarsely crumbled

For this hearty salad, we took a cue from panzanella, an Italian tomato and bread salad. But we swapped out tomatoes for kale and paired it with sweet, earthy beets and bold blue cheese. It's delicious on its own as a light main course, but it's also excellent as a side dish to roasted chicken or pork. We liked the convenience of vacuum-packed cooked baby beets sold in the produce section of the supermarket, but if you prefer, roast and peel your own.

Don't worry if the kale darkens and reduces in volume as you rub it with salt. The salt tenderizes the leaves.

In a small bowl, stir together the shallots and vinegar. Set aside. In a 12-inch nonstick skillet over medium, cook the bacon until browned and crisp, 8 to 10 minutes. Transfer to a paper towel-lined plate, then discard the fat in the skillet.

In the same skillet, heat 2 tablespoons of the oil over medium-high until shimmering. Add the bread and cook, tossing frequently and lowering the heat slightly if the oil smokes, until golden brown, 4 to 5 minutes. Transfer to another plate and let cool until barely warm.

In a large bowl, toss the kale with ¼ teaspoon salt then massage with your hands until the leaves soften and darken, 10 to 20 seconds. Add the bread and beets.

To the shallot mixture, whisk in the remaining 2 tablespoons oil, ½ teaspoon salt, ¼ teaspoon pepper and the honey. Add to the kale mixture and toss. Add the cheese and bacon, then toss gently. Taste and season with salt and pepper.

Thai Grapefruit Salad

with Shrimp (Som Tom O)

START TO FINISH:
45 minutes

SERVINGS:
4

4 grapefruits (preferably red), segmented (see note) and seeded

6 tablespoons fish sauce, divided

8 ounces large shrimp, peeled, deveined, tails removed

3 tablespoons lime juice

3 tablespoons light brown sugar

2 Thai chilies, seeded and minced

1 medium garlic clove, grated

4 ounces small shallots, sliced into thin rings, layers separated

1 cup lightly packed fresh cilantro

½ cup roasted cashews, roughly chopped, divided

Our take on som tom o, Thai pomelo salad, uses grapefruit as a stand-in for the highly seasonal pomelo. Traditional versions include dried shrimp as a flavoring, but we use fresh shrimp and include enough to turn the salad into a light main dish. To segment grapefruit, cut off the top and bottom and set the fruit on a cut end. Working from top to bottom and following the fruit's contour, cut away the peel and white pith. Slide the knife along each side of the membranes separating the segments. If your roasted cashews are only lightly browned, toast them in a dry skillet for a few minutes to crisp them and bring out their flavor.

Don't use shallots that are at all soft or spongy; they need to be fresh and crisp because they're used raw—and because there's a good amount in the salad. If you can't find decent shallots, substitute ½ medium red onion, thinly sliced.

Cut any large grapefruit segments in half. Put the segments in a colander to drain and set aside while you prepare the shrimp.

In a small saucepan, bring 2 cups water to a boil. Add 3 tablespoons of the fish sauce and the shrimp, remove from the heat and cover. Let stand until the shrimp are opaque throughout, 3 to 4 minutes. Drain, transfer to a plate and let cool until barely warm. Cut each shrimp in half lengthwise.

In a small bowl, combine the remaining 3 tablespoons fish sauce, the lime juice, sugar, chilies and garlic. Stir until the sugar dissolves. In a large bowl, combine the grapefruit, shrimp, shallots, cilantro and ¼ cup of the cashews. Pour the fish sauce mixture over and gently toss. Transfer to a platter and scatter the remaining ¼ cup cashews on top.

For nights when only pizza, tacos and burgers will suffice

Pizza Night

Weeknight Pizza

Store-bought fresh pizza dough or homemade dough that you've made in advance makes freshly baked pizza doable as a weeknight dinner. Store-bought dough sometimes is half-hearted in flavor, but the right toppings and baking method can make up for many shortcomings. We start with an overview of how to get the most out of your dough, followed by some of our favorite toppings as well as a quick pizza dough-based stuffed flatbread. You'll need a pizza steel or stone for these recipes. A pizza peel is the best tool for getting the pie into and out of the oven, but a baking sheet will work in a pinch.

Don't let your assembled, unbaked pizza sit on the pizza peel for more than a few minutes. The dough's moisture will soften the semolina, and the pizza won't slide off easily.

SHAPING PIZZA DOUGH

At least 1 hour before baking, heat the oven to 550°F (or 500°F if that's your oven's maximum temperature), with a baking steel or stone on the upper-middle rack.

Warming the dough to 75°F before shaping it makes it easy to work with. For two, 10-inch pizzas, we recommend dividing one pound of dough into two 8-ounce balls, putting the dough balls into oiled bowls, covering them with plastic wrap, then setting the bowls into a larger bowl containing 100°F water. Check the temperature of the dough with an instant thermometer after about 30 minutes and change the water as needed. Make sure you have all of your toppings ready before you begin shaping the dough.

For two, 10-inch pizzas, turn one ball of dough out onto a counter dusted with all-purpose flour. Flour your hands and, using your fingers and starting at the center and working out to the edges, press the dough into a 10-inch round, turning the dough over once, leaving the perimeter slightly thicker than the center. If the dough stretches but shrinks back, let it rest for 5 minutes to relax the gluten, then try again.

Set the first round aside on the counter and cover it with a clean kitchen towel. Shape the second portion of dough in the same way. Top and bake according to one of the recipes on the following pages.

Three-Cheese Pizza

START TO FINISH:
40 minutes

MAKES:
Two 10-inch pizzas

14½-ounce can diced tomatoes

½ teaspoon dried oregano

1 medium garlic clove,
finely grated

¼ teaspoon red pepper flakes

1 tablespoon extra-virgin
olive oil

Kosher salt

3 ounces shredded whole-milk
mozzarella cheese (¾ cup)

1½ ounces shredded fontina
cheese (⅓ cup)

1 ounce finely grated
Parmesan cheese (½ cup)

Semolina flour, for dusting
pizza peel

2 pizza dough rounds
(see page 279)

This is the simple, classic cheese pizza. We use a quick, no-cook tomato sauce
and a mixture of three cheeses for full flavor. Straining the sauce after pureeing
removes excess moisture that otherwise would prevent the crust from crisping.

At least 1 hour before baking, heat oven to 550°F (or 500°F if that's your
oven's maximum temperature), with a baking steel or stone on the upper-
middle rack.

In a food processor, process the tomatoes, oregano, garlic and pepper flakes
until smooth, about 30 seconds. Transfer to a fine mesh strainer set over
a medium bowl. Let stand without stirring until liquid no longer drains
off, about 15 minutes. Discard the liquid. Add the strained tomatoes to the
now-empty bowl and stir in the oil and ½ teaspoon salt. In a medium bowl,
toss all 3 cheeses until combined.

Dust a baking peel, inverted baking sheet or rimless cookie sheet with
semolina. Transfer the first dough round to the peel and, if needed, reshape
into a 10-inch circle. Using the back of a spoon, spread half of the tomato
mixture over the dough, leaving a ½-inch border at the edge. Sprinkle with
half of the cheese mixture. Slide the pizza onto the baking steel and bake until
well browned and the cheese is bubbling and spotted brown, 7 to 10 minutes
(9 to 12 minutes in a 500°F oven).

Using the peel, transfer the pizza to a wire rack. Let cool for a couple minutes.
Meanwhile, repeat with the second dough round, using the remaining tomato
sauce and cheese mixture.

Roasted Eggplant Pizza

with Za'atar and Feta

START TO FINISH:	MAKES:
30 minutes	**Two 10-inch pizzas**

12-ounce eggplant, sliced
into ½-inch-thick rounds

¼ cup extra-virgin olive oil

1½ cups grape or cherry
tomatoes, halved

1 large shallot, peeled and
cut into ¼-inch wedges

6 medium garlic cloves,
minced

Za'atar seasoning

Kosher salt

Semolina flour, for dusting
the pizza peel

2 pizza dough rounds
(see page 279)

4 ounces feta cheese,
finely crumbled (1 cup)

2 tablespoons pine nuts

For efficiency, roast the eggplant once the oven has come to temperature but while the pizza steel or stone is still heating. Look for za'atar, a Middle Eastern sesame, herb and spice blend, in well-stocked grocery stores and spice shops.

At least 1 hour before baking, heat oven to 550°F (or 500°F if that's your oven's maximum temperature), with a baking steel or stone on the upper-middle rack. Place a second rack in the lower-middle position. Line a rimmed baking sheet with foil.

Arrange the eggplant slices in an even layer on the prepared baking sheet. Brush both sides with oil, using all of the oil. Roast on the lower-middle rack until soft and golden brown on both sides, about 10 minutes (12 minutes in a 500°F oven). Let cool slightly, then chop the eggplant into 1-inch pieces. In a medium bowl, combine the eggplant, tomatoes, shallot, garlic, 2 tablespoons za'atar and 1 teaspoon salt.

Dust a baking peel, inverted baking sheet or rimless cookie sheet with semolina. Transfer the first dough round to the peel and, if needed, reshape into a 10-inch circle. Spread half of the eggplant mixture evenly over it, leaving a ½-inch border at the edge. Sprinkle with half the feta and 1 tablespoon of pine nuts. Bake until the crust is well browned, 7 to 10 minutes (9 to 12 minutes in a 500°F oven).

Using the peel, transfer the pizza to a wire rack. Let cool for a couple of minutes. Meanwhile, repeat with the second dough round and remaining ingredients.

White Pizza with Arugula

START TO FINISH:
35 minutes

MAKES:
Two 10-inch pizzas

¾ cup cold heavy cream

4 ounces shredded fontina cheese (1 cup)

½ ounce finely grated Parmesan cheese (¼ cup)

Kosher salt and ground black pepper

1 tablespoon extra-virgin olive oil

1 teaspoon grated lemon zest plus 2 teaspoons lemon juice

Semolina flour, for dusting the pizza peel

2 pizza dough rounds (see page 279)

4 cups lightly packed baby arugula

A whipped cream-fontina mixture makes the "sauce" for these pies. During baking, it melts to a creamy consistency, so be sure to crimp the edge of the dough to create a slight retaining wall for the sauce. Lightly dressed arugula is the perfect finishing touch.

At least 1 hour before baking, heat oven to 550°F (or 500°F if that's your oven's maximum temperature), with a baking steel or stone on the upper-middle rack.

Using an electric mixer, whip the cream until it holds stiff peaks. Fold in the fontina, Parmesan, ½ teaspoon pepper and ¼ teaspoon salt. In a large bowl, whisk the oil, lemon zest and juice, and a pinch of salt. Set aside.

Dust a baking peel, inverted baking sheet or rimless cookie sheet with semolina. Transfer the first dough round to the peel and, if needed, reshape into a 10-inch circle. Using the back of a spoon, spread half of the cream mixture on the dough, leaving a 1-inch border around the edge. Using your fingers, crimp the outer ½ inch of the dough to form a raised edge to contain the sauce and cheese. Slide the pizza onto the baking steel and bake until well browned and the cream mixture is bubbling, 7 to 10 minutes (9 to 12 minutes in a 500°F oven).

Using the peel, transfer the pizza to a wire rack. Repeat with the second dough round using the remaining cream mixture. After the second pizza has cooled for a few minutes, toss the arugula with the oil mixture. Top the pizzas with the arugula, dividing it evenly.

Fig and Blue Cheese Pizza
with Prosciutto

START TO FINISH:	MAKES:
25 minutes	**Two 10-inch pizzas**

Semolina flour, for dusting the pizza peel

2 pizza dough rounds (see page 279)

2 tablespoons extra-virgin olive oil

6 ounces fresh figs, stemmed and sliced into ¼-inch rounds

3 ounces blue cheese, crumbled (¾ cup)

2 ounces prosciutto (about 4 slices), cut into 2-inch ribbons

1 teaspoon aged balsamic vinegar

2 scallions, thinly sliced on diagonal

Ground black pepper

This pizza is defined by a balance of sweet, savory and salty—provided by a classic combination of fresh figs, prosciutto and blue cheese. The prosciutto becomes crisp and adds a welcome textural contrast. If possible, use a good, aged balsamic vinegar, one that is dark and syrupy.

At least 1 hour before baking, heat oven to 550°F (or 500°F if that's your oven's maximum temperature), with a baking steel or stone on the upper-middle rack.

Dust a baking peel, inverted baking sheet or rimless cookie sheet with semolina. Transfer the first dough round to the peel and, if needed, reshape into a 10-inch circle. Brush the round with 1 tablespoon of olive oil. Arrange half the fig slices on the dough, then sprinkle with half the blue cheese. Arrange half of the prosciutto between the figs. Bake until the crust is browned and the prosciutto is crisp, 7 to 10 minutes (9 to 12 minutes in a 500°F oven).

Using the peel, transfer the pizza to a wire rack. Let cool for a couple of minutes, then sprinkle with ½ teaspoon of the vinegar, half of the scallions and black pepper. Repeat with the second dough round, using the remaining figs, blue cheese, prosciutto, vinegar, scallions and pepper.

This stuffed flatbread came to us from Puglia by way of Boston. We were inspired by a longtime menu item at Lydia Shire's Scampo restaurant in Boston. Shire, in turn, learned the recipe from a chef in Puglia.

Ricotta Salata-Stuffed Flatbread

with Shallots (Ciccio)

START TO FINISH:	SERVINGS:
30 minutes, plus cooling	**4**

3 tablespoons extra-virgin olive oil, divided

2 large shallots, halved lengthwise and thinly sliced (about ½ cup)

2 medium garlic cloves, thinly sliced

1 teaspoon minced fresh rosemary

Two 8-ounce portions pizza dough, warmed to 75°F

4 ounces shredded ricotta salata cheese (1 cup)

½ ounce Parmesan cheese, finely grated, plus more to serve (¼ cup)

Bread flour, for dusting

Semolina flour, for dusting

Kosher salt and ground black pepper

1 tablespoon flat-leaf parsley

Ricotta salata is a firm, dry white cheese with a mild flavor and a distinct saltiness; do not substitute regular (fresh) ricotta cheese, which contains too much moisture and too little salt for this recipe. If you cannot find ricotta salata, queso fresco is a good substitute. The shallot mixture can be made a day ahead and refrigerated for up to two days; bring to room temperature before using.

Don't use the shallot mixture until it is fully cooled. If it is even a bit warm, it will soften the dough, making it difficult to shape and handle. And don't completely seal the edges of the two rounds of dough; this will cause the bread to puff up during baking.

In a small saucepan over medium, combine 2 tablespoons of the oil and the shallots. Cook, stirring occasionally, until softened and lightly golden, 8 to 12 minutes. Add the garlic and rosemary, then cook, stirring, until the garlic just begins to color, about 1 minute. Transfer to a heatproof bowl and cool to room temperature.

At least 1 hour before baking, heat oven to 550°F (or 500°F if that's your oven's maximum temperature), with a baking steel or stone on the upper-middle rack.

On a counter dusted generously with bread flour, use a rolling pin to roll each portion of dough into a 10-inch round. Spoon the shallot mixture evenly over one of the dough rounds, including the oil, leaving a ½-inch border. Sprinkle with the ricotta salata and Parmesan. Gently press the cheese into the dough and season with pepper.

Lay the second dough round on top, leaving a few spots unsealed, aligning the edges, and press ½ inch from the edge to lightly seal. Using the rolling pin, gently roll the filled dough to a 12-inch round.

Lightly dust a pizza peel, rimless cookie sheet or inverted baking sheet with semolina. Transfer the filled dough to the peel and reshape as needed. Using the tip of a paring knife, cut a few steam vents in the top dough layer, making sure not to cut through to the bottom. Brush the surface with the remaining 1 tablespoon oil and sprinkle with salt. Slide the pie onto the baking steel and bake until well browned, 7 to 8 minutes (9 to 10 minutes in a 500°F oven).

Using the peel, transfer the pie to a wire rack. Let cool for several minutes, then sprinkle with the parsley and additional Parmesan.

Lahmajoun

START TO FINISH:
25 minutes

MAKES:
Two 10-inch pizzas

1 small yellow onion, roughly chopped

¼ cup chopped drained roasted red peppers

2 tablespoons tomato paste

1 teaspoon sweet smoked paprika

1 teaspoon ground cumin

¾ teaspoon red pepper flakes

½ teaspoon kosher salt

½ pound 80 percent lean ground beef or ground lamb

Semolina flour, for dusting the pizza peel

2 pizza dough rounds (see page 279)

½ cup lightly packed flat-leaf parsley, torn

Lahmajoun is a meat-topped Armenian flatbread. After adding the ground meat to the food processor, pulse only three or four times, just until combined. Over-working the mixture will cause the meat to toughen. A generous scoop of Greek yogurt mixed with a few teaspoons of lemon juice and dolloped onto the baked pie is a delicious final flourish.

At least 1 hour before baking, heat oven to 550°F (or 500°F if that's your oven's maximum temperature), with a baking steel or stone on the upper-middle rack.

In a food processor, pulse the onion until finely chopped, about 5 pulses. Add the peppers, tomato paste, paprika, cumin, red pepper flakes and salt, then process until smooth, about 10 seconds. Add the beef or lamb and pulse just until incorporated, 3 or 4 pulses.

Dust a baking peel, inverted baking sheet or rimless cookie sheet with semolina. Transfer the first dough round to the peel and, if needed, reshape into a 10-inch circle. Top with half of the meat mixture, leaving a ½-inch border at the edge. Bake until well browned, 7 to 10 minutes (9 to 12 minutes in a 500°F oven).

Using the peel, transfer to a wire rack. Let cool for a couple of minutes, then top with half the parsley. Repeat with the second dough round and remaining meat mixture and parsley.

Fish Tacos

with Lime-Pickled Jalapeños

START TO FINISH:	SERVINGS:
30 minutes	**4**

2 teaspoons grated lime zest, plus 5 tablespoons lime juice, divided

Kosher salt and ground black pepper

3 jalapeño chilies, 2 stemmed and sliced into thin rounds, 1 stemmed, halved and seeded

⅓ cup fresh oregano

6 medium garlic cloves, smashed and peeled

¼ cup sour cream

¼ cup mayonnaise

⅓ cup cornstarch

1½ pounds skinless white fish fillets (see note), cut into 1-by-2-inch strips

4 tablespoons grapeseed or other neutral oil, divided

8 corn tortillas, warmed

For these tacos, choose a firm, meaty white fish—we liked cod and tilapia. Coating the fish with seasoned cornstarch before frying gave the pieces a delicately crisp crust that contrasted nicely with the tender, flaky interior. To add bright notes and pull all the flavors together, we made a creamy dressing laced with jalapeños, fresh oregano and lime. Offer shredded cabbage, thinly sliced radishes and fresh cilantro as additional fillings.

Don't fry the fish in a single batch. *Cooking in two batches ensures the pieces aren't crowded in the pan so they cook quickly and crisp nicely.*

In a small bowl, whisk together 4 tablespoons of the lime juice and ¼ teaspoon salt. Stir in the sliced jalapeños and set aside.

In a food processor, combine the lime zest, the halved jalapeño, the oregano, garlic, 1 teaspoon salt and ½ teaspoon pepper. Process until the garlic is finely chopped, about 10 seconds. Add the remaining 1 tablespoon lime juice and process until smooth, another 20 seconds, scraping the bowl as needed. Transfer to a medium bowl and stir in the sour cream and mayonnaise.

In a large bowl, whisk together the cornstarch, 2 teaspoons salt and 1 teaspoon pepper. Add the fish and toss to coat. Set a wire rack in a rimmed baking sheet.

In a 12-inch nonstick skillet over medium-high, heat 2 tablespoons of the oil until barely smoking. Add half of the fish in a single layer and cook without disturbing until light golden brown, 2 to 3 minutes. Carefully flip each piece and cook until light golden brown on the second sides, another 2 to 3 minutes. Transfer to the prepared wire rack and tent with foil. Repeat with the remaining 2 tablespoons oil and remaining fish.

Smear some of the sour cream mixture onto one side of each tortilla. Divide the fish among the tortillas and top with pickled jalapeños.

Chili Chicken Tacos

START TO FINISH:
45 minutes

SERVINGS:
4

1 ounce guajillo chilies
(5 medium), stemmed, seeded
and torn into 1-inch pieces

1½ cups orange juice

5 medium garlic cloves, peeled

2 tablespoons white vinegar

2 teaspoons ground coriander

2 teaspoons honey

1 teaspoon dried oregano

Kosher salt

2 pounds boneless, skinless
chicken thighs, trimmed

Chilorio, a pulled pork from the Mexican state of Sinaloa, inspired this dish. But instead of the traditional pork shoulder, we used faster-cooking chicken thighs. Fresh orange juice amplified the fruity notes of the guajillo chilies while giving the sauce a natural sweetness; a little vinegar and honey helped balance the flavors. Serve the chicken with Mexican rice or tortillas, or use it as a filling for tacos. Diced white onion, sliced radishes and/or crumbled queso fresco are excellent garnishes.

Don't forget to trim any excess fat *from the chicken thighs before cooking to prevent the dish from being greasy.*

In a 12-inch skillet over medium-high, toast the chilies, pressing with a wide metal spatula and flipping halfway through, until fragrant, about 1 minute. Transfer to a small bowl and pour in the juice; press on the chilies to submerge. Let stand until the chilies have softened, about 10 minutes. Set the skillet aside.

In a blender, combine the chilies and juice, garlic, vinegar, coriander, honey, oregano and 1 teaspoon salt. Puree until smooth, about 30 seconds. Pour the puree into the same skillet and bring to a boil over medium-high. Nestle the chicken into the sauce, cover and cook over medium-low, stirring and flipping the chicken halfway through, until a skewer inserted into the chicken meets no resistance, about 20 minutes.

Using tongs, transfer the chicken to a large plate and set aside until cool enough to handle, 10 to 15 minutes. Using 2 forks, shred into bite-size pieces. While the chicken cools, bring the sauce to a simmer over medium-high and cook, stirring, until thickened and reduced to 1 cup, about 10 minutes. Stir the shredded chicken into the sauce, then taste and season with salt.

Chickpea Flour Flatbread

(Socca)

START TO FINISH:	MAKES:
30 minutes	**Four 10-inch crepes**

165 grams (1½ cups)
chickpea flour

2 teaspoons kosher salt

¼ teaspoon ground
black pepper

1½ cups warm (100°F) water

¼ cup extra-virgin olive oil,
plus more to cook

Chickpea flatbreads are known as socca in France, or as farinata in Italy. Some versions are thicker than others, but all are made with chickpea flour and olive oil. Ours are thin and get great flavor from the rich browning they attain in the skillet. You can serve socca hot from the pan, but they're also delicious at room temperature. To turn them into a light meal, offer an olive and roasted pepper relish or spinach, grape and feta salad alongside.

Don't use cool water. We found that warm water created a thicker batter, which resulted in better-textured flatbreads. After adding the oil to the batter, don't overmix; you should be able to see beads of oil suspended in the batter.

In a large bowl, whisk together the chickpea flour, salt and pepper. Pour in half of the water and whisk until smooth. While whisking, slowly pour in the remaining water. Gently whisk in the oil just until incorporated but small beads of oil remain visible.

In a 10-inch nonstick skillet over medium-high, heat 2 teaspoons oil until shimmering. Pour ¼ of the batter (about ½ cup) into the center of the skillet and tilt so the batter completely covers the surface. Cook until the bottom is well browned, 1½ to 2 minutes. Using a spatula, carefully flip and cook until the second side is dark spotty brown, about another minute. Transfer to a wire rack. Repeat with remaining batter and 2 teaspoons oil for each flatbread.

Cut each flatbread into 4 wedges and serve with one of the following toppings:

OLIVE AND ROASTED PEPPER RELISH

In a medium bowl, stir together 1 cup chopped pitted green olives, ¼ cup drained and chopped roasted red peppers, ¼ cup chopped fresh flat-leaf parsley, 1 tablespoon drained and rinsed capers, 1 finely grated garlic clove, ¼ teaspoon red pepper flakes and 1 teaspoon red wine vinegar. Let stand for 15 minutes.

SPINACH, GRAPE AND FETA SALAD

In a large bowl, combine 1 tablespoon minced shallot and 2 teaspoons sherry vinegar; let stand for 10 minutes. Whisk in ½ teaspoon Dijon mustard, ¼ teaspoon kosher salt and ⅛ teaspoon ground black pepper. Whisk in 2 tablespoons extra-virgin olive oil. Add 8 cups loosely packed baby spinach, 1 cup halved seedless red grapes and ⅓ cup crumbled feta cheese. Gently toss to combine.

Fritas traditionally are topped with a handful of shoestring fries. At Milk Street, we sometimes (guiltily) serve our Cuban-spiced burger with Potato Stix mounded on top.

Cuban-Spiced Burgers

START TO FINISH:
1 hour (20 minutes active)

SERVINGS:
4

1½ pounds 85 percent lean ground beef

2 teaspoons Spanish smoked paprika

2 teaspoons ground cumin

1¼ teaspoons kosher salt

½ teaspoon ground black pepper

1 tablespoon grapeseed or other neutral oil

4 burger buns, toasted

The southern Florida tradition of the frita—thin beef patties that began as street food in Havana—inspired the spice mixture we used to add flavor to these burgers. Partially freezing the ground beef before mixing in the spices helped prevent the meat from becoming compacted during mixing and shaping, a common problem with preground beef. Even with chilling, it's important to use a light touch when handling the beef. This recipe can easily be doubled. For a quick and tangy topping, try our 3-minute spicy sauce (recipe below).

Don't knead or overwork the ground beef when mixing in the seasonings. This will make the texture of the burgers dense.

Line a baking sheet with kitchen parchment. Set the beef on the sheet, then use 2 forks to gently spread the meat. In a small bowl, combine the paprika, cumin, salt and pepper. Sprinkle over the beef. Freeze until the meat is very cold and beginning to firm up at the edges, about 20 minutes.

Use a rubber spatula to gently fold the spice mixture into the beef without compacting it; it's fine if the spices are not completely blended. If the beef is still partially frozen, let stand 10 to 15 minutes until slightly softened. Divide the beef into 4 even portions. Shape each into a 4-inch patty about ½ inch thick.

In a large skillet over medium-high, heat the oil until barely smoking. Add the patties and cook until well browned, about 5 minutes; flip and continue to cook until the center is 125°F for medium-rare, another 4 to 5 minutes. Transfer to a plate and let rest for 5 minutes. Set each burger on a bun and top as desired.

For the Spicy Sauce

1 cup mayonnaise

4 tablespoons Cholula Hot Sauce

2 tablespoons yellow mustard

¼ teaspoon cayenne pepper

SPICY SAUCE

START TO FINISH:
3 minutes

MAKES:
1⅓ cups

In a medium bowl, whisk all ingredients until smooth. Cover and refrigerate for up to 1 week.

Parmesan and Herb Turkey Burgers

START TO FINISH:
35 minutes

SERVINGS:
4

¾ cup panko breadcrumbs

10 tablespoons mayonnaise, divided

½ cup chopped fresh mint, divided

½ cup chopped fresh cilantro, divided

6 scallions, thinly sliced, white and green parts reserved separately

Kosher salt and ground white pepper

1 pound ground dark meat turkey

2 ounces Parmesan cheese, finely grated (1 cup)

3 tablespoons lime juice

1 tablespoon grapeseed or other neutral oil

4 hamburger buns, toasted

Mayonnaise and plenty of herbs turn ground turkey into moist and flavorful patties in this take on the classic burger. For our panade—a hydrating binding mixture of dairy and breadcrumbs—we use creamy mayonnaise and crisp panko along with fresh mint, cilantro and scallions. Parmesan cheese adds a salty-savory note. For an extra layer of flavor, more herbs and mayonnaise are stirred together with lime juice for a simple topping. We preferred the flavor and texture of these burgers when made with ground dark meat turkey, but if you prefer, ground breast meat works, too. Instead of using buns, you could serve the burgers sandwiched between Bibb or Boston lettuce leaves spread with the herbed mayonnaise.

Don't cook the burgers without first refrigerating them for 15 minutes. Chilling helps the patties hold together during cooking.

Line a plate with kitchen parchment and mist with cooking spray. In a food processor, combine the panko, 5 tablespoons of the mayonnaise, ¼ cup each of the mint and cilantro, the scallion whites, and 1 teaspoon each salt and pepper. Process until smooth, about 1 minute. Transfer to a large bowl, then add the turkey, ¼ cup water and the cheese. Mix with your hands, form into four ½-inch-thick patties, then set on the prepared plate and refrigerate for 15 minutes.

Meanwhile, in a small bowl, stir together the remaining 5 tablespoons mayonnaise, the remaining ¼ cup each mint and cilantro, the scallion greens, the lime juice and ½ teaspoon each salt and pepper. Set aside.

In a 12-inch nonstick skillet over medium-high, heat the oil until barely smoking. Add the patties, reduce to medium and cook until well browned on the bottoms, about 5 minutes. Flip and cook until the second sides are well browned and the centers reach 165°F. Transfer to a wire rack set in a rimmed baking sheet and let rest for 5 minutes.

Meanwhile, spread the cut sides of each bun with some of the mayonnaise mixture. Sandwich the burgers in the buns and serve with any remaining mayonnaise on the side.

Mushroom, Poblano Chili
and Refried Bean Tortas

START TO FINISH:	SERVINGS:
40 minutes	**6**

7 tablespoons extra-virgin olive oil, divided

8 ounces portobello mushrooms, stemmed, gills removed, caps sliced ¼ inch thick

2 poblano chilies, stemmed, seeded, quartered and thinly sliced

1 medium yellow onion, halved and thinly sliced

Kosher salt and ground black pepper

15½-ounce can pinto beans, drained, ¼ cup liquid reserved

2 teaspoons ground coriander

¼ cup drained sliced pickled jalapeños, chopped, plus 1 tablespoon pickling liquid

2 ripe avocados, halved, pitted and peeled

2 tablespoons lime juice

6 kaiser rolls (see note)

6 deli slices or 4 ounces shredded pepper jack cheese

Tortas, a type of Mexican sandwich, come in classic versions—and multiple variations of those classics—but they can be built any way you please. We make a hearty vegetarian version filled with sautéed mushrooms and chilies, refried beans, mashed avocado and cheese. You also could add lettuce, sliced tomatoes and cilantro. A flattish roll called telera is used for making tortas, but you can use any type of round roll with a soft interior and a thin, lightly crisp crust.

Don't use soft, fluffy rolls, such as hamburger rolls. They won't hold up under the weight of the fillings.

Heat the oven to 450°F with a rack in the middle position. Line a rimmed baking sheet with foil, then brush with 2 tablespoons of the oil. In a nonstick 12-inch skillet over medium, heat 2 tablespoons of the remaining oil until shimmering. Add the mushrooms, chilies, onion and 1 teaspoon salt. Cook, stirring, until the vegetables are light golden brown and have softened, about 8 minutes. Transfer to a medium bowl and tent with foil to keep warm.

Return the skillet to medium-high, add 2 tablespoons of the remaining oil and heat until shimmering. Add the beans and coriander and cook, mashing, until the mixture forms a coarse, dry puree and begins to brown at the edges, about 3 minutes. Stir in the bean liquid and cook, stirring constantly, until the beans are once again dry, about 1 minute. Off heat, stir in ¼ teaspoon each salt and pepper, the pickled jalapeños and pickling liquid. Set aside.

Meanwhile, in a medium bowl mash the avocados with ½ teaspoon each salt and pepper and the lime juice. Set aside. Place the top and bottom halves of the rolls cut side down on the prepared baking sheet. Brush with the remaining 1 tablespoon oil and sprinkle with ¼ teaspoon salt. Bake until crisp and golden brown, 3 to 5 minutes. Transfer the tops to a large plate and turn the bottom halves cut side up. Leave the oven on.

Divide the bean mixture evenly among the bottom halves of the rolls. Top with the mushroom mixture, followed by the cheese. Bake until the cheese begins to melt, 3 to 5 minutes. Remove from the oven. Spread the avocado mixture on the cut sides of the top halves of the rolls, then place on top of the tortas.

The banh mi is arguably the most prominent example of Vietnam's adaptations and innovations of French cuisine. Others include Vietnamese coffee and bahn flan, a type of crème caramel.

Vietnamese Skirt Steak Sandwiches

START TO FINISH:
50 minutes

SERVINGS:
4

¾ cup white vinegar

¼ cup white sugar

Kosher salt and ground black pepper

2 medium carrots, peeled and shredded (1 cup)

1 pound skirt steak, cut crosswise into 3- to 4-inch pieces, patted dry

⅓ cup mayonnaise

3 tablespoons Sriracha

Four 7- to 8-inch French bread rolls (see note), split horizontally

½ English cucumber, sliced into ⅛-inch-thick rounds

1 cup lightly packed cilantro sprigs

Vietnamese sandwiches, called banh mi, combine savory, sweet, spicy and herbal flavors, as well as a blend of crunchy and chewy textures. For our weeknight version, we streamline the ingredient list and use quick-cooking skirt steak. The best type of bread to use here is a supermarket baguette or French rolls with a light, airy crumb and thin, brittle crust, not a chewy, rustic bread. You'll need four 7- to 8-inch pieces of bread; you can cut one or two baguettes into sections or simply use individual rolls. For added heat, include a few thin slices of jalapeño chilies in each sandwich. This is also excellent made with the meatballs from our Vietnamese meatball lettuce wraps (see page 151).

Don't forget to remove some of the interior crumb of the bread. Slightly hollowed bread halves make constructing—and eating!—the sandwiches easier.

In a medium bowl, stir together the vinegar, sugar and 1 teaspoon salt. Stir in the carrots and set aside. Heat the broiler with one rack about 4 inches from the element and another in the middle. Line a rimmed baking sheet with foil.

Season the steak on both sides with 2 teaspoons salt and 1 teaspoon pepper. Place in an even layer on the prepared baking sheet and let stand at room temperature for 15 minutes.

Meanwhile, in a small bowl, stir together the mayonnaise and Sriracha; set aside. Pull out some of the interior crumb of each piece of bread; the remaining crust and crumb should be about ¾ inch thick. Set aside.

Broil the steak until the center of the thickest piece reaches 125°F for medium-rare or 130°F for medium, 3 to 5 minutes, flipping once halfway through. Turn off the broiler, transfer the steak to a plate and tent with foil. Let rest for 10 minutes.

Meanwhile, arrange the bread halves cut sides down on the now-empty baking sheet; it's fine if they overlap a bit. Place in the still-warm oven on the middle rack and heat until the bread is warm, about 5 minutes. Strain the carrots.

Spread the cut sides of the bread evenly with the mayonnaise. Cut the steak against the grain on the bias into thin slices. Taste and season with salt and pepper. Evenly divide the steak and any accumulated juices among the bottom halves of the bread, then top with the carrots, cucumber slices and cilantro. Top with the remaining bread.

The chivito is said to have been invented when an Argentinian diner ordered a plate of roasted young goat (chivo) and, having none, the enterprising restaurateur slapped together a multi-ingredient sandwich and dubbed it "chivito," little goat.

Uruguayan-Style Steak
and Cheese Sandwich

START TO FINISH:	SERVINGS:
35 minutes	**4**

Four 6- to 8-inch hoagie or sub rolls, halved lengthwise

5 tablespoons grapeseed or other neutral oil, divided

10 ounces shredded mozzarella cheese (3½ cups)

½ large red onion, minced

4 large pimento-stuffed green olives, minced

1 jalapeño chili, stemmed and minced

½ cup lightly packed fresh cilantro, finely chopped

4 teaspoons red wine vinegar, divided, plus more if needed

Kosher salt and ground black pepper

2 tablespoons soy sauce

1 pound beef tenderloin, trimmed of silver skin and cut crosswise into 8 medallions (each about ½ inch thick)

The chivito is the national sandwich of Uruguay, and it served as our inspiration for this recipe. Ours is a pared-down version of the classic, which typically includes mayonnaise, lettuce, tomato, sliced hard-cooked eggs, ham and/or bacon. Olives are another common filling, but we opted instead to make an onion-olive-cilantro relish that keeps the flavors fresh and bright. We liked the buttery tenderness of beef tenderloin, but pork tenderloin is a less pricey alternative. If using pork tenderloin, trim off the silver skin, cut the tenderloin crosswise into ½-inch-thick slices and cook similar to the beef tenderloin, but increase timing to about 2 minutes per side.

Don't use preshredded mozzarella, as it's usually coated with anti-caking agents. Purchase a chunk and shred your own. Also, don't use the variety packed in water, as it has a high moisture content and is not a good melting cheese.

Heat the oven to 450°F with the rack in the middle position. Line a rimmed baking sheet with foil. Brush the outsides of the rolls with 1 tablespoon of the oil, then arrange the halves cut side up on the prepared baking sheet. Divide the cheese evenly among the 4 top halves.

In a heavy-bottomed 12-inch skillet over medium, heat 2 tablespoons of the remaining oil until shimmering. Add the onion and cook, stirring, until softened, 2 to 3 minutes. Transfer to a small bowl and let cool slightly; set the skillet aside. Stir in the olives, jalapeño, cilantro, 2 teaspoons of the vinegar and 1 teaspoon salt. Taste and season with salt and additional vinegar if needed, then set aside.

In a medium bowl, combine the remaining 2 teaspoons vinegar, the soy sauce and ½ teaspoon pepper. Add the steak and turn to coat. Let stand at room temperature for 5 minutes, then remove the pieces and pat dry with paper towels.

Transfer the rolls to the oven and bake until the cheese has melted, about 5 minutes. Meanwhile, in the same 12-inch skillet, heat 1 tablespoon of the oil over high until barely smoking. Add half the beef in an even layer and cook undisturbed until well browned and the meat releases easily from the pan, 1 to 3 minutes. Using tongs, flip the meat and cook just until the second side is no longer pink, about 1 minute. Transfer to a plate and repeat with the remaining 1 tablespoon oil and the remaining beef.

Evenly distribute the onion mixture among the bottom halves of the rolls, then layer 2 pieces of beef on each. Cover with the tops of the rolls.

Buttermilk Biscuits

START TO FINISH:
45 minutes

MAKES:
10 biscuits

1¼ cups buttermilk, chilled

¼ cup heavy cream, chilled

20 tablespoons (2½ sticks) salted butter, cut into ½-inch cubes, plus 2 tablespoons melted

480 grams (4 cups) unbleached cake flour (see note), plus more for dusting

2 tablespoons baking powder

½ teaspoon baking soda

¾ teaspoon kosher salt

This is our adaptation of the crisp-on-the-outside-fluffy-on-the-inside biscuits made by Sarah Dodge at 8ARM in Atlanta. They're great alongside hearty soups and stews, and are big and sturdy enough to split and fill with crisp bacon and a fried egg for a savory breakfast-for-supper sandwich. We found that unbleached cake flour worked best to get the texture we were after; King Arthur and Bob's Red Mill are two widely available brands. A good substitute is 455 grams (3½ cups) all-purpose flour mixed with 33 grams (¼ cup) cornstarch. Avoid bleached cake flour, the type of cake flour sold in most supermarkets—it yielded bland biscuits with poor texture. High-fat butter, such as Plugra, gave the biscuits an especially rich flavor, but they were perfectly delicious made with regular butter.

Don't forget to freeze the butter before making the dough. If the butter softens as the dough is processed and handled, the biscuits won't rise well. If your kitchen is warm or if the butter begins to soften, place the dough in the refrigerator for a few minutes to cool. When stamping out the biscuits, press the cutter straight down through the dough. Don't twist.

Heat the oven to 475°F with a rack in the middle position. Line a baking sheet with kitchen parchment. In a small bowl or 2-cup liquid measuring cup, stir together the buttermilk and cream. Refrigerate until needed. Put the cubed butter on a plate and place in the freezer for 10 minutes.

In a food processor, process the flour, baking powder, baking soda and salt for 10 seconds. Scatter in the butter and pulse until the pieces are about ¼ inch, about 15 pulses. Transfer to a large bowl. Pour in the buttermilk mixture, then use a rubber spatula to fold the ingredients until a shaggy dough forms and no powdery flour bits remain.

Turn the dough out onto a counter lightly dusted with flour. Using your hands and working quickly, gently knead the dough just until cohesive, about 5 times. Pat into a 6-by-11-inch rectangle about 1¼ inches thick. Using a 2½-inch round biscuit cutter, cut out 8 biscuits. Gently knead the remaining dough to bring it together, pat it into a 1¼-inch-thick round and cut out 2 more biscuits. Evenly space the biscuits on the prepared baking sheet. Discard the scraps. Refrigerate on the baking sheet for 10 minutes.

Brush the tops of the biscuits with the melted butter. Bake until well risen and deep golden brown, 12 to 16 minutes. Cool on the baking sheet on a wire rack for 5 minutes. Serve warm.

One-stop pot, quick-step clean

One Pot

In Morocco, tangia evolved from a meal bachelors made en masse, pooling their cash to buy ingredients and collectively cooking them in the furnaces that fuel Marrakech's bathhouses. Today, it is enjoyed by all manner of Moroccans.

Moroccan-Style Braised Chicken
with Lemon (Tangia)

START TO FINISH:
1 hour (25 minutes active)

SERVINGS:
4

5 teaspoons ground cumin, divided

Kosher salt and ground black pepper

3 pounds boneless, skinless chicken thighs, trimmed and patted dry

5 tablespoons salted butter, divided

2 medium yellow onions, finely chopped

12 medium garlic cloves, chopped

2 teaspoons ground turmeric

2 teaspoons ground ginger

2 teaspoons ground coriander

½ cup pimento-stuffed green olives, chopped

3 tablespoons grated lemon zest, plus ¼ cup lemon juice

This simple chicken braise loaded with high-flavor ingredients is modeled on tangia, a slow-cooked lamb dish from Marrakech. For a more approachable version, we used boneless, skinless chicken thighs, which have a similar richness. In Morocco, preserved lemons lend the dish a gentle acidity, but we got similar flavor from lemon zest and juice—as well as chopped green olives for brininess—added at the end of cooking. Serve with warmed, halved pita bread for scooping up the tender meat and thickened sauce.

Don't reduce the lemon zest or juice. The zest provides both flavor and fragrance, and the juice adds tang and acidity. You'll need 3 to 4 lemons to get 3 tablespoons grated zest; a wand-style grater works best.

In a small bowl, stir together 2 teaspoons of the cumin and 2 teaspoons salt. Set aside. Season the chicken on both sides with salt and pepper.

In a large Dutch oven over medium-high, heat 2 tablespoons of the butter. When the foaming subsides, add the onions and garlic and cook, stirring occasionally, until lightly browned, about 5 minutes. Add the remaining 3 teaspoons cumin, the turmeric, ginger and coriander. Cook, stirring constantly, until fragrant, about 30 seconds. Stir in 1½ cups water, scraping up any browned bits. Nestle the chicken in the liquid, turning to coat. Cover, reduce to medium-low and cook for 20 minutes, adjusting the heat as needed to maintain a gentle simmer.

Using tongs, turn the chicken. Cover and continue to cook until tender, another 25 minutes. Using tongs, transfer the chicken to a plate. Bring the liquid in the pot to a simmer over medium-high and cook, stirring frequently, until the liquid is thickened, 10 to 14 minutes.

Return the chicken to the pot and stir, roughly breaking up the pieces. Off heat, add the remaining 3 tablespoons butter, stirring until melted, then stir in the olives and lemon zest and juice. Taste and season with salt and pepper. Transfer to a platter and serve with the cumin-salt mixture for sprinkling to taste.

Pork and Chorizo

with Piquillo Peppers (Carcamusa)

START TO FINISH:	SERVINGS:
50 minutes	**4**

6 ounces Spanish chorizo, casing removed, halved lengthwise and thinly sliced, divided

8 medium garlic cloves, peeled

2½ teaspoons dried oregano

2½ teaspoons ground cumin

Kosher salt and ground black pepper

28-ounce can whole peeled tomatoes, drained, juices reserved

1¼-pound pork tenderloin, trimmed of silver skin and cut into ½-inch pieces

3 tablespoons grapeseed or other neutral oil, divided

1 large yellow onion, finely chopped

½ cup dry sherry

10.4-ounce jar piquillo peppers (see note), drained and cut into ½-inch pieces (1 cup)

1 cup lightly packed flat-leaf parsley, roughly chopped

Carcamusa, a Spanish tapas dish, traditionally calls for three varieties of pork—fresh pork, cured ham and chorizo—all simmered with seasonal vegetables in tomato sauce. To simplify, we skipped the ham and opted for jarred roasted piquillo peppers, which are heat-free, meaty red peppers from Spain. If you can't find them, jarred roasted red bell peppers are a fine substitute. Serve with slices of toasted rustic bread.

Don't use Mexican chorizo, which is a fresh sausage, in place of the Spanish chorizo. Spanish chorizo is dry-cured and has a firm, sliceable texture similar to salami.

In a food processor, combine half the chorizo, the garlic, oregano, cumin, 1 teaspoon pepper and 3 tablespoons of the tomato juices. Process until smooth, about 2 minutes, scraping the bowl as needed. Transfer 3 tablespoons of the chorizo paste to a medium bowl and stir in 1 teaspoon salt and another 1 tablespoon of the tomato juices. Add the pork and toss, then let marinate at room temperature for 15 minutes. Meanwhile, add the drained tomatoes to the chorizo paste in the processor and process until smooth, about 1 minute; set aside.

In a 12-inch skillet over medium-high, heat 1 tablespoon of the oil until barely smoking. Add the pork in a single layer and cook without stirring until well-browned, 4 to 6 minutes. Return the pork to the bowl. Add the remaining 2 tablespoons oil to the skillet and heat over medium until shimmering. Add the onion, cover and cook, stirring occasionally, until softened, about 8 minutes.

Add the sherry and cook, scraping up any browned bits, until most of the liquid evaporates, 2 to 4 minutes. Stir in the tomato-chorizo mixture and remaining tomato juice. Bring to a simmer, then reduce to medium-low. Cover and cook for 10 minutes.

Uncover and continue to cook, stirring occasionally, until slightly thickened, another 5 minutes. Return the pork and any accumulated juices to the skillet and add the remaining chorizo and piquillo peppers. Cook, stirring occasionally, until the pork is heated through, about 5 minutes. Stir in the parsley, then taste and season with salt and pepper.

Eggs with Linguiça and Peas

START TO FINISH:
50 minutes

SERVINGS:
4

2 tablespoons extra-virgin olive oil

4 ounces linguiça sausage (see note), quartered and thinly sliced

1 medium red onion, finely chopped

6 medium garlic cloves, thinly sliced

2 teaspoons sweet paprika

28-ounce can fire-roasted crushed tomatoes

Kosher salt

½ cup frozen peas, divided

4 large eggs

2 ounces feta cheese, crumbled (½ cup)

¼ cup lightly packed fresh cilantro or finely chopped fresh chives

This recipe is our version of Portuguese ervilhas guisadas com ovos, a homey dish of peas and poached eggs with sausage. If you can't find linguiça, a cured Portuguese sausage seasoned with garlic and paprika, use Spanish dry-cured chorizo. Serve with slices of rustic bread for dipping into the savory sauce and egg yolks.

Don't use regular crushed tomatoes *unless that's all that's available. We greatly preferred the subtly smoky flavor of fire-roasted tomatoes.*

In a 12-inch nonstick skillet over medium, heat the oil until shimmering. Add the sausage and cook, stirring, until browned, about 5 minutes. Using a slotted spoon, transfer to a paper towel–lined plate, leaving the fat in the pan. Add the onion and garlic and cook, stirring, until the onion has softened, about 7 minutes. Stir in the paprika, tomatoes and ¾ teaspoon salt.

Return the sausage to the pan and cook, uncovered, stirring occasionally, until slightly thickened, 10 to 15 minutes. Stir in ¼ cup of peas. Using the back of a large spoon, make 4 evenly spaced indentations in the tomato mixture. Crack 1 egg into each. Scatter the remaining ¼ cup peas over the sauce, around the eggs. Cover and cook until the egg whites are set but the yolks are still runny, about 5 minutes. Sprinkle with feta and cilantro.

Rigatoni Carbonara with Ricotta

START TO FINISH:
35 minutes

SERVINGS:
4

1 cup whole-milk ricotta cheese

2 ounces Parmesan cheese, finely grated (about 1 cup), plus more to serve

2 large eggs, plus 2 large egg yolks, beaten

4 cups warm water, divided

Kosher salt and ground black pepper

6 slices bacon cut into ½-inch pieces (about 6 ounces)

4 medium garlic cloves, thinly sliced

½ teaspoon red pepper flakes

12 ounces rigatoni pasta

1 cup frozen peas, thawed

This one-pot meal inspired by Zuni Café's Judy Rodgers is a refreshing take on classic Italian pasta carbonara. (Rodgers called it her "rogue" version.) Look for a good-quality ricotta cheese without stabilizers. Rodgers used fresh peas, but we call for the more readily available frozen. To streamline the process, we cook the bacon in the same Dutch oven that later is used for the rigatoni. And when the pasta goes in we use a minimal amount of water, which concentrates the starch to help thicken the sauce and also saves the trouble of draining. Parmesan is common in this dish and we include it along with the ricotta. Avoid pre-grated Parmesan; it typically is too coarse and won't blend well with the sauce.

Don't stop stirring the pasta as the ricotta mixture is added; this prevents it from clumping.

In a medium bowl, whisk together the ricotta, Parmesan, eggs and yolks, ¼ cup of the water, and ½ teaspoon each salt and pepper. Set aside.

In a large Dutch oven over medium, cook the bacon until just crisp, 7 to 10 minutes. Use a slotted spoon to transfer to a paper towel-lined plate. Pour off all but 2 tablespoons of fat from the pot. Stir in the garlic and pepper flakes, then cook until fragrant, about 30 seconds.

Stir in the remaining 3¾ cups water and 1½ teaspoons salt and bring to a boil over medium-high. Stir in the pasta, reduce heat to medium and cook, covered and stirring occasionally, until al dente, 10 to 13 minutes.

Off heat, stir in the peas and reserved bacon. Let pasta sit for 5 minutes. Stir in the ricotta mixture, tossing to coat the pasta and form a creamy sauce. Taste and season with salt and black pepper.

Cilantro-Dill Bean
and Noodle Soup

START TO FINISH:
45 minutes

SERVINGS:
4

3 tablespoons salted butter

1 large yellow onion, finely chopped

Kosher salt and ground black pepper

4 medium garlic cloves, minced

1 teaspoon ground turmeric

15½-ounce can chickpeas, rinsed and drained

¾ cup red lentils

1 quart low-sodium chicken broth

2 ounces linguini, broken into 1-inch pieces

15½-ounce can kidney or cannellini beans, rinsed and drained

½ cup fresh cilantro, roughly chopped

½ cup fresh dill, roughly chopped

Ash reshteh, an Iranian soup served at the Persian new year, was the inspiration for this dish. With chickpeas, kidney beans, red lentils and noodles, this is a quick, yet hearty meal. A generous dose of fresh herbs added at the end helps keep the flavors bright. If you like, garnish each portion with a spoonful of yogurt and serve with lemon wedges.

Don't substitute brown or green lentils for the red lentils; they take too long to soften. After the lentils are added to the pot, don't forget to stir occasionally to ensure the lentils on the bottom don't scorch.

In a large saucepan over medium, melt the butter. When the foaming subsides, stir in the onion and ½ teaspoon salt. Cook, stirring, until the onion is light golden and softened, about 5 minutes. Stir in the garlic and turmeric, then cook until fragrant, about 30 seconds.

Stir in the chickpeas, lentils and broth. Bring to simmer over medium-high, then cover and reduce to low. Cook, stirring occasionally, until the lentils have broken down, about 15 minutes.

Stir in the linguini and kidney beans, then return to a simmer over medium-high. Cook, uncovered, stirring occasionally, until the linguini is al dente, about 9 minutes. Off heat, stir in both herbs. Taste and season with salt and pepper.

Miso-Marinated Pork Soup

START TO FINISH:	SERVINGS:
40 minutes	**4**

4 tablespoons white miso, divided

2 tablespoons soy sauce, divided

1-pound pork tenderloin, trimmed of silver skin

4 ounces dried udon noodles

1½ quarts low-sodium chicken broth

1 tablespoon finely grated fresh ginger

1 jalapeño chili, stemmed and sliced into thin rings

8 scallions, sliced thinly on diagonal, whites and greens reserved separately

8 ounces (10 cups) baby spinach

3 tablespoons unseasoned rice vinegar

Chewy Japanese udon noodles make this a light but satisfying meal. We used white miso and soy sauce to quickly marinate the pork before cooking and to add deep, savory flavors to the simple chicken broth base. Check instructions on the udon package for cooking times, but make sure to test a noodle for doneness at least a minute or two before they're supposed to be done.

Don't rinse the drained noodles under cold water. Use lukewarm water to prevent them from cooling completely and keep the soup hot.

In a large pot, bring 4 quarts of water to a boil. Meanwhile, in a medium bowl, mix 1 tablespoon each of the miso and soy sauce. Cut the tenderloin in half lengthwise, then slice each half crosswise about ¼ inch thick. Add the pork to the bowl and stir. Set aside at room temperature.

While the pork marinates, add the noodles to the boiling water and cook until tender. Drain, rinse under lukewarm water, drain again, then divide among 4 serving bowls. Set aside.

In the pot used to cook the noodles, bring the broth to a boil over medium-high. In a small bowl, whisk the remaining 3 tablespoons miso with 2 tablespoons of the broth. Add the mixture to the pot along with the remaining 1 tablespoon soy sauce, the ginger, half of the jalapeños and the scallion whites. Reduce to medium and simmer gently for 10 minutes.

Return the broth to a boil over medium-high. Add the pork and cook, stirring occasionally, until cooked through, about 2 minutes. Off heat, stir in the spinach and vinegar. Ladle the soup over the noodles, then sprinkle with the scallion greens and the remaining jalapeños.

Many of the most familiar Indian dishes—butter chicken, rogan josh, tikka masala—are wet curries, which usually rely on coconut milk or yogurt as conduits for flavor. Dry curries deliver equal impact with little to no liquid thanks to low-heat cooking.

Ginger-Turmeric Potatoes
and Green Beans (Aloo Faliyan)

START TO FINISH:	SERVINGS:
45 minutes	**6**

3 tablespoons grapeseed or other neutral oil

1 large shallot, finely chopped

1 tablespoon finely grated fresh ginger

2 teaspoons yellow or brown mustard seeds

1½ teaspoons cumin seeds

⅛ to ¼ teaspoon red pepper flakes

½ teaspoon ground turmeric

12 ounces small Yukon Gold potatoes, cut into ½-inch cubes

12 ounces green beans, trimmed and cut into 1-inch pieces

Kosher salt

1 tablespoon lemon juice

½ cup halved grape tomatoes

⅓ cup cashews, toasted and roughly chopped

½ cup chopped fresh cilantro

½ to 1 serrano chili, minced (optional)

The vegetables stay crisp and each bite delivers fully spiced flavor in this take on a vegetarian classic from India, aloo faliyan, or potatoes and green beans. Cooked in the dry curry style—less liquid, lower heat—string beans are mixed with chopped potatoes, which soak up seasonings exceptionally well. Cumin seeds, red pepper flakes, mustard seeds and turmeric plus shallot and fresh ginger provided a flavorful masala for the vegetables. Halved grape tomatoes are added at the end to keep the acid in the tomatoes from dulling the color of the beans. We liked small or baby Yukon Gold potatoes because they are waxier and hold their shape better than larger potatoes; if small Yukons aren't available, use small red potatoes. We preferred the flavor and texture of brown mustard seeds, but if you have difficulty finding them, yellow mustard seeds work, too. Make sure your skillet has a tight-fitting lid.

Don't use russet or other starchy potatoes. They will turn mealy and break down too easily.

In a large skillet over medium, heat the oil until shimmering. Add the shallot, ginger, mustard and cumin seeds, and the pepper flakes. Cook, stirring frequently, until the shallot has softened and is just beginning to brown, about 2 minutes.

Stir in the turmeric, potatoes, green beans and 1½ teaspoons salt. Add ¾ cup water, then cover and cook until the potatoes are just barely tender, about 8 minutes. Uncover the pan; if all of the water has cooked off, add 1 to 2 tablespoons, then continue to cook, stirring occasionally, until the vegetables are tender and the pan is dry, another 2 to 5 minutes.

Off heat, stir in the lemon juice, then taste and season with salt. Fold in the tomatoes, cashews, cilantro and serrano, if using.

Creamy Fennel
and Bean Soup

START TO FINISH:	SERVINGS:
1 hour (20 minutes active)	**4**

8 ounces bacon, finely chopped

2 medium yellow onions, finely chopped

1 medium fennel bulb, trimmed, halved, cored and finely chopped

5 medium garlic cloves, smashed and peeled

2 teaspoons fennel seeds, finely ground

Three 15½-ounce cans cannellini beans, rinsed and drained, divided

5 cups low-sodium chicken broth

4-inch sprig fresh rosemary

Kosher salt and ground black pepper

3 tablespoons extra-virgin olive oil, plus more to serve

3 tablespoons finely chopped fresh chives

Lemon wedges, to serve

Fennel—both the fresh bulbs and the dried seeds—is under-appreciated for the savory-sweet, slightly anise flavor it brings to a dish. Paired and pureed with white beans to form the base of this hearty, speedy soup, fennel adds interest to what otherwise could be one-note flat. For contrast, as well as a smoky-savory counterpoint, we top the soup with crisped bacon. Chopped fresh chives and a squeeze of lemon juice are a finishing touch of freshness. Warm, crusty bread is the perfect accompaniment.

Don't fill the blender jar more than a third full of the hot soup mixture; hot liquids tend to splash out when the blender is turned on because of the rapid release of heat and steam. To help prevent this, remove the cap from the blender lid and then cover the lid tightly with a kitchen towel. Start the blender on low and gradually increase the speed.

In a large Dutch oven over medium, cook the bacon, stirring occasionally, until crisp, about 10 minutes. Using a slotted spoon, transfer to a paper towel-lined plate. Pour off all but 2 tablespoons fat from the pot.

Add the onions, fennel, garlic and ground fennel to the pot and cook over medium-low, stirring occasionally, until the vegetables are tender, about 8 minutes. Measure out 1½ cups of the beans and set aside. Add the remaining beans to the pot along with the broth, rosemary, ½ teaspoon salt and 1 teaspoon pepper. Bring to a simmer over medium-high. Cover, reduce to medium-low and simmer for 15 minutes.

Remove and discard the rosemary sprig. Let the soup cool slightly, about 15 minutes. Transfer about ⅓ of the soup to a blender. Add 1 tablespoon of the oil and puree until smooth. Transfer to a large saucepan, then repeat with the remaining soup and oil, working in batches. Add the reserved beans and heat over medium-low, stirring, until the soup is heated through, about 10 minutes. Taste and season with salt and pepper. Serve drizzled with oil, sprinkled with the bacon and chives, and with lemon wedges on the side.

Paprika-Caraway Kielbasa Soup

START TO FINISH:
45 minutes

SERVINGS:
4

2 tablespoons grapeseed
or other neutral oil

12 ounces Yukon Gold
potatoes, peeled and cut into
1-inch cubes

8 ounces kielbasa, quartered
lengthwise and cut into ½-inch
pieces

1 medium yellow onion,
finely chopped

3 medium garlic cloves, thinly
sliced

1 tablespoon caraway seeds

¼ cup tomato paste

1½ teaspoons hot Hungarian
paprika

2 cups drained fresh
sauerkraut, roughly chopped
(10 ounces)

1½ quarts low-sodium chicken
broth

Kosher salt and ground black
pepper

¼ cup finely chopped fresh dill

Sauerkraut, kielbasa and Yukon Gold potatoes simmered in a tomato- and
paprika-enriched chicken broth yield a hearty, satisfying one-pot meal. If you
don't have hot paprika, substitute 1¼ teaspoons regular paprika plus ¼ teaspoon
cayenne pepper. Serve with thick slices of buttered rye or pumpernickel bread.

*Don't use canned or jarred sauerkraut. Look for fresh, or "raw," sauerkraut in
the refrigerated aisle, near the refrigerated pickles. Fresh sauerkraut has not been
pasteurized, so its flavors are bright and clean.*

In a large Dutch oven over medium, heat the oil until shimmering. Add the
potatoes, kielbasa, onion and garlic. Cook, stirring occasionally, until the onion
is lightly browned, about 7 minutes. Stir in the caraway seeds and cook until
fragrant, about 30 seconds.

Add the tomato paste and paprika and cook, stirring, until the tomato paste
begins to brown, about 1 minute. Add the sauerkraut and broth and bring to
a boil over medium-high. Reduce to medium-low, cover and simmer, stirring
occasionally, until the potatoes are tender, about 25 minutes. Taste and season
with salt and pepper. Serve sprinkled with the dill.

Cape Malay Chicken Curry

START TO FINISH:
1 hour

SERVINGS:
6

1 tablespoon fennel seeds

1 tablespoon cumin seeds

Kosher salt and ground black pepper

1 teaspoon turmeric

2 pounds boneless, skinless chicken thighs, trimmed

2 tablespoons grapeseed or other neutral oil

2 medium yellow onions, chopped

4-ounce piece fresh ginger, peeled and cut into 5 pieces

4 medium garlic cloves, minced

2 serrano chilies, stemmed and halved lengthwise

2 cups low-sodium chicken broth or water

1 pint grape or cherry tomatoes

Two 3-inch cinnamon sticks

2 bay leaves

1 pound Yukon Gold potatoes, cut into 1-inch cubes

2 tablespoons lemon juice, plus lemon wedges, to serve

½ cup lightly packed fresh mint, torn

Cooked basmati or jasmine rice, to serve

Lemony and richly savory, Cape Malay curry is a chicken and vegetable one-pot from South Africa. Its ingredients are similar to those in Indian curries, but the techniques are different, creating a refreshingly light curry. Spices, for instance, aren't ground but are dropped, whole, into the broth and often discarded just before serving. We started our curry with a flavor base of lightly browned onions, then used fennel and cumin seeds to add texture and flavor. Fresh ginger and lemon juice kept flavors bright. A whole chicken is sometimes used for this dish, but we liked the ease of boneless, skinless thighs, which stay moist and taste richer than chicken breasts.

Don't forget to remove the ginger, cinnamon sticks, bay leaves and chili halves from the cooking liquid after removing the chicken. Also, don't cut the potatoes smaller than 1-inch chunks; smaller pieces will overcook and break apart.

In a bowl, mix the fennel, cumin, 2 teaspoons salt, 1 teaspoon pepper and the turmeric. Use 1 tablespoon of the mixture to season the chicken.

In a large Dutch oven over medium-high, heat the oil until barely smoking. Add the onions and cook, stirring occasionally, until lightly browned, 8 to 10 minutes. Stir in the ginger, garlic and chilies, then cook, stirring, until fragrant, about 30 seconds. Stir in the broth or water, tomatoes, cinnamon, bay leaves and remaining spice mixture, then submerge the chicken thighs.

Bring to a simmer, then cover and cook for 25 minutes, adjusting the heat to maintain a steady but gentle simmer. Stir in the potatoes, cover and return to a simmer. Cook until the potatoes are tender and a skewer inserted into the largest piece of chicken meets no resistance, another 12 to 15 minutes.

Transfer the chicken to a large plate. Remove and discard the ginger, cinnamon sticks, bay leaves and chili halves, then continue to simmer over medium until the liquid is slightly reduced, about 5 minutes.

Meanwhile, using 2 forks, pull the chicken into bite-size pieces, then return to the pot and stir to combine, taking care not to break up the potatoes. Stir in the lemon juice, then taste and season with salt and pepper. Transfer to a serving bowl and sprinkle with mint. Serve with rice and lemon wedges.

Jollof Rice

START TO FINISH:
45 minutes

SERVINGS:
6

1 pound plum tomatoes, cored and quartered

1 red bell pepper, stemmed, seeded and cut into quarters

2 medium garlic cloves, peeled

Kosher salt and ground black pepper

¼ cup extra-virgin olive oil

1 medium yellow onion, finely chopped

1½ cups basmati rice, rinsed and drained

3 medium carrots, peeled and finely chopped

1 tablespoon curry powder

1½ teaspoons smoked paprika

1 teaspoon dried thyme

1 cup frozen green peas

For our take on Nigerian jollof, a one-pot rice dish, we use nutty, fragrant basmati rice seasoned with paprika, curry powder and thyme. To ensure the rice cooks evenly, use a large skillet with a tight-fitting lid. A 14½-ounce can of diced tomatoes can be used in place of the plum tomatoes; no need to drain the juices.

Don't forget to rinse and drain the rice. This washes away surface starch and decreases stickiness in the finished dish.

In a food processor, combine the tomatoes, bell pepper, garlic and 1 teaspoon salt. Process until smooth, about 1 minute. Set aside.

In a large skillet over medium, heat the oil until shimmering. Add the onion and cook, stirring, until beginning to brown, 6 to 8 minutes. Stir in the rice, then the carrots, curry powder, paprika, thyme, 1½ teaspoons salt and ½ teaspoon pepper. Cook, stirring, until the rice is fragrant, 1 to 2 minutes. Stir in 1½ cups water, bring to a simmer and cook, stirring occasionally, until most of the water has been absorbed, about 2 minutes.

Stir in the tomato puree and return to a simmer, then reduce to medium-low. Cover and cook until almost dry and the rice is tender, 12 to 15 minutes.

Scatter the peas over the rice, then cover the pan. Remove from the heat and let stand until the remaining moisture has been absorbed and the peas are heated through, about 5 minutes. Stir the peas into the rice. Taste and season with salt and pepper.

Posole Rojo with Chicken

START TO FINISH:
45 minutes

SERVINGS:
4

1 tablespoon grapeseed or other neutral oil

1 medium white onion, chopped, plus thinly sliced white onion, to serve

6 medium garlic cloves, minced

3 tablespoons ancho chili powder

2 teaspoons ground cumin

14½-ounce can diced fired-roasted tomatoes

2 quarts low-sodium chicken broth

1½ pounds boneless, skinless chicken thighs, trimmed

29-ounce can hominy, drained and rinsed

½ cup finely chopped fresh cilantro

3 tablespoons lime juice, plus lime wedges, to serve

Kosher salt

Tortilla chips or warmed tortillas, to serve

A key ingredient in the hearty Mexican soup known as posole is hominy, or dried corn kernels cooked in an alkali solution. Hominy has a satisfying and subtle chewiness and a mild sweetness. It's sold in cans, often in the Latin foods section of the supermarket. If you're up for offering more garnishes for your posole, shredded cabbage or radishes add color and crunch.

Don't use regular chili powder, which is a blend of ground chilies, herbs and spices. Ancho chili powder, the type called for here, is simply ground ancho chilies, without any added ingredients. It gives the pozole a pure, deep chili flavor.

In a large Dutch oven over medium-high, heat the oil until shimmering. Add the onion and cook until lightly browned, about 5 minutes. Add the garlic, ancho powder and cumin, then cook, stirring constantly, until fragrant, about 30 seconds. Add the tomatoes and cook, stirring, until most of the liquid has evaporated, 3 to 5 minutes. Add the broth and bring to a simmer. Stir in the chicken and hominy, then bring to a simmer. Reduce to medium, cover and cook until a skewer inserted into the largest piece of chicken meets no resistance, about 20 minutes.

Transfer the chicken to medium bowl. Cover the pot and reduce to low to keep hot. Using 2 forks, shred the chicken into bite-size pieces. Stir the chicken back into the pot and cook until heated through, 2 to 3 minutes. Off heat, stir in the cilantro and lime juice. Taste and season with salt. Serve with sliced white onion, lime wedges and tortilla chips.

Recipes that let you walk away from the cooking

Roast and Simmer

Coriander-Roasted Chicken

START TO FINISH:	SERVINGS:
50 minutes	**4**

3 tablespoons ground coriander

2 teaspoons ground ginger

1¼ teaspoons white sugar

Kosher salt and ground black pepper

3 pounds bone-in, skin-on chicken parts, trimmed and patted dry

10 medium garlic cloves, peeled

1 tablespoon finely grated lemon zest, plus ¼ cup lemon juice

2 tablespoons extra-virgin olive oil

¼ cup finely chopped fresh cilantro

A whole chicken can take quite some time to roast, which can be a challenge on weeknights. But chicken parts cook quickly and taste equally good. If you use a combination of breasts and legs or thighs, begin checking the breast for doneness after about 30 minutes of roasting, as white meat is done at 160°F while dark meat needs to reach 175°F. We came up with three variations on this supper, using coriander, spicy Scotch bonnet and tangy za'atar to add flavor and depth. In this take, the citrusy, floral notes of the coriander in the spice rub pair well with the lemon zest and juice in the accompanying sauce. These flavorful chicken dishes are a great match for the earthy sweetness of root vegetables such as roasted or mashed sweet potatoes or winter squash drizzled with tangy yogurt. They're also excellent with our herbed bulgur pilaf with fried chickpeas (page 123).

Don't use a roasting pan. The low sides of a sturdy rimmed baking sheet allow the chicken to cook quickly and brown evenly.

Heat the oven to 450°F with a rack in the middle position. In a small bowl, combine the coriander, ginger, sugar, 1 tablespoon salt and 2 teaspoons pepper.

Place the chicken parts on a rimmed baking sheet and evenly season both sides with the spice mixture. Place the garlic cloves in a single layer down the center of the baking sheet, then arrange the chicken parts, skin up, around the garlic; this prevents the garlic from scorching during roasting.

Roast the chicken until the thickest part of the breast (if using) reaches 160°F and the thickest part of the largest thigh/leg (if using) reaches 175°F, 30 to 40 minutes. A skewer inserted into the thickest part of the chicken should meet no resistance. Transfer to a platter; leave the garlic on the baking sheet.

Using a fork, mash the garlic to a paste on the baking sheet. Carefully pour ⅓ cup water onto the baking sheet and use a wooden spoon to scrape up any browned bits. Pour the mixture into a small bowl and whisk in the lemon zest and juice, oil and cilantro. Taste and season with salt and pepper. Serve the sauce with the chicken.

Jerk-Roasted Chicken

START TO FINISH:
50 minutes

SERVINGS:
4

1 tablespoon packed brown sugar

2 teaspoons ground allspice

2 teaspoons dried thyme

2 teaspoons dried oregano

½ teaspoon cinnamon

Kosher salt and ground black pepper

3 pounds bone-in, skin-on chicken parts, trimmed and patted dry

10 medium garlic cloves, peeled

1 Scotch bonnet or habanero chili, stemmed

¼ cup lime juice, plus 1 tablespoon finely grated lime zest

2 tablespoons extra-virgin olive oil

4 scallions, thinly sliced

Typical Jamaican jerk seasoning packs a big punch of heat from Scotch bonnet chilies. Here, we call for just one chili; it roasts along with the chicken and garlic and becomes part of the sauce. If you like, you can use a milder chili, such as serrano or jalapeño. Use chicken breasts, legs, thighs or a combination.

Don't use a roasting pan. *The low sides of a sturdy rimmed baking sheet allow the chicken to cook quickly and brown evenly*

Heat the oven to 450°F with a rack in the middle position. In a small bowl, combine the sugar, allspice, thyme, oregano, cinnamon, 1 tablespoon salt and 2 teaspoons pepper.

Place the chicken parts on a rimmed baking sheet and evenly season both sides with the spice mixture. Place the garlic cloves and chili in a single layer down the center of the baking sheet, then arrange the chicken parts, skin up, around the garlic; this prevents the garlic from scorching during roasting.

Roast the chicken until the thickest part of the breast (if using) reaches 160°F and the thickest part of the largest thigh/leg (if using) reaches 175°F, 30 to 40 minutes. A skewer inserted into the thickest part of the chicken should meet no resistance. Transfer the chicken to a platter; leave the garlic on the baking sheet.

Using a fork, mash the garlic and chili to a paste on the baking sheet. Carefully pour ⅓ cup water onto the baking sheet and use a wooden spoon to scrape up any browned bits. Pour the mixture into a small bowl and whisk in the lime zest and juice, oil and scallions. Taste and season with salt and pepper. Serve the sauce with the chicken.

Za'atar-Roasted Chicken

START TO FINISH:
50 minutes

SERVINGS:
4

3 tablespoons za'atar seasoning

2 teaspoons dried oregano

1¼ teaspoons white sugar

Kosher salt and ground black pepper

3 pounds bone-in, skin-on chicken parts, trimmed and patted dry

10 medium garlic cloves, peeled

1 tablespoon finely grated lemon zest, plus ¼ cup lemon juice

2 tablespoons extra-virgin olive oil

2 tablespoons minced fresh oregano

Za'atar is a Middle Eastern blend of herbs and sesame seeds; look for it in well-stocked markets, Middle Eastern grocery stores or online. We mix za'atar with dried oregano to boost its herbal flavor. Use chicken breasts, legs, thighs or a combination.

Don't use a roasting pan. The low sides of a sturdy rimmed baking sheet allow the chicken to cook quickly and brown evenly.

Heat the oven to 450°F with a rack in the middle position. In a small bowl, combine the za'atar, dried oregano, sugar, 1 tablespoon salt and 2 teaspoons pepper.

Place the chicken parts on a rimmed baking sheet and evenly season both sides with the za'atar mixture. Place the garlic cloves in a single layer down the center of the baking sheet, then arrange the chicken parts, skin up, around the garlic; this prevents the garlic from scorching during roasting.

Roast the chicken until the thickest part of the breast (if using) reaches 160°F and the thickest part of the largest thigh/leg (if using) reaches 175°F, 30 to 40 minutes. A skewer inserted into the thickest part of the chicken should meet no resistance. Transfer the chicken to a platter; leave the garlic on the baking sheet.

Using a fork, mash the garlic to a paste on the baking sheet. Carefully pour ⅓ cup water onto the baking sheet and use a wooden spoon to scrape up any browned bits. Pour the mixture into a small bowl and whisk in the lemon zest and juice, oil and fresh oregano. Taste and season with salt and pepper. Serve the sauce with the chicken.

For a homemade green chili sauce, use an immersion blender and a tall, narrow vessel to emulsify 1 plum tomato (cored and quartered), 5 serrano chilies (stemmed and chopped), 3 tablespoons lime juice, 2 peeled garlic cloves and 1-1/2 teaspoons salt.

Somali Chicken Soup

START TO FINISH:	SERVINGS:
50 minutes	**4**

1 tablespoon grapeseed or other neutral oil

2 large yellow onions, chopped

Kosher salt and ground white pepper

2 serrano chilies, stemmed and sliced into thin rounds

4 medium garlic cloves, smashed and peeled

4 teaspoons ground coriander

2 teaspoons ground cardamom

1 bunch fresh cilantro, stems chopped, leaves finely chopped, reserved separately

4 plum tomatoes, cored, seeded and chopped, divided

1½ quarts low-sodium chicken broth or water

Four 12-ounce bone-in, skin-on chicken breasts

2 tablespoons lime juice, plus lime wedges, to serve

Thinly sliced radishes and/or chopped red cabbage, to serve (optional)

Green chili sauce, or other hot sauce, to serve

Floral cardamom, earthy coriander and bright cilantro by the handful punch up the flavor of this brothy soup. It's great for serving family style—bring the pot to the table along with the radishes, cabbage and lime wedges, then have diners fill and garnish their bowls as they like. Offer a simple homemade or store-bought hot sauce alongside. For a more robust meal, hot steamed rice, added to bowls before the soup is ladled in, is a satisfying addition.

Don't use boneless, skinless chicken breasts. Both the bones and skin contribute flavor to the broth.

In a large Dutch oven over medium, heat the oil until shimmering. Add the onions and ½ teaspoon salt and cook, stirring, until beginning to brown, about 5 minutes. Add the chilies, garlic, coriander, cardamom, cilantro stems and half of the tomatoes. Cook, stirring constantly, until fragrant, about 30 seconds.

Add the broth and bring to a simmer over high. Submerge the chicken breasts, cover and cook over low until the chicken registers 160°F and a skewer inserted into the thickest part meets no resistance, about 30 minutes.

Transfer the chicken to a large plate and set aside to cool. Use a mesh strainer to strain the broth into a large heatproof bowl, discarding the solids, then return the broth to the pot. When the chicken is cool enough to handle, shred the meat into bite-size pieces, discarding the skin and bones.

Add the chicken to the broth and bring to a simmer over medium-high. Remove from the heat and stir in the remaining tomatoes, the cilantro leaves and lime juice. Taste and season with salt and pepper. Serve with lime wedges, radishes or cabbage (if using), and hot sauce.

Tamarind Chickpeas with Greens

START TO FINISH:
1 hour (20 minutes active)

SERVINGS:
4

¼ cup tamarind paste
(2 ounces)

⅓ cup grapeseed or
other neutral oil

1 medium yellow onion,
finely chopped (1 cup)

1 tablespoon cumin seeds

¼ cup packed dark
brown sugar

5 medium garlic cloves,
minced

1 tablespoon finely grated
fresh ginger

5 teaspoons garam masala

1 teaspoon ground turmeric

Kosher salt

1 pound collard greens,
stemmed and cut into
1-inch pieces (3 cups)

Two 15½-ounce cans
chickpeas, drained

Lime wedges, to serve

Khatta chana, stewed chickpeas in a tart tamarind sauce, is a popular street food from the Punjab region of northern India. We learned to make it from Meeru Dhalwala, co-owner of Vij's restaurant in Vancouver. Dhalwala adds heft to the chickpea curry by spooning it over sautéed brown sugar greens, a non-traditional side dish. Our version combines chickpeas and collard greens in a delicious one-pot braise that dials down the sweetness and uses canned chickpeas for convenience. If you prefer kale, it's a fine substitute for the collards. Serve this dish spooned over steamed white or brown rice and finished with a dollop of plain yogurt spiked with chopped fresh cilantro and mint.

Don't rinse the chickpeas after *draining them; the starchy liquid that coats them helps to lightly thicken the sauce.*

In a 4-cup glass measuring cup or medium microwave-safe bowl, combine the tamarind paste and 2 cups hot water. Microwave on high for 1 minute, then whisk to combine. Set aside.

In a large Dutch oven over medium, heat the oil until shimmering. Add the onion and cook, stirring, until golden brown, about 10 minutes. Add the cumin and cook until fragrant, about 30 seconds. Add the brown sugar, garlic, ginger, garam masala, turmeric and 2 teaspoons salt. Cook, stirring, until fragrant, 45 to 60 seconds.

Add the collards and turn to coat. Cook, stirring occasionally, until the collards begin to wilt and turn bright green, about 2 minutes. Strain the tamarind mixture into the pot, pressing the solids to extract as much liquid as possible; discard the solids. Stir to combine, then cover, reduce to medium-low and cook, stirring occasionally, until the collards are tender, about 40 minutes.

Stir in the chickpeas. Cover and cook until heated through, about 5 minutes. Taste and season with salt. Serve with lime wedges.

Chickpea and Harissa Soup

(Lablabi)

START TO FINISH:
45 minutes

SERVINGS:
8

5 tablespoons extra-virgin olive oil, divided, plus more to serve

1 large yellow onion, chopped

Kosher salt and ground black pepper

6 medium garlic cloves, minced

2 tablespoons tomato paste

3 tablespoons ground cumin, toasted, divided

6 tablespoons harissa, plus more to serve

Two 15½-ounce cans chickpeas, ⅓ cup liquid reserved, drained

2 quarts low-sodium chicken broth

8 ounces crusty white bread, sliced ½ inch thick and torn into bite-size pieces

2 tablespoons lemon juice, plus lemon wedges, to serve

½ cup chopped fresh cilantro

Chopped pitted green olives, to serve

This brothy-bready Tunisian chickpea soup gets punches of flavor from garlic, tomato paste and toasted cumin. To toast the cumin, in a small, dry skillet over medium, stir it constantly, until fragrant, about 1 minute, then transfer to a small bowl. Store leftover soup and croutons separately for up to three days; refrigerate the soup and keep the croutons in an airtight container at room temperature. We also like to top this soup with halved soft-cooked eggs.

Don't forget to reserve ⅓ cup of the chickpea liquid before draining. *The starchy liquid gives the soup a rich body.*

In a large Dutch oven over medium-high, heat 2 tablespoons of the oil until shimmering. Add the onion and ½ teaspoon salt and cook, stirring occasionally, until lightly golden, about 5 minutes. Stir in the garlic and cook until fragrant, about 30 seconds. Add the tomato paste and cook, stirring, until it browns, about 2 minutes.

Stir in 2 tablespoons of the cumin and the harissa and cook until fragrant, about 1 minute. Add the chickpeas, the reserved liquid and the broth. Stir to combine, then bring to a boil over high. Reduce to medium and simmer, uncovered, for about 30 minutes.

Meanwhile, in a 12-inch nonstick skillet over medium, combine the bread, the remaining 3 tablespoons oil and 1 teaspoon salt. Cook, stirring occasionally, until the bread is crisp and light golden brown, 4 to 6 minutes. Remove from the heat and let the croutons cool in the pan, then transfer to a bowl.

When the soup is ready, stir in the lemon juice. Taste and season with salt and pepper. Place 2 to 3 tablespoons croutons in each serving bowl. Ladle the soup around them, then drizzle with oil. Garnish to taste with some of the remaining cumin, additional harissa, chopped cilantro and olives.

Sweet Soy–Braised Pork

START TO FINISH:
50 minutes

SERVINGS:
4

3 tablespoons grapeseed or other neutral oil, divided

3 large shallots, finely chopped (1 cup)

4 medium garlic cloves, minced

1 tablespoon finely grated fresh ginger

2 serrano chilies, stemmed and sliced into thin rings, divided

2 pounds boneless country-style pork ribs, trimmed and cut into 1-inch pieces

3 tablespoons soy sauce

Kosher salt and ground black pepper

3 tablespoons molasses

1 tablespoon lime juice, plus lime wedges, to serve

Steamed jasmine rice, to serve

½ cup lightly packed fresh cilantro

The combination of soy sauce and molasses—inspired by Charmaine Solomon's Balinese-style pork from "Encyclopedia of Asian Food"—mimics the flavor and consistency of kecap manis, or Indonesian sweet soy sauce. Boneless country-style pork ribs provide rich, meaty flavor, but be sure to trim off excess fat so the dish won't be greasy. Serve with steamed rice, topping each portion with cilantro and sliced chilies and offering lime wedges on the side.

Don't use blackstrap molasses; *its flavor is too bitter.*

In a 12-inch skillet over medium-high, heat 2 tablespoons of oil until shimmering. Add the shallots, garlic, ginger and half of the chilies, then reduce to medium and cook, stirring, until golden, about 7 minutes. Transfer to a small bowl and set aside. Return the skillet to medium-high and heat the remaining 1 tablespoon oil until shimmering. Add the pork in an even layer and cook, stirring, until lightly browned, 6 to 8 minutes. Transfer to a paper towel–lined plate and discard any fat in the skillet.

In the same skillet over medium-high, add 1 cup water, the soy sauce and ¼ teaspoon black pepper, scraping up any brown bits. Pour off and discard any oil in the bowl with the shallot mixture. Stir the shallot mixture and the pork into the skillet. Cover and simmer over medium-low until the pork is tender, about 35 minutes, stirring once halfway through.

Stir in the molasses and cook, uncovered, until the sauce is thick enough to lightly coat the pork, about 2 minutes. Off heat, stir in the lime juice, then taste and season with salt and pepper.

Cider-Braised Lentils

with Apple-Radish Pickles

START TO FINISH:
1 hour (15 minutes active)

SERVINGS:
6

4 tablespoons (½ stick) salted butter, divided

4 large shallots, sliced into thin rings, layers separated

2 medium garlic cloves, minced

2 sprigs fresh thyme, plus 2 teaspoons chopped fresh thyme

1 cup apple cider

1 tablespoon plus 2 teaspoons whole-grain mustard

Kosher salt and ground black pepper

1½ cups French green lentils, rinsed and drained

3 tablespoons cider vinegar, divided

4 medium radishes, thinly sliced (about 1 cup)

1 Granny Smith apple, cored, thinly sliced and cut into rough ½-inch squares

5 ounces chèvre (fresh goat cheese), crumbled (1¼ cups)

French green lentils hold their shape with cooking and retain a firm, meaty bite. In this recipe their earthy, slightly peppery flavor pairs perfectly with the sweetness of apple cider and butter-sautéed shallots. For efficiency, prep the radishes and apple while the lentils simmer. You could serve this as a vegetarian meal, or for added savoriness garnish with ribbons of prosciutto. It's also a great accompaniment to garlicky sausages.

Don't substitute brown lentils for the French green lentils. Brown lentils have a milder flavor and softer texture, and cook much more quickly than green lentils.

In a large saucepan over medium-high, melt 3 tablespoons of the butter, occasionally swirling the pan, until the milk solids at the bottom begin to brown, about 2 minutes. Add ¾ of the shallots and cook, stirring, until lightly browned, about 5 minutes. Stir in the garlic and thyme sprigs, then cook until fragrant, 30 to 60 seconds.

Stir in the cider, mustard, 2½ teaspoons salt and ¾ teaspoon pepper. Bring to a boil over high and cook, stirring occasionally, until the cider has almost completely reduced, about 6 minutes. Add 3½ cups water and the lentils, then bring to a simmer. Reduce to low, cover and cook, stirring occasionally, until the lentils are tender, 45 to 50 minutes.

Meanwhile, in a small bowl, combine 2 tablespoons of the vinegar and 2 teaspoons salt and stir until the salt dissolves. Add the radishes, apple and the remaining shallots. Toss to combine and set aside.

Taste the lentils and season with salt and pepper. Remove and discard the thyme sprigs, then stir in the remaining 1 tablespoon butter, the chopped thyme and the remaining 1 tablespoon cider vinegar. Transfer to a bowl and serve with the apple-radish mixture and goat cheese on the side.

Turkish Red Lentil Soup

START TO FINISH:
45 minutes

SERVINGS:
4

3 tablespoons salted butter

1 medium yellow onion cut into ½-inch dice (about 1 cup)

1 medium garlic clove, finely grated

1 tablespoon tomato paste

1 tablespoon sweet paprika

½ teaspoon ground cumin

1 cup red lentils, rinsed and drained

2 tablespoons long-grain white rice

Kosher salt

3 tablespoons extra-virgin olive oil

2 teaspoons Aleppo pepper (see note)

Chopped fresh mint, to serve (optional)

Lemon wedges, to serve

This simple, yet substantial Turkish soup is made from red lentils, which soften and break down during cooking, adding texture. The Aleppo pepper brings gentle heat to the dish. If you can't find it, order online or substitute with an additional teaspoon of paprika and ½ teaspoon red pepper flakes. The soup can be made vegan by substituting olive oil for the butter.

Don't omit the rice. The grains help thicken the soup.

In a large saucepan over medium, melt the butter. Once it has stopped foaming, add the onion then cook until softened and translucent, about 5 minutes. Add the garlic and cook until fragrant, 30 seconds. Add the tomato paste, paprika and cumin, then sauté for 1 minute.

Add the lentils, rice, 5 cups of water and 2 teaspoons salt, then bring to a boil. Adjust heat to maintain a steady simmer, cover and cook until the lentils and rice are tender and broken down, about 30 minutes. Taste and season with salt.

Meanwhile, in a small skillet over medium, heat the oil, swirling to coat the pan. Add the Aleppo pepper and cook until a few bubbles appear and the oil is bright red. Remove from the heat and set aside.

Serve the soup with Aleppo pepper oil drizzled over each serving. Serve with mint, if using, and lemon wedges.

The simple, bold flavors of this soup stand up well to additions. Try wilted spinach or arugula and a dollop of yogurt with grated garlic. Or stir in crumbled cauliflower, chopped tomatoes, diced cooked beets, or crispy bits of sautéed ground lamb.

Roasted Chicken Breasts

with Grapes and Sherry Vinegar

START TO FINISH:	SERVINGS:
1 hour (20 minutes active)	**4**

12 ounces seedless red grapes, halved

4 tablespoons sherry vinegar, divided

2 teaspoons white sugar

Kosher salt and ground black pepper

4 teaspoons fennel seeds, finely ground

Four 12-ounce bone-in, skin-on chicken breasts, patted dry

2 medium red onions, root ends intact, peeled, each cut into 8 wedges

1 tablespoon extra-virgin olive oil

2 tablespoons salted butter

1 tablespoon whole-grain mustard

6 tablespoons finely chopped fresh tarragon

Melissa Clark understands that pairing contrasting flavors—as in the French bistro classic of roasted chicken and red grapes—easily elevates everyday meals. We were inspired by her version for this weeknight riff using chicken breasts. Try to purchase breasts of similar size so they cook at the same rate. We preferred 12-ounce breasts, which take 30 to 35 minutes in the oven. Breasts weighing about 1 pound each will require 40 to 50 minutes. If you can find ground fennel, use 2 teaspoons in place of grinding your own. We liked the flavor and texture of grainy mustard, but regular Dijon worked, too. The chicken breasts should fit comfortably in a single layer in the center of the roasting pan with the onion wedges around the perimeter; if your pan is too small, a broiler pan without the slotted top is a good alternative.

Don't completely cut off the root ends of the onions. Just shave off the dry, fibrous outer layers. This helps the onion wedges hold together.

Heat the oven to 475°F with a rack in the middle position. In a small bowl, stir together the grapes, 2 tablespoons of the vinegar, the sugar, and ½ teaspoon each of salt and pepper. Set aside. In a separate small bowl, combine the fennel, 1 teaspoon salt and ½ teaspoon pepper, then use to season the chicken breasts on all sides. In a medium bowl, toss the onion wedges with the oil and ½ teaspoon each of salt and pepper.

Arrange the onion wedges around the perimeter of a roasting pan and place the chicken breasts in a single layer in the center. Roast until the thickest part of the breasts reaches 160°F, or a skewer inserted into the thickest part of the chicken meets no resistance, 30 to 35 minutes. Transfer the chicken to a platter and let rest for 10 minutes.

Meanwhile, drain the grapes, reserving the liquid. Add the grapes to the center of the roasting pan and return the pan to the oven. Cook until the grapes just begin to soften, about 5 minutes. Transfer the roasting pan to the stovetop, add the reserved grape liquid and cook over medium-high, scraping up any browned bits, until most of the liquid has evaporated, about 2 minutes.

Off heat, add the remaining 2 tablespoons vinegar, the butter, mustard and tarragon. Stir until the butter melts. Taste and season with salt and pepper. Spoon the mixture over the chicken.

Spicy Pork with Leeks

and Roasted Red Peppers (Tigania)

START TO FINISH:	SERVINGS:
45 minutes	**4**

¾ teaspoon red pepper flakes

Kosher salt and ground black pepper

2¾ teaspoons dried oregano, divided

2 pounds boneless country-style pork ribs, trimmed and cut into 1½-inch chunks

3 tablespoons grapeseed or other neutral oil

2 tablespoons extra-virgin olive oil

6 large leeks, white and light green parts sliced ½-inch thick, rinsed and dried

4 medium garlic cloves, roughly chopped

1 cup dry white wine

7-ounce jar roasted red peppers, drained and chopped (about 1 cup)

½ cup pitted green olives, chopped

2 tablespoons fresh oregano, minced

Lemon wedges, to serve

Tigania is the Greek cook's simple—and flavorful—solution to leftovers. It means "from the frying pan" and is a catchall term for a braised dish traditionally made with scraps of pork and whatever vegetables are on hand. They are seared, then simmered, though what happens next depends on where you are. The dish might come swimming in lemon juice and olive oil in Crete or flavored with honey and thyme in the Peloponnese. Our version was inspired by Diane Kochilas' take in "The Glorious Foods of Greece," which uses white wine and leeks, the way tigania is done in the northern region of Macedonia. Kochilas seasons pork shoulder with paprika before simmering; we found boneless country-style pork ribs cooked more quickly and stood up well to the bold Mediterranean ingredients. We use six large leeks, which seems like a lot, but they reduce to a creamy, rustic sauce that pairs well with the tender meat. Serve with pita bread, rice or roasted potatoes.

***Don't forget to wash and dry the leeks** after slicing them. Their layers trap sand and grit. After adding the pork to the skillet, don't stir the pieces until they've formed a nice brown crust on the bottom.*

In a large bowl, stir together the pepper flakes, 1 teaspoon each salt and pepper, and ¾ teaspoon of the dried oregano. Add the pork and toss.

In a 12-inch skillet over medium-high, heat the grapeseed oil until barely smoking. Add the pork in a single layer and cook without disturbing until dark golden brown on the bottom, about 5 minutes. Stir and cook until no longer pink, about another 2 minutes. Using a slotted spoon, transfer to a large plate.

Pour off and discard the fat from the pan, then return to medium-high. Add the olive oil, leeks, garlic, the remaining 2 teaspoons dried oregano and ½ teaspoon salt. Cook, stirring and scraping up any browned bits, until the leeks begin to soften, 3 to 4 minutes. Stir in the pork, then the wine. Bring to a simmer and cover, then reduce to low and cook until the pork is tender, about 30 minutes.

Stir in the roasted red peppers and olives. Taste and season with salt and pepper. Transfer to a serving plate and sprinkle with fresh oregano. Serve with lemon wedges.

Chicken en Cocotte

START TO FINISH:
1 hour 35 minutes (15 minutes active)

SERVINGS:
4

5 tablespoons salted butter, divided

1 large yellow onion, cut into 8 wedges

8 medium garlic cloves, peeled and halved

1½ cups dry white wine

10 thyme sprigs

4- to 4½-pound whole chicken, wings tucked and legs tied

Kosher salt and ground black pepper

3 tablespoons lemon juice

2 tablespoons Dijon mustard

½ cup finely chopped fresh tarragon

For chicken en cocotte with apricots and shallots: Substitute 8 large shallots (peeled and halved) for the onion, omit the mustard and decrease the tarragon to ¼ cup. When the shallots and garlic are lightly browned, after about 5 minutes, add 3 ounces dried apricots (thinly sliced), ½ teaspoon red pepper flakes and ¼ teaspoon saffron threads (optional), then cook until fragrant, about 30 seconds. Add the wine and proceed with the recipe.

There is little prep involved in this chicken en cocotte—or chicken in a pot—and most of the cooking is hands-off. Cooking the chicken breast side down allows the delicate white meat to gently poach in the wine while the legs bake up above, a technique that helps equalize the cooking of the white meat (done at 160°F) and dark meat (done at 175°F). Allowing the chicken to rest breast side up afterward prevents the white meat from overcooking. The chicken pairs well with mashed or roasted potatoes, sautéed greens with garlic, or sugar snap peas cooked with garlic and chili flakes.

Don't use a Dutch oven smaller than 7 quarts or a chicken larger than 4½ pounds. If the bird fits too snugly, there won't be enough space for heat to circulate, hindering even cooking.

Heat the oven to 400°F with a rack in the lower-middle position. In a large Dutch oven over medium, heat 1 tablespoon of the butter. When the foaming subsides, add the onion and garlic and cook until lightly browned, about 5 minutes. Pour in the wine and bring to a simmer. Lay the thyme sprigs on the onion mixture.

Using paper towels, pat the chicken dry then season with salt and pepper. Set the chicken, breast down, over the thyme and onions. Cover and bake until the thickest part of the breast reaches 160°F and the thighs reach 175°F, 55 to 65 minutes. A skewer inserted into the thickest part of the chicken should meet no resistance. Using tongs inserted into the cavity of the chicken, carefully transfer it to a large baking dish, turning it breast up. Let rest for at least 15 minutes.

Meanwhile, remove and discard the thyme sprigs. Tilt the pot to pool the liquid to one side and use a wide spoon to skim off and discard the fat. Bring to a simmer over medium and cook until thickened and reduced to about 1 cup (with solids), about 5 minutes. Off heat, whisk in the remaining 4 tablespoons butter, the lemon juice and mustard. Taste and season with salt and pepper.

Remove the legs from the chicken by cutting through the hip joints. Remove and discard the skin from the legs, then separate the thighs from the drumsticks. Remove the breast meat from the bone, remove and discard the skin, then cut each crosswise into thin slices. Arrange the chicken on a platter. Transfer the sauce to a bowl, stir in the tarragon and serve with the chicken.

Cocotte pans were named for a child's nickname for hens (the feminine derivative of coq). But a cocotte is simply a covered oven-safe dish or casserole similar to a Dutch oven.

Piri Piri Chicken Thighs

START TO FINISH:
50 minutes

SERVINGS:
4

3 tablespoons New Mexico or California chili powder

1 tablespoon ground cumin

1 tablespoon ground coriander

1 tablespoon smoked paprika

Kosher salt

3 pounds bone-in, skin-on chicken thighs, trimmed

2 tablespoons white sugar

8 medium Fresno chilies, stemmed and quartered

3 medium garlic cloves, peeled

⅓ cup lemon juice

¼ cup red wine vinegar

1 cup lightly packed fresh cilantro, finely chopped

Piri piri can refer to a finger-staining chili pepper sauce—usually spiked with garlic, sugar and plenty of cayenne, lemon and paprika—or to whatever the sauce douses. Its origins are Portuguese, but it's found today in South Africa, Mozambique and Namibia. To make our version of the tangy-sweet sauce, we use pure New Mexico or California chili powder. If you can't find either, use ¼ cup regular (not smoked) sweet paprika. Avoid standard chili powder, which is a blend of ground chilies and other herbs and spices. Fresno chilies are fresh red chilies similar in size and shape to jalapeños, but with pointy tips. If they are unavailable, fresh cherry peppers are a good substitute. The thighs can be a bit spicy, so we like to serve them with a simple rice pilaf to soak up the heat and sauce, or a cooling cucumber salad. If you have leftovers, shred the meat and make chicken salad with mayonnaise and a dollop of the sauce.

Don't reduce the number of Fresno chilies; all are needed for flavor and color. To reduce spiciness, remove some or all of the seeds and ribs from the chilies before processing. Don't substitute Thai chilies for the Fresnos; they pack far more heat.

Heat the oven to 450°F with a rack in the middle position. In a small bowl, stir together the chili powder, cumin, coriander, paprika and 1½ tablespoons salt. Set aside 2 tablespoons of the mixture; add the remaining mixture to a food processor and set aside. Sprinkle the 2 tablespoons over the skin sides of the chicken and rub it in. Place the thighs on a rimmed baking sheet. Roast until the thickest part of the largest thigh reaches 175°F, a skewer inserted into the thickest part of the chicken should meet no resistance, 30 to 35 minutes. Remove from the oven and let rest for 10 minutes.

Meanwhile, add the sugar, chilies and garlic to the spice mixture in the processor. Pulse until finely chopped, scraping the bowl as needed. With the machine running, pour in the lemon juice and vinegar, then process until smooth, scraping the bowl once or twice. Transfer to a serving bowl and stir in the cilantro. Transfer the chicken to a platter and serve with the sauce.

Whole Roasted Cauliflower

START TO FINISH:
1 hour (10 minutes active)

SERVINGS:
4

2-pound head cauliflower, leaves trimmed

Kosher salt and ground black pepper

3 tablespoons extra-virgin olive oil

A head of cauliflower roasted whole and brought to the table uncut makes a striking, centerpiece-like dish. Blanching it in heavily salted water before roasting ensures the vegetable is seasoned to its core and reduces roasting time. Cooking times are for a 2-pound cauliflower; larger ones retained more water and took longer to roast. To serve more people, cook two 2-pounders rather than a jumbo-size head. We like this served as is, but it's also delicious drizzled with tahini, Sriracha, a blend of both, or basbaas, a spicy cilantro-yogurt sauce (see recipe below) from Somalia.

Don't wait for the water to return to a boil after adding the cauliflower before you start timing the 5-minute blanch. If the cauliflower is left in the water for longer, it will absorb too much water.

Heat the oven to 475°F with a rack in the upper-middle position. In a 6- to 8-quart pot, bring 4 quarts of water to a boil. Add ½ cup salt to the water, then carefully lower the cauliflower into the pot. Cook for 5 minutes (start timing immediately), flipping the cauliflower with a spoon after 2 minutes. Transfer to a colander, stem down, and drain for 10 minutes.

Transfer, stem down, to a baking dish. Rub the top with the oil and sprinkle with 1 teaspoon pepper. Roast, spooning any oil that accumulates in the dish over the cauliflower and rotating the dish once or twice, until golden brown and a skewer inserted into the center meets no resistance, 20 to 25 minutes.

Let cool for 5 minutes, then serve directly in the baking dish, with a spoon for scooping portions.

For Spicy Cilantro-Yogurt Sauce (Basbaas)

½ cup whole-milk Greek yogurt

½ cup packed fresh cilantro

¼ cup unseasoned rice vinegar

3 serrano chilies, stemmed and seeded

1 medium garlic clove, smashed and peeled

¼ teaspoon kosher salt

SPICY CILANTRO-YOGURT SAUCE (BASBAAS)

START TO FINISH:
1 hour (5 minutes active)

MAKES:
1 cup

This simple yogurt-based Somali hot sauce packs a spicy, herbal punch. It's delicious on just about anything, from fried eggs to grilled chicken. If you're a fan of chili heat, use the seeds of some—or all—of the serranos.

Don't use fat-free or low-fat Greek yogurt. The flavor is best with the richness of whole-milk yogurt.

In a blender, puree all ingredients until smooth and bright green, about 1 minute. Refrigerate, covered, for at least 1 hour or up to 3 days.

Colombian Coconut Chicken

START TO FINISH:
40 minutes

SERVINGS:
4

1½ cups unsweetened shredded coconut

2 tablespoons grapeseed or other neutral oil

1 teaspoon ground turmeric

1 medium yellow onion, finely chopped

8 medium garlic cloves, minced

1 tablespoon tomato paste

1½ teaspoons ground allspice

1 tablespoon soy sauce

Kosher salt

2 pounds boneless, skinless chicken thighs, trimmed

1 tablespoon lime juice, plus lime wedges to serve

1 pint cherry or grape tomatoes, quartered

Traditionally, pollo con leche de coco is made with fresh coconut milk. We found that canned coconut milk—both regular and light—lacked the clean, bright flavor of homemade coconut milk. We opted instead to make our own with unsweetened shredded coconut and hot water. The process took only a few minutes and yielded a light, flavorful coconut milk that worked wonderfully. If you require a shortcut, 1½ cups coconut water is an acceptable option, but the flavor will be less complex. We liked this paired with rice made with half coconut milk and half water, but plain rice is good, too.

Don't use cold water when pureeing the shredded coconut. Warm water slightly softens the shreds so they break down and release their flavor more easily.

In a blender, combine the coconut and 2 cups warm water. Let stand until the coconut begins to soften, about 1 minute. Blend on high until creamy, 1 to 2 minutes. Strain through a fine mesh strainer set over a large measuring cup or medium bowl, pressing on the solids; you should have 1½ cups strained coconut milk. Discard the solids; set the coconut milk aside.

In a large Dutch oven over medium, heat the oil until shimmering. Stir in the turmeric and cook until fragrant and the oil has turned yellow, about 30 seconds. Add the onion and garlic and cook, stirring occasionally, until softened, about 3 minutes. Stir in the tomato paste and allspice, then stir in the coconut milk, soy sauce and 1 teaspoon salt. Bring to a simmer, nestle the chicken in an even layer in the liquid, then cover and reduce to medium-low. Cook until a skewer inserted into the largest thigh meets no resistance, 18 to 22 minutes, flipping the pieces halfway through.

Using tongs, transfer the chicken to a bowl. Bring the liquid to a simmer over medium and cook, stirring frequently, until thickened and reduced by about half, about 12 minutes. Pour in any accumulated chicken juices and simmer another minute. Off heat, stir in the lime juice and tomatoes. Taste and season with salt, then return chicken to the pot, turning to coat. Cook until heated through, 2 to 3 minutes. Transfer to a serving bowl and serve with lime wedges.

Colombian cooks use a convex metal grater called a rallador de coco to shred coconut. The shreds are soaked, then wrung out several times, making different strengths of milk. The first and richest batch is normally used to cook fish or chicken; the second is for rice.

A little something sweet

Sweets

Raspberry-Pistachio Meringue
with Spiced Whipped Cream

START TO FINISH:	SERVINGS:
25 minutes	**4**

Three 6-ounce containers raspberries

5 tablespoons white sugar, divided

Kosher salt

2 teaspoons finely grated lemon zest plus 4 teaspoons lemon juice

2 ounces vanilla meringue cookies, broken into rough ½-inch bits (about 2 cups)

¾ cup heavy cream

⅔ cup sour cream

½ teaspoon ground cardamom

¼ cup roasted, salted shelled pistachios, chopped

Traditional Eton mess is like a simplified trifle—strawberries, cream and meringue cookies, folded together in a large bowl. For our version, we used raspberries and spiked the whipped cream with sour cream to lend a subtle tang. Store-bought meringue cookies made this recipe a breeze to assemble; Trader Joe's carries a good version. Layering the berries and cream gave us a more attractive final dish.

Don't walk away from the oven *while the meringues are under the broiler, as they can scorch in a matter of seconds.*

In a small saucepan over medium-high, mash together half of 1 container of raspberries (about ½ cup), 4 tablespoons of the sugar and a pinch of salt. Heat, stirring, just until the berries have broken down and the sugar has dissolved, about 3 minutes. Transfer to a fine-mesh strainer set over a medium bowl. Press on the solids to extract as much liquid as possible; discard the solids. Let cool to room temperature, about 5 minutes, then stir in the lemon zest and juice. Gently stir the remaining berries into the puree.

Heat the broiler with a rack about 4 inches from the element. Spread the meringue pieces in an even layer on a rimmed baking sheet. Broil until browned, 30 to 60 seconds. Let cool to room temperature.

In a large bowl, use a stand mixer on medium-high to beat the heavy cream, sour cream, cardamom, remaining 1 tablespoon sugar and ⅛ teaspoon salt until the mixture holds peaks, about 2 minutes.

Spoon about ¼ cup of the whipped cream into each of four glasses or serving bowls. Spoon about ⅓ cup of the berry mixture into each glass, then top with several spoonfuls of meringue pieces, reserving 1 tablespoon. Layer in the remaining whipped cream, dividing it evenly, then spoon in the remaining berry mixture. Sprinkle with the reserved meringue pieces and the pistachios.

For a brandy-flavored cherry compote to go with these or any pancake, combine 1 cup finely chopped dried cherries with 1/4 cup brandy and 1/4 cup water in a small saucepan. Simmer over medium-high until the cherries have softened, about 5 minutes. Stir in 1/4 cup maple syrup.

Buckwheat Apple Pancakes

START TO FINISH:
35 minutes

SERVINGS:
6

3 Granny Smith apples, peeled, cored and cut into rough ¼-inch cubes (3 cups)

1 tablespoon lemon juice

5 tablespoons white sugar, divided

2 teaspoons cinnamon, divided

195 grams (1½ cups) all-purpose flour

70 grams (½ cup) buckwheat flour

2½ teaspoons baking powder

2 teaspoons kosher salt

½ teaspoon ground allspice

2 large eggs

1½ cups whole milk

1 cup sour cream, divided

2 tablespoons vanilla extract

Grapeseed or other neutral oil, for cooking

Powdered sugar, to serve

Inspired by a traditional Polish snack, these apple-studded pancakes get full, rich flavor from buckwheat flour, warm spices, sour cream and a good dose of vanilla. We liked them made with tart Granny Smith apples, but if you prefer a combination of tart and sweet, use a mix of Granny Smiths and Golden Delicious. We macerated the apples with sugar, lemon juice and cinnamon to boost flavor. Instead of mixing the apples into the batter, we mimicked a blueberry pancake technique, scattering the cubed apple into the poured pancakes.

Don't prep the apples in advance; the fruit will discolor if left to stand. Dry the drained apples well to keep the pancakes from becoming soggy.

Heat the oven to 350°F with a rack in the middle position. Set a wire rack in a rimmed baking sheet. In a medium bowl, stir together the apples, lemon juice, 1 tablespoon of the white sugar and ½ teaspoon of the cinnamon. Set aside.

In a second medium bowl, whisk together both flours, the baking powder, salt, allspice, the remaining 1½ teaspoons cinnamon and the remaining 4 tablespoons white sugar. In a third medium bowl, whisk together the eggs, milk, ½ cup of the sour cream and the vanilla. Add the milk mixture to the flour mixture and whisk just until the batter is evenly moistened; do not overmix.

Drain the apples and transfer to a paper towel–lined plate; discard the liquid. With additional paper towels, press the apples as dry as possible; return them to the bowl.

Heat a 12-inch nonstick skillet over medium-low until hot, 3 to 4 minutes. Add ½ teaspoon oil to the skillet, then use a wad of paper towels to spread an even film of it over the skillet, wiping out any excess. Using 2 heaping tablespoons of batter per pancake, form 3 pancakes in the pan, using the back of a spoon to spread each into a 4-inch round. Working quickly, scatter about 1 heaping tablespoon of apple cubes onto each and gently press into the batter.

Cook until the edges begin to look set and the bottoms are golden brown, 2 to 3 minutes; lower the heat if they brown too quickly. Using a wide spatula, flip each pancake and cook until the second sides are well browned, another 1 to 2 minutes. Transfer the pancakes apple-side down to the wire rack. Repeat with the remaining batter, coating the skillet with oil for each batch.

Place the baking sheet with the pancakes in the oven and heat until warmed through, about 5 minutes. Transfer to plates. Put a spoonful of powdered sugar in a fine mesh strainer and lightly dust the pancakes. Serve warm, with the remaining ½ cup sour cream on the side.

Maple-Whiskey Pudding Cakes

START TO FINISH:
45 minutes (20 minutes active)

SERVINGS:
4

6 tablespoons maple syrup

1 teaspoon cider vinegar

6 tablespoons whiskey, divided

8 tablespoons (1 stick) salted butter, divided

Kosher salt

107 grams (½ cup) white sugar

¼ cup whole milk

1 large egg

1 teaspoon vanilla extract

90 grams (¾ cup) pecans, toasted

65 grams (½ cup) all-purpose flour

1 teaspoon baking powder

These individual desserts bake up with a gooey sauce beneath a layer of rich, tender cake. We tried a few different types of whiskey here: Our favorites were Jameson for its clean, bright flavor and Rittenhouse rye for its spicy depth. This recipe can easily be doubled to serve eight. Serve the pudding cakes warm, with vanilla ice cream or lightly sweetened whipped cream.

Don't stir the maple-whiskey syrup into the batter after dividing it among the batter-filled ramekins. During baking, the syrup forms a sauce at the bottom.

In a small saucepan over medium, combine ½ cup water, the maple syrup, vinegar, 4 tablespoons of whiskey, 2 tablespoons of butter and ¼ teaspoon of salt. Bring to a boil, stirring occasionally. Reduce to low and simmer for 5 minutes. Remove from the heat and set aside.

In another small saucepan over medium, melt the remaining 6 tablespoons butter. Cook, swirling the pan, until the milk solids at the bottom are deep golden brown and the butter has the aroma of toasted nuts, about 5 minutes. Transfer to a medium bowl and cool to room temperature.

Meanwhile, heat the oven to 325°F with a rack in the middle position. Mist four 6-ounce ramekins with cooking spray and place on a rimmed baking sheet. When the butter is cool, whisk in the sugar, milk, egg, vanilla and remaining 2 tablespoons whiskey. Set aside.

In a food processor, process the pecans until finely ground and beginning to clump, 30 to 40 seconds. Add the flour, baking powder and ½ teaspoon salt, then pulse until combined, about 5 pulses. Add the butter mixture and pulse until a smooth, thick batter forms, about 5 pulses, scraping down the bowl once.

Divide the batter among the prepared ramekins. Gently pour the maple mixture over the batter in each ramekin. Do not stir. Bake until the cakes are puffed and the centers jiggle only slightly, 25 to 30 minutes. Let cool on the baking sheet for 10 minutes before serving; the cakes will fall slightly as they cool.

Sesame-Oat Crumble

START TO FINISH:
40 minutes (15 minutes active)

MAKES:
3 cups

60 grams (¼ cup) tahini

½ teaspoon vanilla extract

¼ teaspoon toasted sesame oil

98 grams (¾ cup) all-purpose flour

43 grams (½ cup) old-fashioned rolled oats

82 grams (6 tablespoons) packed light brown sugar

23 grams (2 tablespoons) pumpkin seeds

13 grams (1½ tablespoons) black sesame seeds

13 grams (1½ tablespoons) white sesame seeds

¼ teaspoon kosher salt

6 tablespoons (¾ stick) salted butter, cut into ¼-inch cubes and chilled

Sprinkle this baked topping on yogurt for breakfast, on ice cream for dessert, or on any sweet to which you'd like to add nutty flavor and crunchy texture. If you prefer, instead of pumpkin seeds, use raw sunflower seeds or chopped nuts. And if you can't find black sesame seeds, simply increase the white sesame seeds to 3 tablespoons. As always with tahini, be sure to stir well before measuring to reincorporate the oil that separates to the top. The crumble will stay fresh in an airtight container at room temperature for up to three days.

Don't stir the crumble vigorously as it bakes. A gentle hand will preserve the nubby, clumpy texture that makes the crumble so appealing.

Heat the oven to 350°F with a rack in the middle position. Line a rimmed baking sheet with kitchen parchment. In a small bowl, whisk together the tahini, vanilla and sesame oil. Set aside.

In a large bowl, stir together the flour, oats, sugar, pumpkin seeds, both sesame seeds and the salt. Scatter the butter over the dry ingredients and, using your fingertips, rub in the butter until the mixture resembles wet sand and holds together when pinched. Drizzle with the tahini mixture, then fold with a rubber spatula until combined and the mixture forms marble-sized clumps; smaller and larger bits are fine.

Spread the mixture in an even layer on the prepared sheet. Bake until the crumble is golden brown, 25 to 30 minutes, using a metal spatula to scrape up and flip the mixture 2 or 3 times during baking. Let cool to room temperature.

Chocolate-Tahini Pudding

START TO FINISH:
25 minutes

SERVINGS:
4

¼ cup plus 1½ teaspoons white sugar, divided

3 tablespoons Dutch-processed cocoa

5 teaspoons cornstarch

½ teaspoon kosher salt

2 cups half-and-half, divided

2 large egg yolks

3 ounces semisweet chocolate, chopped

2 tablespoons salted butter, cut into 4 pieces

2 tablespoons plus 2 teaspoons tahini, plus more to serve

½ cup heavy cream

Cocoa nibs or toasted black or white sesame seeds, to serve

This stovetop dessert pairs dark chocolate with the earthy, nutty notes of toasted sesame. Slightly warm, the pudding is creamy; chilled, it has the consistency of firm custard. We preferred Dutch-processed cocoa for its rich, dark color, but natural cocoa, which has a lighter hue, worked, too. For a little more chocolate intensity and slightly less sweetness, use bittersweet chocolate instead of semisweet.

Don't forget to stir the tahini. The oil in tahini separates and must be mixed in before use.

In a medium saucepan, whisk the ¼ cup sugar, cocoa, cornstarch and salt, breaking up any large clumps of cocoa; it's fine if some small lumps remain. Add ¼ cup of half-and-half and whisk until smooth. Whisk in the yolks. Gradually whisk in the remaining half-and-half.

Bring the mixture to a simmer over medium-high while whisking continuously. Once it reaches a simmer, cook for 1 minute, whisking constantly; the pudding will be thick and glossy. Off heat, whisk in the chocolate until smooth, then whisk in the butter and 2 tablespoons tahini.

Set a fine mesh strainer over a medium bowl. Scrape the pudding into the strainer and push it through with a silicone spatula; scrape the bottom of the strainer to collect all of the pudding. Divide the pudding evenly among 4 serving dishes and set aside until barely warm, about 15 minutes.

In a medium bowl, combine the cream, 2 teaspoons tahini and remaining 1½ teaspoons sugar. Beat with an electric mixer until it holds stiff peaks. Dollop the whipped cream onto the puddings. Drizzle each with additional tahini and sprinkle with cocoa nibs or sesame seeds.

Before there was trendy chocolate and tahini there was tahini and carob molasses, a classic Levantine pairing. Carob has long been an essential Middle Eastern ingredient, used as a syrup in pastries and on bread, as well as a powder in cookies.

Sherry-Soaked French Toast

(Torrijas)

START TO FINISH:	SERVINGS:
25 minutes	**4**

Four 1-inch-thick slices challah bread, halved on the diagonal

1 cup dry sherry

120 grams (1 cup) powdered sugar

2 teaspoons grated orange zest, divided, plus ¼ cup orange juice

¼ cup white sugar

¼ teaspoon ground cinnamon

⅛ teaspoon ground cloves

4 large eggs

65 grams (½ cup) all-purpose flour

½ cup grapeseed or other neutral oil

This is our take on torrijas, Spain's version of French toast. Cinnamon and citrus are typical flavorings. Dry sherry infuses the bread with a subtle nuttiness and caramel undertones. Challah isn't typical for torrijas, but we liked its eggy richness and tender crumb. Torrijas are especially good warm from the oven, when the outsides are delicately crisp and the insides are soft and custardy, but they're also great at room temperature. Unlike regular French toast, the bread for torrijas is sweetened throughout, so skip syrup for serving—berries or a fresh fruit compote are the best accompaniments. You'll need a thermometer to gauge the temperature of the oil for frying.

Don't use stale challah. *Stale bread will soak up too much of the sherry mixture.*

Heat the oven to 350°F with a rack in the middle position. In a large baking dish, arrange the challah in a single layer. In a medium bowl, whisk the sherry, powdered sugar, 1 teaspoon of the zest and the orange juice. Pour the mixture over the bread; do not wash the bowl. Let stand for 5 minutes, then flip each piece of bread. Let stand until the bread absorbs most of the liquid, another 5 minutes.

Meanwhile, in a small, shallow bowl, stir together the remaining 1 teaspoon zest, the white sugar, cinnamon and cloves. In the same bowl used for the sherry mixture, whisk together the eggs, flour and 1 tablespoon of the sugar-spice mixture. One at a time, remove the soaked bread slices from the baking dish and dunk in the egg mixture, coating on both sides, then return them to the baking dish.

In a 12-inch skillet over medium, heat the oil to 350°F. Set a wire rack in a rimmed baking sheet. When the oil is ready, place half of the slices in the pan and cook until golden brown, about 1 minute. Using a thin metal spatula, flip each piece and cook until the second sides are golden brown, about 1 minute longer. Transfer to the prepared baking sheet. Repeat with the remaining slices of bread. Place the baking sheet in the oven and bake until the centers are cooked through, about 5 minutes.

Using tongs, dip each slice into the remaining sugar-spice mixture, turning to coat, then transfer to a serving plate. Serve warm.

Puddings Chômeur

START TO FINISH:
1 hour (15 minutes active)

SERVINGS:
4

6 tablespoons (¾ stick) salted butter, softened, plus more for ramekins

1 cup maple syrup (see note)

6 tablespoons heavy cream

2 tablespoons cider vinegar

130 grams (1 cup) all-purpose flour

¾ teaspoon baking powder

½ teaspoon ground cinnamon

⅛ teaspoon kosher salt

93 grams (7 tablespoons) white sugar

1 large egg

Vanilla ice cream, to serve

This gooey Québecois dessert is said to have been created during the Great Depression, when many people were au chômage, or unemployed. The individual "puddings" have the texture of a cake-like biscuit, with crusty edges moistened by maple and cream. The vanilla ice cream may seem unnecessary, but its cold creaminess is the perfect foil for the rich, warm puddings. You'll need four 6-ounce ramekins for this recipe. If you like, it can be doubled to serve eight.

Don't use maple-flavored syrup. This dessert gets its flavor from pure maple syrup. We especially liked the puddings made with darker syrups, which tend to have a deeper, richer taste. But lighter "amber" syrups were good, too.

Heat the oven to 400°F with a rack in the middle position. Line a rimmed baking sheet with foil. Generously butter four 6-ounce ramekins; place on the baking sheet. In a medium saucepan over medium, whisk together the maple syrup and cream. Bring to a simmer and cook for 1 minute. Off heat, whisk in the vinegar. Set aside.

In a medium bowl, whisk together the flour, baking powder, cinnamon and salt. With a stand mixer, in another medium bowl beat the 6 tablespoons of butter and sugar on medium-high until light and fluffy, 2 to 4 minutes, scraping the bowl as needed. With the mixer on low, beat in the egg, 1 to 2 minutes. With the mixer running, gradually add the flour mixture and beat until incorporated, about 30 seconds, scraping the bowl as needed; the mixture will resemble sticky cookie dough. Cover and refrigerate for 15 minutes.

Into each prepared ramekin, spoon 2 tablespoons of the maple mixture. Scoop the dough into the ramekins, dividing it evenly (about ⅓ cup in each). Spoon another 2 tablespoons of the maple mixture over each.

Bake until the puddings are deep golden brown and bubbling at the edges, about 25 minutes. Transfer the ramekins to a wire rack and cool for 10 minutes. Serve warm, topped with ice cream and with the remaining maple mixture on the side.

Triple-Chocolate Almond Cookies

START TO FINISH:
30 minutes (20 minutes active)

MAKES:
30 cookies

8 ounces milk chocolate, chopped

130 grams (1 cup) all-purpose flour

160 grams (¾ cup packed) dark brown sugar

16 grams (3 tablespoons) cocoa powder

¾ teaspoon kosher salt

3 large eggs

⅔ cup roasted almond butter, stirred well

1 teaspoon vanilla extract

6 ounces semisweet chocolate, chopped

¾ cup sliced almonds, lightly toasted

1 large egg white, lightly beaten

2 teaspoons flaky sea salt (such as Maldon Sea Salt Flakes)

Almond butter keeps these chocolate cookies moist, fudgy and almost brownie-like. We liked them with sliced almonds pressed onto the tops, but they can be left off, if you prefer. If the dough is very sticky when you try to shape the cookies, allow it to sit for 5 to 10 minutes. As the milk chocolate solidifies, the dough becomes easier to work with.

Don't forget to stir the almond butter before measuring. And don't use inexpensive milk-chocolate candy bars, which will make these cookies too sweet and not chocolaty enough. Opt for good-quality bar or chip milk chocolate; we liked Guittard. Don't forget to stir the chocolate as it melts, and take care not to overheat it, which causes the chocolate to seize.

Heat the oven to 350°F with racks in the upper- and lower-middle positions. Line 2 baking sheets with kitchen parchment.

Put the milk chocolate in a medium microwave-safe bowl. Microwave at 50 percent power, stirring every 30 seconds, until completely smooth and melted. Set aside.

In a medium bowl, whisk together the flour, sugar, cocoa powder and salt. Add the eggs and mix thoroughly with a rubber spatula. Stir in the melted chocolate, almond butter, vanilla and chopped semisweet chocolate.

Spread the almonds on a large plate. Divide the dough into 1-tablespoon balls, then lightly press into the almonds, coating one side and slightly flattening them. Arrange 15 of the balls, almond side up, on each of the prepared baking sheets, spaced about 2 inches apart. Brush the tops lightly with the egg white and sprinkle with sea salt.

Bake until the center is set and the edges are no longer glossy, 10 to 13 minutes, rotating the sheets and switching racks halfway through. Let cool completely on the sheets. Store in an airtight container at room temperature for up to 5 days.

Coconut-Saffron Macaroons

START TO FINISH:
45 minutes (20 minutes active)

MAKES:
about 20 cookies

4 large egg whites

½ teaspoon kosher salt

½ teaspoon saffron threads, crumbled

2 tablespoons salted butter

¾ teaspoon ground cardamom

¾ teaspoon ground ginger

225 grams (3 cups) unsweetened shredded coconut

50 grams (½ cup) almond flour

143 grams (⅔ cup) white sugar

2 tablespoons honey

1 teaspoon vanilla extract

Cardamom and ground ginger infuse these macaroons with alluring fragrance and flavor, and the saffron adds a golden hue. They're the perfect sweet to pair with hot tea or coffee. The cooled cookies can be stored in an airtight container at room temperature for up to three days; their exteriors will lose their crispness but the flavors will still be fantastic.

Don't use sweetened shredded coconut *or the macaroons will be too sweet.*

Heat the oven to 350°F with a rack in the upper- and lower-middle positions. Line 2 baking sheets with kitchen parchment. In a large bowl, whisk the egg whites, salt and saffron until the whites turn bright yellow, 1 to 2 minutes. Let stand for 5 minutes, whisking occasionally, to allow the saffron to bloom.

In a small skillet over medium, combine the butter, cardamom and ginger. Cook, stirring occasionally, until the butter begins to sizzle, about 1 minute. Remove from the heat and let cool slightly. In a medium bowl, whisk the coconut and almond flour to break up any clumps.

To the egg mixture, whisk in the sugar, honey and vanilla. Whisk in the butter mixture. Add the coconut mixture and fold with a rubber spatula until evenly moistened. Drop 1½-tablespoon portions of batter onto the prepared baking sheets, spacing them evenly.

Bake until golden brown and firm when gently pressed, about 20 minutes, switching and rotating the baking sheets halfway through. Let cool on the baking sheets for 5 minutes, then transfer to a wire rack. Cool for another 10 minutes. Serve warm or at room temperature.

There's little that tahini—or sesame paste—can't improve, be it sweet or savory. Drizzle it over roasted fish or vegetables, spoon it into yogurt for a quick dip, or swirl it over chocolate ice cream. Or rethink the classic PBJ and use it in place of peanut butter.

Benne Seed Cookies

80 grams (½ cup) white sesame seeds

84 grams (½ cup) black sesame seeds

½ cup (1 stick) salted butter

130 grams (1 cup) all-purpose flour

¼ teaspoon baking soda

60 grams (¼ cup) tahini

210 grams (1 cup) turbinado sugar

¼ teaspoon kosher salt

1 large egg

Sesame seeds are known as benne seeds in the South, and these cookies are a nod to traditional Southern benne wafers. The addition of tahini reinforced the nutty notes of the toasted sesame seeds; be sure to stir the tahini well before measuring. We liked these made with a mixture of black and white sesame seeds. Black sesame seeds are sold in natural foods stores, Asian markets and in the international aisle of well-stocked supermarkets. If you cannot find black sesame seeds, you can make the cookies with twice the amount of white seeds. Turbinado sugar is a coarse raw sugar with a light golden color; it gives the cookies interesting texture as well as hints of molasses.

Don't toast the black and white sesame seeds separately. Since the black sesame seeds won't darken as they cook, the color of the white seeds will help you gauge doneness. As you toast, stir frequently and pay attention, as the seeds burn easily.

Heat the oven to 350°F with racks in the upper- and lower-middle positions. Line 2 baking sheets with kitchen parchment.

In a 12-inch skillet over medium, combine both sesame seeds and toast, stirring, until the white seeds are golden brown, 8 to 10 minutes. Transfer to a small bowl and let cool completely; wipe out but do not wash the skillet.

Set the empty skillet over medium and melt the butter. Cook, swirling the pan frequently, until the milk solids at the bottom are browned and the butter has a nutty aroma, 1 to 3 minutes. Immediately pour into a medium heatproof bowl and let cool for 10 to 15 minutes. Meanwhile, in a small bowl, whisk together the flour and baking soda; set aside.

Into the cooled butter, whisk the tahini, sugar and salt; the sugar will not fully dissolve. Whisk in the egg. Using a silicone spatula, stir in the sesame seeds. Add the flour mixture and stir until combined.

Form the dough into thirty 1-inch balls (1 rounded tablespoon each), rolling the dough between the palms of your hands. Arrange 15 balls on each prepared baking sheet, spacing them evenly. Using the palm of your hand, flatten each into a ¼-inch-thick disc.

Bake until the cookies are light golden brown at the edges, 12 to 14 minutes, switching and rotating the baking sheets halfway through. Let cool on the sheets for 5 minutes, then transfer to wire racks and let cool completely.

Venetian Cornmeal Cookies
with Currants (Zaletti)

START TO FINISH:
30 minutes (10 minutes active)

MAKES:
About 40 cookies

75 g (½ cup) dried currants

3 tablespoons orange liqueur, such as Cointreau

12 tablespoons (1½ sticks) salted butter, softened

107 grams (½ cup) white sugar

1 tablespoon grated orange zest

½ cup (73 grams) fine yellow cornmeal

½ teaspoon kosher salt

1 large egg yolk

1 teaspoon vanilla extract

195 grams (1½ cups) all-purpose flour

Zaletti are buttery, crisp Italian cornmeal cookies studded with raisins or currants. The dried fruit usually is first plumped in grappa, a fiery Italian brandy, but we opted instead to use orange liqueur for its more nuanced flavor. We then upped the citrus notes with grated orange zest. The cooled cookies will keep in an airtight container for up to one week.

Don't use coarsely ground cornmeal or polenta. *Their rough texture will result in crumbly, rather than crisp, cookies*

Heat the oven to 350°F with racks in the upper- and lower-middle positions. Line 2 baking sheets with kitchen parchment. In a small saucepan over medium, bring the currants and orange liqueur to a simmer. Cover, remove from the heat and set aside.

Meanwhile, in a stand mixer with the paddle attachment, beat the butter and sugar on medium until light and fluffy, 1 to 2 minutes, scraping the bowl as needed. Beat in the zest for about 30 seconds. Mix in the cornmeal, salt, egg yolk and vanilla until combined, about 30 seconds. Add the flour and mix on low until incorporated, another 30 seconds, then mix in the currants and their liquid.

Form the dough into 1-tablespoon balls (each about 1 inch in diameter) and space evenly on the prepared baking sheets. Using your hand, flatten each to a 2-inch round about ¼ inch thick. Bake until golden brown at the edges, 15 to 20 minutes, switching and rotating the sheets halfway through. Cool on the sheets for 5 minutes, then transfer to a wire rack and cool completely.

Brazilian Chocolate Fudge
Candies (Brigadeiros)

START TO FINISH:	MAKES:
50 minutes (20 minutes active)	**18 candies**

14-ounce can sweetened condensed milk

¼ cup Dutch-processed cocoa powder, sifted

2 teaspoons instant espresso powder

1 teaspoon cinnamon

½ teaspoon kosher salt

2 tablespoons salted butter, cut into 4 pieces

¼ cup unsalted, dry-roasted cashews, finely chopped

¼ cup chocolate sprinkles, chopped

Sweet and simple, these chocolate confections are a staple at Brazilian parties. Typically, they're made with sweetened condensed milk, cocoa powder and butter, but our version includes cinnamon and instant espresso for heightened flavor. Classic brigadeiros are coated with only chocolate sprinkles. To add nuttiness, we mixed chopped cashews into the sprinkles.

Don't turn up the heat to rush the cooking; the chocolate mixture can easily scorch. Medium heat and constant stirring yield a perfectly smooth, silky texture.

In a 10-inch nonstick skillet, whisk the condensed milk, cocoa, espresso, cinnamon and salt. Add the butter then set over medium and cook, stirring constantly with a silicone spatula and scraping along the sides, until the mixture reaches 225°F, about 10 minutes; it will appear matte and slide around freely in the pan. Immediately pour into a wide, shallow baking dish. Let cool to room temperature, about 30 minutes.

Line a rimmed baking sheet with kitchen parchment. In a small bowl, stir together the cashews and sprinkles.

Scoop the chocolate mixture into 1-tablespoon portions and roll each into a ball. A few at a time, drop into the cashew mixture and roll around, pressing so that the mixture adheres evenly. Transfer to the prepared baking sheet. Store in an airtight container at room temperature for up to 3 days.

Index

U

udon (Japanese wheat noodles), 81, 86–87, 97, 181, 322

umami, 115, 119, 237

Unger, Diane, 17

Uruguayan-style steak and cheese sandwich, 306–7

V

vanilla, 373

Venetian cooking, 8–9, 140–41

cornmeal cookies with currants, 390–91

vermouth, 113

Vietnamese cooking, 5, 72, 73, 245

meatball lettuce wraps, 150–51, 305

meatball soup with watercress, 16–17

shaking beef, ix, 138–39

skirt steak sandwiches, 151, 304–5

turmeric fish with wilted herbs and peanuts, 82–83

Vij's restaurant (Vancouver), 347

vinaigrette, 135, 227, 249

vinegar, 175, 265, 295

balsamic, 287

onion-infused, 259

red wine, 194

rice, 55, 67, 86

sherry, 194, 357

white balsamic, 111, 220

W

walnuts, 46, 249, 255

cilantro sauce, 12–13

watercress, 16, 139, 189

whipped cream, 284, 371, 375, 378

whiskey, 375

whole-wheat penne with Broccolini and chèvre, 60–61

wine, 15, 235, 359

sake, 67, 121, 165

sherry, 43, 381

wonton strips, fried, 225

Worcestershire sauce, 159

Y

yakiudon with pickled ginger, 86–87

Yanagihara, Dawn, 58

"Yashim Cooks Istanbul" (Goodwin), 239

yellow aji chilies, 109, 167

yogurt, 25, 209, 225, 291, 324, 355, 388

and chickpea soup, 160–61

flatbreads with flavored butters, 240–41

pasta with browned butter, herbs and, 146–47

spicy cilantro sauce, 365

Z

za'atar, 149, 241, 283, 339

roasted chicken, 342–43

zaletti (Venetian cornmeal cookies with currants), 390–91

zucchini, 52

salad with Parmesan and herbs, 216–17

Zuni Café (San Francisco), 176, 319

"Zuni Café Cookbook, The" (Rodgers), 176, 177

Acknowledgements

Milk Street is located at 177 Milk Street in Boston. It is a real place with a small crew, a cooking school, and a mission—to change how we cook at home. To that end, we produce a magazine, cookbooks such as this one, television and radio shows, kitchen tools and cookware, and live events.

The essence of Milk Street, however, is not its mission; it's the people. For leading the charge on conceiving, developing and editing *Tuesday Nights*, I want to acknowledge J.M. Hirsch, our tireless editorial director; Matthew Card, food editor; and Michelle Locke, books and special editions editor. Additional thanks for exacting editorial help from Jenn Ladd, Milk Street's managing editor.

Also, Jennifer Baldino Cox, our art director; and the entire creative team who deftly captured the look and feel of Milk Street Tuesday Nights. A special thank you to our photo team: Brianna Coleman, associate art director (and props stylist!); Connie Miller, our photographer; and Christine Tobin, our food stylist. This trio of talent created page after page of beautiful images. And a big thank you to Gary Tooth, our book designer.

Also, our team of production cooks and recipe developers kept the bar high, throwing out recipes that did not make the cut and improving those that did. Our in-house team includes Erin Register, Diane Unger, Courtney Hill, Julie Rackow, Phoebe Maglathin and Sarah Gabriel. Our consulting food editors include Dawn Yanighara and Erika Bruce, as well as Guy Crosby, our science editor. Our consulting recipe developers also are a big part of Milk Street, including Elizabeth Germain, Lynn Clark, Bianca Borges, Sandra Rose Gluck, Alison Ladman, Kemp Minifie, Laura Russell, Jeanne Maguire, Joanne Smart, Cristin Walsh and Yvonne Ruperti.

A very special thanks as well to Deborah Broide, Milk Street's director of media relations. She has done a spectacular job of introducing Milk Street to the world.

We also have a couple of folks to thank who work outside 177 Milk Street. Michael Szczerban, editor, and everyone at Little, Brown and Company have been superb and inspired partners in this project. Yes, top-notch book editors still exist! And my long-standing book agent, David Black, has been instrumental in bringing this project to life both with his knowledge of publishing and bourbon. Thank you, David.

Finally, a sincere thank you to my business partner and wife, Melissa Baldino, who manages our media department, from television to radio to social media. Melissa has nurtured the Milk Street brand from the beginning so that we ended up where we thought we were going in the first place! Thanks.

And, last but not least, to all of you who have supported the Milk Street project. Everyone has a seat at the Milk Street table, so pull up a chair and dig in.

Christopher Kimball

About the Author

Christopher Kimball is founder of Christopher Kimball's Milk Street, a food media company dedicated to discovering and sharing bold, easy cooking from around the world. It produces the bimonthly *Christopher Kimball's Milk Street Magazine*, as well as *Christopher Kimball's Milk Street Radio*, a weekly public radio show and podcast heard on over 200 stations nationwide. Kimball is also host of public television's *Christopher Kimball's Milk Street Television*. He founded *Cook's Magazine* in 1980 and the Who's Who of Cooking in America in 1983. Through 2016, Kimball was host and executive producer of public television's *America's Test Kitchen* and *Cook's Country*. Kimball is the author of five books, including *Fannie's Last Supper*. *Christopher Kimball's Milk Street* also provides free cooking classes to the Big Sister Association of Greater Boston and the Boys and Girls Clubs of Dorchester as part of Milk Street's community education outreach.